T0082239

WALES ON THIS DAY

WALES ON THIS DAY

366 Facts You Probably Didn't Know

Huw Rees & Sian Kilcoyne

2022

www.uwp.co.uk

British Library Cataloguing-in-Publication Data
A catalogue record for this book is available from the
British Library.

ISBN: 978-1-91527-911-8

The right of Huw Rees and Sian Kilcoyne to be identified
as authors of this work has been asserted in accordance
with sections 77 and 79 of the Copyright, Designs and
Patents Act 1988.

Cover artwork and illustrations by David Wardle
Typeset by Agnes Graves
Printed by CPI Antony Rowe, Melksham, United Kingdom

The publisher acknowledges the financial support of the
Books Council of Wales

To our parents,
who inspired in us a love of the culture,
history and language of Wales

1 JANUARY

The Welsh have a number of traditional New Year customs.

Calennig can trace its roots back to the Middle Ages and is still active in many areas of Wales today, especially the south-west. Children go from house to house, singing rhymes and wishing the occupants a healthy and prosperous new year. In exchange for this goodwill, they receive money, food or the *calennig* apple, which is an apple standing on a tripod of twigs and decorated with holly.

The tradition of 'first footing' involved making sure that the first person invited into the house in the New Year was a dark-haired man bearing specific gifts: salt for seasoning, silver for wealth, coal for warmth, a match for kindling and bread for sustenance.

A visit from the Mari Lwyd was said to bring good luck for the coming year – find out more about this on 23 December.

2 JANUARY

On Sunday, 2 January 1155, Mwnt Bay near Cardigan was the site of an unsuccessful Flemish invasion of the Kingdom of Deheubarth.

Many Flemish people fought for William the Conqueror during the Norman invasion of England in 1066 and were subsequently rewarded with land holdings after William took control. By the early twelfth century, Flanders was becoming overpopulated and this, combined with devastating floods in 1106, saw many more Flemish people move to England. Initially, they were welcomed, but friction soon developed between the new arrivals and the English natives. The then king, Henry I's, solution was to drive out the native Welsh to allow the Flemings to colonise parts of Wales.

Henry I's death in 1135 prompted a succession crisis in England that resulted in a civil war that lasted until Henry II took the throne in 1153. Welsh rulers had taken advantage of this civil war to regain disputed lands. Henry II set about reversing this trend and the invasion at Mwnt was probably part of this process.

The Flemish soldiers that landed at Mwnt were roundly defeated by the native Welsh. The victory was celebrated in later centuries on the first Sunday in January by a festival known as *Sul Coch y Mwnt*, or Red Sunday, a reference to the bloodshed during the invasion. A nearby stream still goes by the name of Nant y Fflymon (Flemings' Brook).

3 JANUARY

Joseph Jenkins Roberts was elected as the first president of the newly created Republic of Liberia on 3 January 1848.

Roberts (1809–76) was born in Virginia, United States. His father is thought to have been a slave-owning planter of Welsh origin and his mother, Amelia, was a slave. Amelia gave all but one of her children the middle name of Jenkins, which suggests that may have been their biological father's name.

Amelia was freed by the planter while she was young – before Joseph was born – and she then married James Roberts, a free Black man who established a successful business transporting goods by flatboat. Joseph Roberts would go on to work in the family business before emigrating to Liberia in 1829 with his wife, mother and five of his six siblings. He became the country's first African-American governor in 1841, paving the way for him to become Liberia's first president after it gained independence in 1847. He served until 1855, but was elected again in 1872.

Roberts' legacy in Liberia remains: Liberia's main airport – Roberts International – and the town of Robertsport are named in his honour; his face is depicted on the Liberian ten-dollar bill introduced in 1997 and his birthday, 15 March, is a national holiday.

4 JANUARY

Griffith Park in Los Angeles – home to the Griffith Observatory – is named for Griffith J. Griffith, who was born in Betws, Bridgend on 4 January 1850.

Griffith emigrated to Pennsylvania in 1865, before moving to San Francisco in 1873, where he became manager of the Herald Publishing Company. In 1878, he became the mining correspondent for a San Francisco newspaper. He gained extensive knowledge of the mining industry on the Pacific Coast which led to him being employed by many mining syndicates where he earned a significant fortune.

In 1882, Griffith moved into property development and also started an ostrich farm near the Los Angeles River. The birds' feathers were used in making women's hats. After the property rush peaked, in 1896, Griffith donated 3,015 acres of land to the City of Los Angeles, which later became Griffith Park. He also provided the money to build the park's Greek Theatre and Griffith Observatory. Griffith's legacy, however, is marred by his shooting of his wife in 1903. She survived but suffered injuries including the loss of her left eye. Griffith served two years in prison for the crime.

5 JANUARY

Traditionally in the Western Church, 5 January is the Twelfth Night.

'Hunting the Wren' is one of Wales's Twelfth Night customs. It usually took place between the 6 and 12 January and involved a party of young men catching a wren and putting it in a cage. They would then carry it through their community, singing songs that acclaimed it as the 'King of the Birds'. The group would be invited into houses and given food and money.

In Pembrokeshire, this custom was called 'Twelfth tide' and the wren's cage was in the form of a wooden cottage adorned with ribbons.

6 JANUARY

On 6 January 1926, Sir Clough Williams-Ellis first published photographs of scale models and preliminary designs in *The Architects' Journal* for Portmeirion in north-west Wales.

Williams-Ellis stated that he wanted to pay tribute to the atmosphere of the Mediterranean and drew inspiration from the Italian village Portofino. He incorporated fragments of demolished buildings. The main building of the hotel and three cottages ('White Horses', 'Mermaid' and 'The Salutation') had previously been a private estate called Aber Iâ (Ice Estuary) , which had been developed on the site of a late eighteenth-century foundry and boatyard in the 1850s. Williams-Ellis changed the name to Portmeirion: 'port' from its position on the coast and 'meirion' from the county of Meirionydd in which it was sited. Hotel Portmeirion was officially opened for the Easter Weekend of 1926.

It's now a popular tourist village, owned by a charitable trust. The majority of hotel buildings are used as hotel rooms or self-catering cottages, together with shops, a café, a tea room and restaurant.

DID YOU KNOW?

Portmeirion has served as the location for numerous films and television shows, most famously the 1960s cult television series *The Prisoner*. It's also thought that Noël Coward wrote the play *Blithe Spirit* while visiting.

7 JANUARY

Born in Merthyr on 7 January 1956 as John Richard Owens, Johnny Owen was bantamweight boxing champion of Great Britain and the Commonwealth and Europe.

Owen began to box aged eight and went on to win several Welsh, British and Commonwealth titles. He was a quiet, reserved and friendly character outside the ring, but inside it he was a formidable opponent with a determination and strength in contrast to his frail-looking body, which earned him nicknames such as 'the Bionic Bantam' and 'the Merthyr Matchstick'. He possessed an impressive stamina, built by long hours running up the steep hills of the south Wales Valleys.

On 19 September 1980, Owen was knocked out by Mexican boxer Lupe Pintor during a challenge for the World Bantamweight title at the Grand Olympic Auditorium, Los Angeles. Owen fell into a coma and never regained consciousness. He died on 4 November that year. Owen's family, far from blaming the World Champion, telegraphed him shortly after the loss and encouraged him to go on fighting. Twenty years later, a memorial to Johnny Owen was unveiled in Merthyr Tydfil and, at the request of the late fighter's father, the unveiling was performed by Lupe Pintor.

8 JANUARY

Born on 8 January 1823, Alfred Russel Wallace (1823–1913) from Llanbadoc, near Usk, was one of the greatest experts in natural history and explorers of the nineteenth century. He was a leading thinker on evolution and his unconventional ideas caused much discomfort to the scientific community.

Wallace was also a biologist and a social activist, but he is best known for independently coming up with the theory of evolution by natural selection and then co-publishing a paper on the subject with Charles Darwin in 1858. Despite this, his fame faded quickly after his death, but he has become a more well-known and respected figure in recent years.

9 JANUARY

Sarah Jane Rees, who was born in Llangrannog on 9 January 1839, was a navigational and nautical trainer, a campaigner for the temperance movement, a supporter of women's rights, a poet and magazine editor.

The daughter of a sea captain, Sarah Jane insisted on working with her father instead of doing chores at home. She ultimately gained a master's certificate in London, which enabled her to command ships anywhere in the world, and Sarah Jane then returned to Wales to establish a renowned school of navigation in Llangrannog.

In 1865, Sarah Jane won the crown for her poetry at the National Eisteddfod, competing under the bardic name of Cranogwen. This victory brought her national fame and encouraged her to publish a book of poems entitled *Caniadau Cranogwen* as well as to edit the woman's journal, 'Y Frythones'. One of her best-known poems, 'Fy Ffrynd' (My Friend) commemorates her romantic rela-tionship with Fanny Rees, who died from tuberculosis in Sarah's arms.

In later life, Sarah Jane became a popular lay preacher and

established the South Wales Women's Temperance Union in 1901, as well as founding a home for destitute girls in Tonypandy.

10 JANUARY

On 10 January 1952, an Aer Lingus aircraft (named 'Saint Kevin') on a London–Dublin flight crashed at the Cwm Edno bog in Snowdonia, killing all twenty passengers and three crew. It took rescue workers and police officers almost an hour to reach the remote site in atrocious weather conditions. The only thing they found unscathed in the wreckage was a child's doll.

11 JANUARY

On 11 January 1970, the last trolleybus ran in Cardiff, on the last such system in Wales. A trolleybus was an electric bus that was run on the electricity supplied from overhead wires, through spring-loaded trolley poles. It differed from a tram in that it didn't need tracks.

The first trolleybuses in Wales came into operation in Aberdare in 1914 and they were introduced to Cardiff in 1942. Before that, transport options included horse-pulled trams, buses and, later, electric-powered trams. Initially, however, the trolleybuses were beset with problems. They suffered damage from the poor road surfaces and the electric collectors (a part nicknamed the 'monkey') were prone to drop off the wires and land in the street. However, passengers liked them because the lack of vibration made them comfortable, and they were quiet – although this earned them the moniker 'the silent death' as pedestrians often didn't hear them coming.

Motor buses have been operating since the early part of the twentieth century, but early journeys would have been uncomfortable as pneumatic tyres were not fitted until 1924. They began to replace the trolleybuses in 1962.

12 JANUARY

On 12 January 1895, Octavia Hill, Sir Robert Hunter and Canon Hardwicke Rawnsley founded the National Trust. Later that year, on 29 March, Dinas Oleu became the charity's first piece of land. The four-and-a-half-acre gorse-covered hillside in the Mawddach Estuary was donated by philanthropist Mrs Fanny Talbot, a friend of Hill and Rawnsley. The hillside also features small areas of sycamore and oak, and rare liverworts and mosses have been recorded there.

Today, the National Trust looks after more than 114,000 acres of land in Wales including the Dolaucothi Gold Mines, the only known Roman gold mine in the UK.

13 JANUARY

The first confirmed case of smallpox in south Wales occurred in a Cardiff hospital on 13 January 1962. Between January and April, the outbreak infected forty-five people in Wales and killed nineteen – six in the Llantrisant and Rhondda area and thirteen in Bridgend. In response, over

900,000 people in south Wales were vaccinated against the disease.

Smallpox was a leading cause of death in the eighteenth century. Most people became infected at some stage during their lifetimes, and approximately thirty per cent of those infected died from the disease. Smallpox also had a major impact on world history and a devastating effect on the native peoples of America, Australia, India and Africa when it arrived with colonising Europeans. A vaccination was developed following Edward Jenner's experiments in 1796 exploring smallpox's connection with the less dangerous disease, cowpox, and after widespread vaccination campaigns, the WHO certified smallpox's global eradication in 1979.

14 JANUARY

Hen Galan (happy old new year)! *Yr Hen Galan* (hen meaning 'old' in Welsh, and 'calan' indicating the first day of the month) is a custom that dates back to the adoption of the Gregorian calendar in 1752. The previously used Julian calendar had, over the years, lost thirteen days, resulting in 1 January in the Julian calendar equating to 14 January in the Gregorian. Many people celebrate on 13 January, or the equivalent of New Year's Eve, and the communities of the Gwaun Valley near Fishguard and Llandysul continue to observe the tradition of the new year according to the Julian calendar.

15 JANUARY

The world's first radio play, *Danger* by Richard Hughes, was broadcast by the BBC on 15 January 1924. The play was set in a collapsed Welsh coal mine and featured the first broadcast words of Welsh when '*Ar Hyd y Nos*' was sung.

Richard Hughes (1900–76) was born in Weybridge, Surrey and was of Welsh descent. Of his four novels, the most well-known is *A High Wind in Jamaica* (1929). Hughes moved to Castle House, Laugharne in 1934 where he wrote the follow-up *In Hazard*. This is also where his friend Dylan Thomas wrote *Portrait of the Artist as a Young Dog* and it was Hughes who influenced Thomas to make a permanent home in Laugharne.

16 JANUARY

On 16 January 1909, Tannatt Edgeworth David from St Fagans led the first expedition to successfully reach the estimated position of the South Magnetic Pole.

In December 1907, Edgeworth David was working as Professor of Geology at the University of Sydney when he joined Sir Ernest Shackleton's British Antarctic (*Nimrod*) Expedition in New Zealand as the party's chief scientific officer. In March 1908, he led the first ascent of Mount Erebus, the only active and the second-highest volcano in Antarctica. In October 1908, when Shackleton decided to make attempts on both the South Pole and the South Magnetic Pole, he appointed Edgeworth David as leader of the latter.

Edgeworth David, along with Douglas Mawson and

Alistair Mackay, trekked on foot, pulling their supply sledges across difficult and icy terrain, made even more laborious by biting winds and low temperatures. In danger of starvation, they were forced to reduce their rations to crumbs of biscuits and hunt for seals and penguins. On 16 January 1909 after covering 1,260 miles, they arrived at their estimated position for the South Magnetic Pole. However, the party now having physically deteriorated and exhausted still faced the arduous task of rendezvousing with the ship, *Nimrod* captained by Frederick Pryce Evans from Newtown, for the return journey home. They endured more heavy blizzards, crevasses concealed by snow and innumerable steep ice ridges before finally meeting up with their colleagues on board the *Nimrod* on 3 February.

17 JANUARY

Following Llywelyn ap Gruffydd's death in 1282, Wales was annexed by King Edward I of England. The next year, Sir Roger de Puleston was appointed High Sheriff of Anglesey and tasked with imposing unpopular new English taxes on the Welsh. On 17 January 1294, during a raid on Caernarfon Borough by de Puleston, a riot ensued during which he was seized and put to death.

The simmering resentment continued and came to a head in September 1294 when it sparked a national revolt. Welsh soldiers, assembling at Shrewsbury where they were due to march to Portsmouth for Edward's military campaign in Gascony, mutinied and killed their English officers. Madog ap Llywelyn, a distant relation of Llywelyn ap Gruffydd, put himself at the fore of the uprising and soon every strategically important castle in Wales was under siege. By December, the Welsh were in control of most of north Wales and had driven the majority of the English back into Chester. In response, Edward I marched multiple armies into Wales and spent Christmas at Conwy Castle. He then marched to the Llŷn Peninsula but suffered a major setback there when the Welsh captured his supplies. He was forced back to Conwy, where he was besieged.

The rebellion was brought to an end following a battle at Maes Moydog, near Montgomery, in March 1295. Madog's army was destroyed, and he barely escaped with his life.

Edward had Beaumaris Castle constructed and triumphantly toured Wales demanding surrender and allegiance. Madog became a fugitive, before surrendering. He avoided execution but was imprisoned in the Tower of London for the rest of his life.

The revolt of 1294–5 elicited a harsh response from Edward I in the form of humiliating and punitive ordinances that further restricted the civil rights and economic and social opportunities of the Welsh.

18 JANUARY

On 18 January 1823, Reverend William Buckland, Professor of Geology at Oxford University, began exploring the Paviland Caves on the Gower Peninsula. He discovered a partial adult skeleton, stained with red ochre and accompanied by shell beads in Goat's Hole Cave. Initially assumed to be female remains from the Roman times, the discovery became known as the 'Red Lady of Paviland'. Later investigations revealed that it was a young male and an estimated 33–34,000 years old: evidence of one of the earliest ceremonial burials of a modern human in Western Europe.

19 JANUARY

The siege of Holt Castle that took place during the English Civil War (1642–51) ended on 19 January 1647.

Situated four miles north-east of Wrexham, the castle is strategically situated on the west bank of the River Dee, where it forms the Welsh–English border. Its construction was begun by Edward I soon after his invasion of north Wales in 1277. In 1282, following his conquest of Wales, Edward gave the castle and surrounding land to John de Warenne, Earl of Surrey and one of his closest supporters. By 1311, de Warenne had finished building the castle and established a town for English settlers next to it (Holt's original town charter was granted in 1285). This town was burned down by the forces of Welsh independence fighter Owain Glyndŵr, during his uprising against the rule of Henry IV, although the castle was not taken.

At the beginning of the English Civil War, Holt was held by the Royalists. Nearby Chester was an important port that Charles I used to bring in Irish forces and control of Holt Bridge was crucial for access to Chester from Wales. The castle was captured by the Parliamentarians in 1643 but retaken by the Royalists the following year when thirteen of the Parliamentarian garrison were executed and their bodies thrown into the moat. On 19 January 1647, after a siege that lasted for nine months, the Parliamentarians regained the castle and it was slighted (deliberately partially destroyed) later that year.

20 JANUARY

On 20 January 1785, Wrexham-born Samuel Ellis bought New York's Oyster Island, which was later renamed Ellis Island after him.

Following Ellis's death in 1794, it seems that his family were not interested in keeping the island and it passed into the possession of the American government. They built an immigration station here, which became the country's busiest entry point. Between 1892 and 1954, more than twelve million immigrants arrived in the United States via Ellis Island – eight million of them between 1855 and 1890.

21 JANUARY

Concorde's first commercial passenger flights took off at 11.40 a.m. on 21 January 1976. One flew from London to Bahrain, and the other travelled from Paris to Rio de Janeiro, via Dakar.

Sir Morien Bedford Morgan (1912–78) from Bridgend is regarded as being the 'Father of Concorde'. In 1948, while working for the Royal Aircraft Establishment, he began researching the possibility of a supersonic passenger airliner, and in 1956, when serving as Chairman of the

Supersonic Transport Aircraft Committee, he selected the Bristol 223 as the basis for the design of what would ultimately become Concorde. After further development, a Concorde jet (built jointly by manufacturers in Britain and France) made its first successful flight in March 1969. In April 1969, the first UK-built Concorde was piloted by Brian Trubshaw from Llanelli.

22 JANUARY

The Brecon-based 24th (2nd Warwickshire) Regiment of Foot (later the South Wales Borderers) were heavily involved in both the Battle of Islandlwana and the Battle of Rorke's Drift, which occurred on 22 January 1879.

The Anglo-Zulu War of 1879 began on 11 January when, in an attempt to extend British control in South Africa, three columns of the British Army invaded the Zulu Kingdom. One column, led by Lord Chelmsford, established a camp at Isandlwana, sixteen kilometres from Rorke's Drift. On 22 January, Chelmsford advanced to engage with what he thought was going to be the main Zulu army but had underestimated their opponents and been tricked: 20,000 Zulu warriors launched a surprise attack and killed the majority of the 1,700 British soldiers left at Isandlwana. The few survivors returned to Rorke's Drift.

The Zulu warriors soon arrived at Rorke's Drift. Here 150 British troops managed to defend the depot during twelve hours of continuous storming by the Zulu fighters. The fighting was fierce and the British were reduced to a mere handful of men. Then when they were almost out of ammunition, the Zulu, who had themselves taken heavy losses, retreated.

Eleven defenders of Rorke's Drift were subsequently awarded the Victoria Cross, including two Welshmen: John Williams (born John Fielding) from Abergavenny and Robert Jones from Penrhos. The Zulu leader King Cetshwayo was captured in August 1879 and Zululand was broken up and annexed.

23 JANUARY

On 23 January 1974 there was a reported sighting of a UFO crashing in the Berwyn Mountains in north Wales.

That night, unusual lights were seen in the sky, then the ground started to startlingly shake. At first, it was thought that it was an aircraft crash or a meteorite hitting the earth, but when the police and RAF found nothing, speculation started that it had been caused by a UFO that had crash-landed. There were rumblings that the area had been cordoned off to prevent the public from seeing the wreckage and further rumours of alien bodies being found.

However, subsequent scientific enquiries found that the area had experienced a force 3.5 earthquake that night which, combined with a reported bright meteor in the sky, had given the false impression of a UFO landing.

24 JANUARY

A homeless man who helped change the course of the Second World War died on 24 January 1943.

In 1943, the Allies planned an invasion of Sicily, but, to make the Germans reduce their defences, they needed to make them believe their target was elsewhere. MI5, in particular agents Ewen Montagu and Charles Cholmondeley, devised Operation Mincemeat. A corpse dressed as a Royal Marines officer was intentionally washed up in Spain, to be found by the Germans. The body was carrying false documents suggesting that the Allies were planning to attack through Greece.

The corpse was thirty-four-year-old Glyndwr Michael from Aberbargoed. Michael was an orphan who had ended up broke and homeless in London. He probably died after inadvertently eating bread smeared with rat poison.

In April, Michael's body, disguised as the (non-existent) Major William Martin, was released into the sea where the tides took it to Huelva in south-western Spain. It was found by a fisherman who gave it to the Spanish authorities where it came to the attention of the Germans. They fell for the deception and the Allied invasion of Sicily was a success.

Michael was buried as Major Martin in Huelva's cemetery, but when the British Government revealed the body's actual identity in 1996, a plaque was added to his gravestone, stating 'Glyndwr Michael; Served as Major William Martin'. There is also a commemorative plaque dedicated to him on Aberbargoed's war memorial, headed *Y Dyn Na Fu Erioed* (The Man Who Never Was).

25 JANUARY

St Dwynwen, the Welsh patron saint of friendship and lovers, is celebrated in Wales on 25 January.

According to stories, the fifth-century King Brychan of Brycheiniog had twenty-four daughters, and Dwynwen was one of the prettiest. She was already betrothed to another when she fell in love with Prince Maelon Dafodrill from Gwynedd. Maelon became annoyed and forced himself upon Dwynwen, who fled into the woods and prayed that God would make her forget all about Maelon. Dwynwen then fell asleep and received a visit from an angel, who gave her a potion to make her forget Maelon, which also turned him into ice.

God then granted Dwynwen three wishes. She asked for Maelon to be thawed, for God to give true lovers all their hopes and dreams, and also that she would never be forced to marry. The three wishes were granted and Dwynwen dedicated the rest of her life to God. The remains of Dwynwen's church are still visible today on Ynys Llanddwyn Island off Anglesey, where there is also a well, allegedly containing a sacred fish, whose movements forecast the romantic future of visiting couples.

26 JANUARY

The Abermule train disaster on the 26 January 1921 resulted in the death of seventeen people.

The crash was a head-on collision between a train from Whitchurch and another from Aberystwyth, caused by a miscommunication that allowed both trains onto a section of the line that was single tracked. The subsequent inquiry resulted in major changes to railway safety procedures.

27 JANUARY

Auschwitz-Birkenau Concentration Camp was liberated on 27 January 1945. Now International Holocaust Remembrance Day is observed on this date, honouring the memories of those murdered in the Holocaust and in subsequent genocides in Cambodia, Rwanda, Bosnia and Darfur.

Ron Jones from Newport, a lance corporal in the 1st Battalion Welch Regiment, was held prisoner at Auschwitz after being captured in Libya in 1942. He was put to work at a factory making synthetic petrol and initially tried to sabotage his work, but after a fellow prisoner of war (POW) was shot, he kept a low profile.

Ron remembered giving a piece of sausage to 'Josef', a Jewish factory worker, who in return, gave Ron a ring he had made from steel pipe. Josef vanished a month later, most likely sent to his death in the gas chambers, and Ron wore the ring in Josef's memory until his death in 2019.

As the Russian army advanced, the camp guards moved the POWs. For seventeen weeks they trudged over the Carpathian Mountains through Czechoslovakia to Austria, enduring freezing temperatures and eating whatever they could find. They were eventually liberated by American forces who found them in a barn. Of the 280 POWs who started the march, only 150 survived. Ron returned to Wales weighing just seven stone and wearing rags on his feet.

Ron subsequently dedicated years of his life to raising

money for the British Legion and was Britain's oldest poppy seller when he died aged 102.

Another Welsh connection to International Holocaust Remembrance Day is Reverend Leslie Henry Hardman. Born in Glynneath, Reverend Hardman was a British Army chaplain when Allied forces entered the notorious Bergen-Belsen concentration camp. Hardman was Jewish himself and was subsequently responsible for providing comfort and support for the survivors and supervised the burial of approximately 20,000 victims.

28 JANUARY

An underground explosion at the Tylorstown Colliery in the Rhondda Valley on 28 January 1896 became the catalyst that led to the practice of using canaries to detect dangerous gases underground.

The explosion killed fifty-seven miners. The subsequent inquest found that the explosion was caused by the firing of an explosive shot into air that was full of dangerous gas and that the explosion was accelerated by coal dust.

Previously, it was believed that miners killed in explosions died from the force of the blasts themselves. John Scott Haldane, a Scottish professor, was a lone voice in his belief that suffocation was a far greater killer in these circumstances. Following the Tylorstown disaster, he insisted on going underground to see the victims before they were moved. He saw that there was hardly a mark on them. Post-mortems discovered that a pink tinge to their skin that was thought to be bruises or burns was caused by the blood's haemoglobin combining with the poisonous carbon monoxide.

Over the next few months, Haldane tested the effects of carbon monoxide on himself and a series of smaller animals, concluding that canaries were twenty times more susceptible to the gas than humans. From 1911, canaries were taken into the pit with miners; if the canary died, the miners knew it was time to evacuate. In 1986, canaries were phased out in favour of electronic carbon monoxide detectors.

29 JANUARY

The 29 January is the feast day of St Gildas, the patron saint of Welsh historians.

Born around AD 500, Gildas was a cleric, historian and writer. He wrote the *De Excidio et Conquestu Britanniae* (*The Ruin and Conquest of Britain*), about the post-Roman history of Britain and is the earliest British writer whose work is still available.

It's generally believed that Gildas was born in Scotland on the banks of the Clyde, to a noble Brythonic family. He possibly studied in south Wales under St Illtud before embracing monastic life at Llancarfan (Glamorgan) with his companion St Samson. He then travelled to Ireland, where he founded monasteries and churches, and then to northern England before returning to Ireland. In a quest for solitude, he retired to Brittany in France, where he established a monastery at Rhuys.

30 JANUARY

The Bristol Channel floods of 30 January 1607 resulted in an estimated 3,000 deaths of people by drowning. It is thought that the floods were caused by a tsunami-like wave as high as twenty-five feet and travelling at thirty-eight miles per hour.

Houses and whole villages were swept away, with the devastation particularly severe along the coast from Laugharne to Chepstow. Cardiff was badly affected, with the foundations of St Mary's Church destroyed. The event is recorded on plaques in the Monmouthshire churches of Goldcliff, St Brides, Redwick and Peterstone.

31 JANUARY

Watched by an estimated 20,000 people, the cremation of William Price took place on 31 January 1893. The man who paved the way for legal cremation in Britain was himself cremated on a pyre of two tons of coal located on a hillside overlooking Llantrisant. The event was overseen by his family, who were dressed in a mix of traditional Welsh and Druidic clothing.

Price was born in Rudry, Caerphilly on 4 March 1800, he trained as a doctor in Caerphilly and, after qualifying from the Royal College of Surgeons in London in 1821, he returned to Wales to practice. He got involved in Chartist politics, becoming a local leader. After the Chartist march on Newport in 1839, he was forced to flee to France disguised as a woman.

Whilst in France, he visited the Louvre, where he became fascinated with a stone with a Greek inscription.

He interpreted it as a prophecy given by an ancient Welsh prince named Alun, foretelling that the secrets of the Welsh language would soon be revealed by a man who would also liberate the people of Wales. Convinced that the prophecy applied to him, Price decided to go home to free Wales from English domination.

Upon returning he began to get increasingly interested in Welsh cultural activities. He scorned orthodox religion and claimed to be an archdruid and began performing ancient rites on the Pontypridd Rocking Stone. He also took to wearing a white tunic over a scarlet waistcoat, green cloth trousers and a huge fox skin hat. He neither shaved nor cut his hair. He later opened a medical practice in Llantrisant.

In 1881, aged eighty-one, Price married twenty-one-year-old Gwenllian Llewelyn, and she bore him a son, whom Price named Iesu Grist (Jesus Christ). However, sadly the infant died at five months of age. Believing that burying corpses polluted the earth, Price decided to cremate his son's body upon the summit of a hill outside Llantrisant. Cremation at the time was unlawful and Price was arrested and put on trial for the illegal disposal of a corpse. However, he successfully argued during the trial that there was no legislation that specifically outlawed it, paving the way for the Cremation Act of 1902. Price returned to Llantrisant to a hero's welcome and in 1892 erected, on top of the hill where the cremation had taken place, a sixty-foot-high pole, with a crescent moon symbol at its peak. The UK's first official cremation took place in 1895.

There is a statue and an exhibition dedicated to Williams in Llantrisant.

1 FEBRUARY

On 1 February 1886, the Cardiff Coal Exchange was formally opened. At one time, it determined the price of coal throughout the world and is reputedly where, in 1901, the world's first million-pound business deal was made.

Cardiff was once the biggest coal port in the world and the Coal Exchange in Mount Stuart Square was where mine owners, agents and ship owners met to conduct their business. Up to 10,000 people passed through its doors every day. However, the decline in the coal industry led to the Coal Exchange closing in 1958. In 1979, it was set to become the home of the proposed Welsh Assembly – however, in a referendum that year devolution was rejected and so the building wasn't required. The coal exchange is now a hotel, restaurant and wedding and events venue.

2 FEBRUARY

The Football Association of Wales is the third-oldest national association in the world. It was founded on 2 February 1876, following a meeting at the Wynnstay Arms Hotel in Wrexham.

DID YOU KNOW?

Pele scored his first World Cup goal against Wales in 1958, when Brazil beat Wales 1–0 in the FIFA Men's World Cup quarter finals. Brazil went on to win the tournament.

In the 2016 UEFA Men's European Football Championships, Wales were knocked out by the eventual winners again. Portugal beat them 2–0.

Wales's highest ever FIFA ranking was 8th in October 2015. Their lowest was 117th in August 2011.

In 1959, Welsh footballer John Charles came third in the *Ballon d'Or* (FIFA's annual award to the best male player).

3 FEBRUARY

On 3 February 1935, 300,000 Welsh people took to the streets to protest about low incomes, poor health, substandard housing and a reduction in unemployment benefits (the Means Test), which had resulted in Wales becoming one of the world's most economically depressed countries.

After the First World War ended in 1918, it was initially thought that the recession which followed was a result of a temporary post-war disruption to the economy. However, things were about to get a lot worse. The danger signals had started to appear in the mid-1920s when twenty-nine per cent of coal miners were unemployed, rising to forty-three per cent by 1932. Other industries such as steel, tinplate, slate and agriculture were also badly affected and resulted in massive emigration: over 440,000 people left Wales, which dealt a devastating blow to the Welsh language.

4 FEBRUARY

In Walbrook stands a famous Inn
Near ancient Watling Street
Well stored with brandy, beer and gin,
Where Cambrians nightly meet.
(David Samwell)

On 4 February 1771, the London-based Gwyneddigion Society held its first formal meeting at the Bull's Head Tavern in Walbrook.

The group was an offshoot of the Cymmrodorion society, which had itself developed from an earlier society – the Most Honourable and Loyal Society of Ancient Britons – to provide for those who were finding its meetings rather too grand and lacking in musical entertainment.

The Gwyneddigion Society was originally an informal social club for Welsh speakers residing in London, who had a fondness for music and singing, but later developed into a literary and cultural society. One member described the Bull's Head between 1790 and 1815 as *'canolfan bywyd llenyddol ein gwlad'* (the 'centre of Welsh literary life'). Among the society's notable members were Iolo Morganwg, creator of the Gorsedd of the Bards, and David Samwell, naval surgeon for Captain James Cook's third and final voyages to the Pacific Ocean, whose journals provide a detailed account of the expeditions.

One of the society's celebrated projects was the funding of an expedition to North America in the 1790s, to find evidence of Madog ab Owain Gwynedd's legendary discovery of America (find out more on 12 October). The society also promoted annual Eisteddfodau in Wales, and published important Welsh literary texts.

Tensions and differences of opinion resulted in all the London-based Welsh societies dissolving by the middle of the nineteenth century. However, the Honourable Society of Cymmrodorion was revived in 1873 and remains active today.

5 FEBRUARY

Joe Calzaghe retired undefeated from boxing on 5 February 2009. At this time of his retirement, he had spent the longest continual time as world champion of any active fighter.

'Super Joe' – also referred to as the 'Pride of Wales' or the 'Italian Dragon' – was born in London in 1972, to a Sardinian father and Welsh mother. The family moved to Newbridge, near Caerphilly in south Wales, when he was two years old. Calzaghe is the longest-reigning world champion in professional boxing history, having held the WBO super middleweight title for over 10 years and defending it against 20 opponents before moving up to the light-heavyweight division. He was voted BBC Sports Personality of the Year in 2007 and became the first person to be awarded the Freedom of Caerphilly, in 2009.

6 FEBRUARY

On 6 February 1958, Swansea-born Kenny Morgans was found unconscious amongst the debris of the Munich air disaster – a devastating crash involving a plane carrying the Manchester United football team that resulted in the death of twenty-three of the forty-four people on board. Morgans was the last survivor to be rescued from the mangled wreckage, five hours after the official search was called off.

Morgans signed for Manchester United in 1955 and was soon the club's first-choice right-winger. After the crash, he was playing for the side before the end of the season, but his form was never the same. He left the club in 1961 to play for Swansea Town and later Newport County. He eventually retired from football and returned to south Wales to run a pub.

7 FEBRUARY

The future Edward II (1284–1327) became the first non-native Prince of Wales when his appointment was formalised on 7 February 1301. He was also given control of Llywelyn ap Gruffydd's lands in Gwynedd and the allegiance of all those lords who owed their titles to Llywelyn. Llywelyn had been killed in 1282 during Edward I's conquest of Wales and the appointment of his conqueror's son as the Prince of Wales was seen as part of the subjugation of the Welsh people. From then on, the title was traditionally and ceremonially granted to the heir apparent of the British throne. (Find out more about Llywelyn ap Gruffyd on 24 June.)

8 FEBRUARY

The 8 February marks the anniversary of the death of St Ciwa in the sixth century.

According to legend, Ciwa was raised by wolves in Gwent and is therefore often referred to as the 'Wolf Girl'. She is credited with founding the church at Llangiwa, near Abergavenny. She also founded a church at Kewstoke in Somerset, while on her way to see her brother Dochau in Cornwall.

On her arrival in Cornwall, it's said that Dochau refused to meet with Ciwa unless she ridded the area of a man-eating bear. Ciwa proceeded to tame the bear and took it as her companion, after which, Dochau welcomed her and she was allowed to set up a hermitage and church at what is now known as St Kew, named in her honour.

9 FEBRUARY

The death of the last Prince of the entire Kingdom of Powys, Madog ap Maredudd, on 9 February 1160, caused a series of dynastic struggles, which resulted Powys being separated into two parts.

The northern portion (Maelor) went to Gruffydd Maelor, eventually becoming known as Powys Fadog. The southern portion (Cyfeiliog) was under the leadership of Owain Cyfeiliog. It was later called Powys Wenwynwyn after Owain Cyfeiliog's son, Gwenwynwyn ab Owain Cyfeiliog, who ruled the area from 1195 until his death in 1216.

Gwenwynwyn's possession of Powys Wenwynwyn, brought him into conflict with Llywelyn ap Iorwerth (Llywelyn the Great), ruler of Gwynedd, who was keen to extend his own jurisdiction. Gwenwynwyn had allied himself with King John of England. However, in 1201, Llywelyn also concluded a treaty with King John in which he agreed to swear fealty and pay homage to the king in return for cases relating to lands he laid claim to, to be heard under Welsh law. Llywelyn made his first move beyond the borders of Gwynedd in August 1202 when he raised a force to attack Gwenwynwyn ab Owain Cyfeiliog, who was now his main rival in Wales. The clergy intervened to make peace and the invasion was called off. Llywelyn later consolidated his position in 1205 by marrying Joan, King John's daughter.

In 1208, Gwenwynwyn ab Owain Cyfeiliog fell out with King John who summoned him to Shrewsbury and then arrested him and stripped him of his lands. Llywelyn took the opportunity to annex southern Powys and northern

Ceredigion and rebuild Aberystwyth Castle. Then in 1216, Llywelyn held a council at Aberdyfi to adjudicate on the territorial claims of the lesser princes, who affirmed their homage and allegiance to him. In response Gwenwynwyn allied himself again with King John, but Llywelyn called up the other princes for a campaign against him and they drove him out of southern Powys. Gwenwynwyn ab Owain Cyfeiliog died in England later that year.

10 FEBRUARY

On 10 February 1557, Robert Recorde (c.1512–58), a physician and mathematician born in Tenby, was imprisoned for failing to pay a debt. Recorde is best known for introducing the equals sign and the plus sign into mathematics in his 1557 textbook, *The Whetstone of Witte*.

Recorde graduated from Oxford University in 1531 and in 1545 he moved to London where he practised medicine. In 1549, he was appointed controller of the Bristol Mint, where he refused to give money to Sir William Herbert, who was guardian to the young King Edward VI. In 1551, Recorde was appointed by the king to be general surveyor of the mines and monies in Ireland and, in this capacity, he was in charge of silver mines in Wexford and technical supervisor of the Dublin Mint.

On his return to London in 1553, he attempted to regain his court position – now overseen by Queen Mary following the death of her young brother – by charging Herbert with misconduct. This was a misjudgement: Recorde was a supporter of the Reformation, so was unlikely to get a positive result against Herbert, who was close to the Catholic queen. Herbert countered Recorde's charges by successfully suing him for libel and Recorde was ordered to pay Herbert £1,000 which he could not afford. He was therefore sent to King's Bench Prison, Southwark, where he died in 1558.

11 FEBRUARY

Fashion designer Mary Quant was born on 11 February 1930. Quant has been immortalised as the originator of the miniskirt and her work has come to epitomise the 1960s fashion era.

Quant was born in Blackheath, London to Welsh parents Jack and Mildred Quant, who both moved to London to work as teachers after graduating from Cardiff University. She spent part of her childhood in Wales when her father was relocated to Pembrokeshire during the Second World War. Her affordable Ginger Group clothing collection, launched in 1963, was manufactured by the Steinbergs in Pontypridd.

12 FEBRUARY

Blanche Parry, nursemaid, personal attendant and confidante to Elizabeth I, died on 12 February 1590.

Blanche Parry was born in 1507 or 1508 in St Faith's, Bacton, in the Welsh Marches. There is a theory that Blanche, who was Welsh speaking, taught Queen Elizabeth I to speak Welsh. It is suggested that Blanche would sing lullabies to baby Elizabeth and that, in later life, they would use Welsh words to disguise their discussions about courtiers and conspirators.

13 FEBRUARY

On 13 February 1962, writer and political activist Saunders Lewis delivered a now famous radio lecture entitled *Tynged yr Iaith* (*The Fate of the Language*) which was instrumental in the formation of Cymdeithas yr Iaith Gymraeg (The Welsh Language Society) and, therefore, the implementation of most of today's bilingual policies.

In the lecture, Lewis predicted the decline and eventual death of the Welsh language if action wasn't taken. He wanted all Welsh speakers to refuse to fill in all types of official forms if it was not possible for them to do so in Welsh – even if it resulted in imprisonment.

Saunders Lewis was born to Welsh family in Wallasey, England in 1893 and was raised amongst the Welsh community on Merseyside. During the First World War he served with the South Wales Borderers. It is thought that this experience and the influence of the Republican Irishmen he was fighting alongside helped to shape his convictions about the importance of Welsh national identity, although he stopped short of condoning violence against representatives of the British state.

Saunders Lewis went on to have a profound influence on twentieth-century Welsh politics and his legacy is immense. As well as being a co-founder of Plaid Cymru (originally Plaid Genedlaethol Cymru) and being instrumental in the creation of Cymdeithas Yr Iaith Gymraeg, he was twice nominated for the Nobel Prize for Literature. Some of his most exciting works include *A School of Welsh Augustans* (1924), *Williams Pantycelyn* (1927), and *Braslun o hanes llenyddiaeth Gymraeg* (*An Outline History of Welsh Literature*) (1932).

14 FEBRUARY

Production at Swansea's first copper works began on 14 February 1717. The Llangyfelach Copperworks near Landore had opened the previous month and hailed the beginning of an era that would see Swansea nicknamed 'Copperopolis'.

The beginning of Swansea's industrial growth commenced in the early eighteenth century when Gabriel Powell, steward to the Duke of Beaufort, promoted its suitability as a centre for copper production. By 1800 Swansea was smelting an estimated ninety per cent of Britain's total copper output and the area's copper works and supporting industries employed 10,000 people out of a population of around 15,000. By 1860, eleven major copper works had been established in the Tawe Valley which produced sixty-five per cent of the world's output.

The boost for the local area had darker implications elsewhere. Originally, the ore came from Anglesey and Cornwall but, as demand for Swansea Copper increased, so did the distances Swansea's ships sailed to get it. Spain, Cuba and the Pacific coast of South America also became regular sources. Slave labour was used at the Cuban copper

mines and Swansea copper work owners were heavily connected to slavers from Bristol and Liverpool. The copper
they produced was used to barter in the slave markets of
the central and western African coasts.

Workers from Swansea were encouraged to migrate to
other countries to share their expertise.

By the 1890s, the US and Australia had set up their own
smelting industries. This reduced the demand for Swansea's copper and the region diversified into other metal
industries. By the 1950s all but one of the copper smelting
works had closed down, with the final one closing in 1980.

DID YOU KNOW?

Swansea's copper was so good and
pure in quality that it was used by
Nelson to 'copper-bottom' his ships.
This process increased the ships'
manoeuvrability and was instrumental
in his victory in the Napoleonic Wars
(1803–15).

---

15 FEBRUARY

15 February 1971 was known as Decimal Day in the United
Kingdom to mark the moment that the old currency of
pounds, shillings and pence (with the pound being worth
two hundred and forty pennies) was replaced with a

currency of pounds and pence (with one hundred pennies in each pound).

The announcement of the change to decimal coinage came in 1966. Hundreds of millions of new coins were needed and expansion at the existing Royal Mint at Tower Hill in London was not practical, so it was decided to find a new location outside London. More than twenty sites were considered. However, in keeping with the government's policy of transferring industry from the capital to developing areas, Llantrisant was chosen as the site for the new Royal Mint. It had a suitable thirty-eight-acre site with a readily available workforce and the backing James Callaghan, Chancellor of the Exchequer, Master of the Mint and an MP for Cardiff.

Work on the new mint began in August 1967 with the first phase opening on 17 December 1968 in time for decimalisation. The second phase of construction began in 1973 involving a progressive transfer from Tower Hill which was completed in 1975. The Royal Mint at Llantrisant now houses some of the most advanced coining machinery in the world and the largest capacity of any mint in Western Europe.

16 FEBRUARY

On 16 February 1953, Usk Castle was made a Grade I listed building.

Thought to have been built in 1120, Usk Castle is situated near to the site where the Romans established a fortress before moving it to Caerleon. The Normans, in an attempt

to consolidate control over the newly taken area, assigned the castle to Norman Marcher Lord, Richard Fitz Gilbert de Clare. The Welsh, however, took the castle repeatedly in 1138, 1174, 1184, and again in 1233 by an alliance of Richard Marshall and Llywelyn the Great.

Owain Glyndŵr's uprising brought significant conflict to the area and the town of Usk was burned down in 1402 and 1405. On 5 May 1405, Owain Glyndŵr suffered his first major defeat at the Battle of Pwll Melyn on land immediately to the north of Usk Castle, a serious setback to his uprising in south-east Wales.

The battle began with an attack on Usk Castle led by Glyndŵr's son, Gruffydd. The castle guards repelled the assault and counter-attacked, driving the Welsh across the River Usk and into the forest of Monkswood towards Mynydd Pwll Melyn – the 'Hill of the Yellow Pool'. According to one report, the Welsh lost 1,500 men. Three hundred were beheaded in front of Usk Castle. Gruffydd was captured as he was ministering to the dying and wounded; he was imprisoned in the Tower of London. Following the uprising, the castle passed to the Duchy of Lancaster and no further redevelopment or refortification was undertaken.

17 FEBRUARY

On this day in 1912 Edgar Evans perished as he made his journey back from the South Pole.

Edgar Evans was born at Middleton on Gower on 7 March 1876. He attended St Helen's Boys' School before joining the Royal Navy in 1891, aged fifteen. His first experience of polar exploration was between 1901 and 1904 when he joined the National Antarctic Expedition whose brief was to seek out mineral wealth for the British Empire. The officer in command, Captain Scott, was so impressed with Evans's ingenuity, strength and courage that he invited him to join their attempt to reach the South Pole (1910–13).

The five-man team reached the Pole on 17 January 1912 only to discover that Norwegian explorer Roald Amundsen had beaten them to it just a month earlier. Demoralised and suffering from the effects of poor diet and inadequate equipment, the team perished on the return journey. Edgar Evans was the first to die. His widow, Lois, had a plaque placed in his memory in the church at Rhossili and Evans is also remembered at the naval shore establishment on Whale Island, Portsmouth, where the Edgar Evans Building was the first to be named after a petty officer rather than an admiral.

18 FEBRUARY

On 18 February 1915, the Imperial German Navy instituted unrestricted submarine warfare in the waters around Great Britain and Ireland. This meant that if neutral ships chose to enter British waters they would be doing so at their own risk. It followed the UK's declaration that the North Sea was a war zone and that any cargo heading to Germany, Austria-Hungary and Turkey would be confiscated.

The first victim of the campaign was the Cardiff-registered steamship *Cambank*, which was carrying a cargo of copper from Huelva in Spain to Liverpool. It was torpedoed without warning ten miles off Point Lynas, Anglesey on 20 February 1915. By the end of the war, it is estimated that 344 U-boats sunk more than 5,000 Allied ships with the resulting loss of 15,000 lives. Ships carrying coal were particularly targeted and much of it was exported from Cardiff, as Welsh coal was highly valued by the Royal Navy because it produced less smoke – important when trying not to give your location away to the enemy. Many of Cardiff's shipping companies lost ships to U-boat attacks – one, Evan Thomas Radcliffe, lost twenty out of a fleet of twenty-eight. The most high-profile victim of the U-boats was the transatlantic liner RMS *Lusitania* which was sunk on 7 May 1915, killing 1,198 passengers and crew.

19 FEBRUARY

On 19 February 1881, Wales played their first ever rugby international, against England at Richardson's Field in Blackheath, London.

This game has become historically notorious for its chaotic organisation. Firstly the Rugby Football Union insisted that the match be played on the same day that Swansea were playing Llanelli in a semi-final cup-tie, depriving the Welsh team of several players. In fact, the players from Wales had never played together before and one player, Major Richard Summers from Haverfordwest, was selected based on his performances at school. No formal invitations to play were sent out, so two of those expected to play didn't turn up and two bystanders with tenuous Welsh links were roped in instead. The final team that took to the pitch consisted of eight Welshmen, four Englishmen, two Irishmen and an Australian.

Major Summers described the playing kit as being light walking boots, high-necked jerseys and buttoned blue knickers. The changing rooms were in a pub and the teams had to walk half a mile to the game, after – rumour has it – the Welsh team had spent some time drinking heavily.

Needless to say, the Welsh team lost – the score was the equivalent of 82–0 in modern scoring values. It could have been worse, though: England had a try disallowed when England captain Lennard Stokes put Robert Hunt in for a score by throwing a colossal pass. The umpires decided that a long pass was not fair play.

20 FEBRUARY

On 20 February 1959, Shirley Bassey (1937–) became the first Welsh person to reach number one in the UK singles chart, with 'As I Love You'.

Born in Cardiff's Tiger Bay to a Yorkshire mother and Nigerian father, Bassey was raised in the working-class neighbourhood of Splott and worked in an enamelware factory before making her professional debut aged sixteen. She found fame in the mid-1950s and has since become one of the world's most popular female vocalists – in 2020 she became the first female artist to chart in the Top 40 of the UK Albums Chart in seven consecutive decades and she was made a Dame in 1999. Some of her best-known records are the theme songs to the James Bond films *Goldfinger*, *Diamonds Are Forever* and *Moonraker*.

21 FEBRUARY

The world's first steam train made its maiden journey on this day in 1804, travelling from Penydarren Ironworks to Abercynon.

Samuel Homfray, the owner of the Penydarren Ironworks in Merthyr Tydfil, tasked his mechanical engineer Richard Trevithick to produce a steam locomotive to transport the ironworks' products. Homfray was so impressed with Trevithick's design that he placed a wager with fellow iron master Richard Crawshay that it could haul ten tons of iron from Penydarren Ironworks to Abercynon, a distance of 9.75 miles (16 km).

On the morning of 21 February 1804, Trevithick's locomotive successfully completed the journey in four hours and five minutes, reaching a top speed of nearly five miles an hour: the world's first locomotive-hauled railway journey.

22 FEBRUARY

On 22 February 1797, 1,400 members of the French Legion Noire of the French Revolutionary Army landed at Carreg Wasted Point near Fishguard. It remains the last time Britain was invaded by a foreign military force.

The French were helping Irish revolutionary leader Wolfe Tone end British rule in Ireland. French invasions of

Britain were planned to divert and weaken British forces, meanwhile carrying out the main aim of sending a much larger force to Ireland to overthrow the British there. However, bad weather and poor organisation meant that the only invasion that went ahead was the one planned through Wales, to target Bristol and the west of England, led by William Tate.

An initial attempt to land was unsuccessful due to the defensive cannons at Fishguard Fort, so the fleet landed three miles away in the bay at Carreg Wasted under the cover of darkness. They established their headquarters at a nearby farmhouse, but many of the men got drunk and ran away. The next morning the French moved inland and occupied strong defensive positions on high rocky ground. Meanwhile, the British, although outnumbered, decided to attack, with many Fishguard locals volunteering to fight. Notably Jemima Nicholas – known as *Jemima Fawr* (Big Jemima) – took twelve French soldiers prisoner in St Mary's Church armed only with a pitchfork.

The force of the resistance convinced Tate that, although he had much superior forces, he had to accept an unconditional surrender. The following afternoon the French laid down their weapons on Goodwick Sands Beach.

23 FEBRUARY

On 23 February 1959, *Y Ddraig Goch* (the Welsh Dragon) was officially recognised as the national flag of Wales.

It is thought that the Romans brought the dragon emblem to what is now Wales in the form of the draco standards carried by Roman cavalry units who were stationed in Britain from the second to fourth centuries.

The oldest known use of the dragon to represent Wales is from the *Historia Brittonum*, which is commonly attributed to the Welsh monk Nennius around AD 830. The text describes a struggle between two serpents who prevent King Vortigern from building a fortress. This story was later adapted by Geoffrey of Monmouth in *Historia Regum Britanniae* (*History of the Kings of Britain*) (c.1136) into a prophecy by Merlin that the white dragon, representing the Saxons, would at first dominate but would eventually be conquered by the red dragon, symbolising the Celts.

Wales and Bhutan are the only countries in the world to have a dragon as a prominent feature of their national flags. Although Malta also has a dragon being slain by St George in a badge on its flag's top left-hand corner.

24 FEBRUARY

On 24 February 1852, *The Times* reported that Robert Stephenson had approved Isambard Kingdom Brunel's design for the railway bridge at Chepstow.

Chepstow Railway Bridge was used for the first time on 19 July 1852, which allowed the Great Western Railway to open its London to Swansea line. It is considered one of Brunel's major achievements due to the complex design. The span of 300 feet needed to be self-supporting, as the Monmouthshire side is low-lying sedimentary deposit that is subject to regular flooding. Also the height requirement of eighty-four feet above high water imposed by the Admiralty ruled out an arched bridge. Brunel therefore designed the bridge to be suspended by chains from two cast iron tubes, nine feet in diameter. The new railway line and bridge reduced the travelling time between London and Swansea from fifteen hours, by rail, road and ferry, to five hours by rail.

Brunel (1806–59) is considered to be the most prolific mechanical and civil engineer of the Industrial Revolution. His other significant work in Wales includes the Taff Vale Railway, the Vale of Neath Railway (including the Dare Valley Viaduct), the Llynvi Valley Railway and South Wales Mineral Railway, the tubular suspension bridge across the River Wye at Chepstow, the viaduct over the River Tawe at Landore, the stone viaduct at Goitre Coed and the flying arches across the track at Llansamlet. Much of the iron-work for the Great Western Railway, Brunel's bridges, and SS *Great Britain* – the first propeller-driven, ocean-going iron ship – was manufactured in Merthyr Tydfil.

25 FEBRUARY

On 25 February 1246, Dafydd ap Llywelyn – also known as the *tarian Cymru* (the shield of Wales) – died.

Dafydd was the son of Llywelyn ap Iorwerth (Llywelyn the Great) and Joan, daughter of King John of England. In 1220, Llywelyn broke with Welsh traditions (which stated that a man's property passed to all his sons equally) and – with the support of King Henry III of England – named Dafydd as his sole heir. This act alienated Dafydd's illegitimate and older half-brother Gruffydd.

In 1228, Dafydd and Llywelyn captured the Marcher lord William de Braose, who held lands in Brecknock, Radnor, Abergavenny and Buellt. During the ransom negotiations, it was agreed that Dafydd would be betrothed to de Braose's daughter, Isabella, and be given Buellt (Builth) Castle.

Llywelyn died in 1240 and Dafydd became Prince of Gwynedd. He captured and imprisoned his brother, Gruffydd, at Criccieth Castle. However, Gruffydd was under the church's protection, and Dafydd was excommunicated. In August 1241, King Henry III, with the support of Gruffydd's wife Senena, invaded Gwynedd. Dafydd was obliged to sign the terms of surrender, the Treaty of Gwerneigron, which included the handing over of Mold Castle, Lower Powys, Meirionydd, Buellt Castle and Ellesmere.

He also had to release Gruffydd into Henry's custody, who imprisoned him in the Tower of London, using the threat of his release as a means of forcing Dafydd to keep the terms of the treaty. On 1 March 1244, Gruffydd fell to his death while trying to escape from the Tower. His death allowed Dafydd to enter into alliances with other Welsh princes, including Gruffydd's son Llywelyn, against the English king in order to regain Welsh lands lost to the English. Dafydd also began a process of diplomacy with Pope Innocent IV, the result of which was the lifting of his excommunication and the recognition by the Vatican of his right to rule over north Wales. He was, for a time, recognised as Prince of Wales.

But in 1245, the Pope needed England's support in his dispute with the Holy Roman Emperor Frederick II, and withdrew his protection from Wales. Henry reacted by sending an army to invade Gwynedd but, when their supply lines were attacked by the Welsh, he was forced to withdraw.

Dafydd died suddenly in the royal home at Abergwyngregyn on 26 February 1246 and was buried with his father at the abbey of Aberconwy. He was succeeded by his nephew, Gruffydd's son, Llywelyn ap Gruffydd.

26 FEBRUARY

On this day in 1942, the film *How Green Was My Valley*, directed by John Ford and based on a novel by Richard Llewelyn, won five Oscars including Best Picture. The film follows the lives of a hard-working Welsh coal mining family at the turn of the twentieth century. None of the leading actors were Welsh, but Clydach-born Rhys Williams made his screen debut in the film in a minor role. Williams had been originally hired by Ford to coach the other actors, who were mainly English and Irish, on their Welsh accents, and subsequently secured an acting role.

27 FEBRUARY

Joseph Jenkins (1818–98), was born on 27 February, at Blaenplwyf farm near Ystrad Aeron, Ceredigion. He was reputedly 'The Jolly Swagman' of the song 'Waltzing Matilda'.

Whilst in Wales, Jenkins was a farmer who also won prizes at Eisteddfodau for his poetry. When he was fifty-one, Joseph famously emigrated to Australia because of a nagging wife, leaving his family behind. He initially became a swagman, travelling from farm to farm to find work, and later worked as a street cleaner in Maldon, Victoria. He returned to Wales aged seventy-six, after becoming homesick.

During his time in Australia, Jenkins kept a diary, which brought him posthumous fame after it was published as the Diary of a Welsh Swagman.

In 1994 a drinking fountain and plaque were unveiled at the railway station in Maldon to celebrate the hundredth anniversary of his departure from the town.

28 FEBRUARY

The first confirmed case of Covid-19 in Wales was recorded on 28 February 2020 in Swansea. On 11 March 2020, the World Health Organization declared the outbreak a pandemic on and the first death in Wales was reported in Wrexham on 16 March. After the UK death toll hit 335 deaths – sixteen in Wales – the first 'lockdown' order (where everyone was ordered stay at home, except for a limited amount of outdoor exercise each day alone or with members of one's household) was announced on 23 March 2020.

29 FEBRUARY

The Pembrokeshire Coast National Park was established on 29 February 1952. It is Britain's only coastal national park and runs from St Dogmaels in the north of the county to Amroth in the south. It also includes the Preseli Hills, the

Daugleddau Estuary, and islands such as Caldey, Ramsey, Skomer and Grassholm. The National Park also includes seven Special Areas of Conservation, a Marine Nature Reserve, six National Nature Reserves, seventy-five Sites of Special Scientific Interest and more Blue Flag beaches than any other county in the country.

DID YOU KNOW?
The 186-mile Pembrokeshire Coast Path trail around the coastline of Pembrokeshire opened in 1970. Its 35,000 feet of ascent and descent is said to be equivalent to climbing Everest.

MARCH

1 MARCH

1 March marks *Dydd Gwyl Dewi* – St David's Day. On this day, Welsh people celebrate the life of St David by wearing a daffodil or a leek and preparing traditional Welsh dishes such as cawl and Welsh cakes. Many children also wear traditional costumes to school. There are church services and the national flag is displayed prominently.

David is thought to have been born towards the end of the fifth century and to have died on 1 March 589. His mother was Non, a nun at Ty Gwyn (Whitesands Bay) and gave birth to David at Caerfai on the coast just south of Mynyw (St Davids) in the middle of a violent storm. It is reported that even from the womb David performed miracles: during her pregnancy Non entered a church to listen the preaching of the local priest, who was immediately struck dumb and unable to continue whilst in David's presence.

David began his education in a monastery called Henfynyw near Aberaeron and then studied under the monk St Paulinus (the disciple of St Germanus of Auxerre), probably at Whitland, where he was a star pupil – even curing Paulinus of his blindness. He is also believed to have studied under St Illtud at Llanilltud Fawr.

David was soon ordained and began to travel the country, founding twelve monasteries and more than fifty churches from Pembrokeshire to Herefordshire. It is claimed that David ate only bread and herbs and drank only water, which resulted in him being known as *Dewi Dyfyrwr* (David the Waterman). However, in spite of his frugal lifestyle, it's said that he was of a lovable and happy disposition, and was tall and physically strong.

David was consecrated as a bishop during a pilgrimage to Jerusalem. On his return, David founded the monastery of Mynyw (St Davids), which became a renowned centre of learning, attracting pupils from many walks of life. David's order at Mynyw was known for its extreme asceticism: the brothers ate only one meal a day of bread with vegetables and salt and, like David, only drank water. They were a silent order and their days were filled with prayer and hard manual labour. They also practised a ministry of hospitality, caring for many pilgrims and travellers who needed lodgings.

One of the most well-known events in David's life is his attendance at the Llanddewi Brefi in around AD 560,

which was reportedly attended by a thousand members of the church. David had initially not intended to attend, but was persuaded by Dyfrig, Bishop of Ergyng (and said to be Archbishop of Wales). When Dyfrig addressed the crowd, his voice could hardly be heard, so he called on David to speak in his place. When David stood up, according to legend 'the ground rose up until everyone could see and hear him, and a white dove settled upon his shoulder'. It is said that Dyfrig was so impressed by the eloquent way in which David addressed the crowd that he resigned his Archbishopric in David's favour.

David is buried in the grounds of his monastery in Pembrokeshire, where the Cathedral of St David now stands.

2 MARCH

On 2 March 1768, Rowland Hughes discovered the 'Great Lode' of copper on Parys Mountain, overlooking Amlwch on Ynys Mon (Anglesey). Hughes was rewarded with a bottle of whisky and a rent-free house for life.

The mountain had previously been mined for copper ore in the early Bronze Age and later by the Romans. Following its rediscovery by Hughes it became Europe's largest copper mine. The area even became known as the 'Copper Kingdom', briefly producing more copper than any other mine in the world. The copper was notably used by the Admiralty to protect the bottom of wooden ships of war from barnacles and wood worms, as well as increasing their speed and manoeuvrability.

3 MARCH

J. G. Parry-Thomas died attempting to break the land speed record on 3 March 1927.

John Godfrey Parry-Thomas was born in Wrexham in April 1884. He was fascinated with engineering from an early age. By 1908, he had designed an infinite ratio electrical transmission – now viewed to be seventy years ahead of its time – which was used in London buses and railcars. Parry-Thomas was also in demand on government advisory boards during the First World War and later became the chief engineer at Leyland Motors.

Thomas then decided to become a professional racing driver. In 1925 he had focused his attention on the land speed record, which he broke the following year, driving his car 'Babs' at 170 miles per hour on Pendine Sands. However, his great rival Malcolm Campbell soon topped that and regained the record for himself. So on 3 March 1927, Parry-Thomas arrived back in Pendine to attempt to retake the record. He was unwell with the flu that day and, during the attempt, he lost control. The car skidded, rolled over, slid along the beach and burst into flames. Parry-Thomas was killed. Following the inquest, 'Babs' was buried on the beach where she had crashed.

4 MARCH

On 4 March 1919, a riot broke out in the Canadian Army Camp at Kinmel Park near Abergele in north Wales.

There had been discontent among the 15,000 Canadian soldiers waiting to be repatriated after the end of World

War One. The place was a sea of mud, sleeping conditions were cramped and blankets were in short supply. On top of this, food rations had been halved and many had not received their pay for over a month.

The tipping point seemed to be when it was announced that the ships designated to take the Canadians home had been allocated to the Americans. After nothing was done following several protests, the mood turned to outrage. Some of the soldiers looted and started fires in the quartermaster's stores and officers' messes. Rifle shots were exchanged with officers which resulted in the deaths of three rioters and two guards, with many others wounded.

The mutiny was put down the following morning and seventy-eight of the Canadian soldiers were arrested; however, the incident was 'hushed up' by the Canadian army. The remaining Canadians were transported home by 25 March.

5 MARCH

Is America named after a Welshman?

On this day in 1496, John Cabot received the letter of authority from Henry VII to make a voyage to the New World. He sailed there the following year on the *Matthew*, a ship owned by a Bristol merchant of Welsh descent, Richard ap Meryk – anglicised to Richard Amerike.

Amerike was born at Meryk Court, Weston under Penyard, near Ross-on-Wye in 1445 and was a descendant of the Earls of Gwent. He met Cabot when he came to Bristol in 1495 hoping to find sponsors for a voyage of discovery.

At that time, Amerike and other Bristol merchants were trying to find new waters to fish and other opportunities. They were so impressed with Cabot that they arranged an audience with King Henry VII, who commissioned Cabot to make the voyage and claim lands on his behalf.

A legend grew that the North American continent had been named for Amerike because he was the main sponsor of the voyage. His coat of arms was also similar to the flag later adopted by the independent United States. However, the more widely held view is that America is named after the Italian explorer, Amerigo Vespucci.

6 MARCH

Porthcawl's railway station was rebuilt and moved near to the seafront on 6 March 1916. This was a contributing factor in transforming the port town into a major coastal resort.

Porthcawl was a thriving coal and iron port in the mid-nineteenth century, but its dock closed in 1906 after more modern and larger facilities were built in nearby Cardiff, Barry and Port Talbot. The town was then developed as a coastal and health resort – partly led by John Brogdon, an industrialist entrepreneur who had previously been instrumental in making improvements to Porthcawl Dock. He and his wife had built the Marine Hotel and Marine Terrace by 1886 and subsequently also developed a considerable amount of housing and infrastructure in the town.

After the end of the First World War, Porthcawl became the destination for the workers' holiday (which became

known as the miners' fortnight) on the last week of July and the first week of August, when typically the entire population of a mining community decamped to Porthcawl. The resort's popularity boomed.

The Coney Beach Amusement Park quickly developed and included a bandstand, an indoor and outdoor skating rink, three cinemas, a Pierrot stage and donkey and pony rides. The first permanent ride was erected in 1920: the Figure 8 had originally been brought to Swansea to entertain US troops waiting to be shipped home after the First World War. This also gave Coney Beach its name, named after the New York amusement park on Coney Island.

In the early days, the park's entertainment was the Grand Pavilion Theatre which hosted concerts, dances and recitals, and part of the harbour was enclosed to create 'Salt Lake', an area popular with wild swimmers and where small boats could be hired. During the Second World War, Coney Beach Amusement Park was used for billeting troops and the beach was used as a training ground for military exercises. Following the Second World War, the park experienced a boom in popularity with events such as aerial acrobat shows, boxing matches and firework displays drawing hundreds of visitors from all over Britain. By the late 1980s, thousands of people visited the park from all over the world as further events, such as open-air markets, circuses, and professional darts and snooker tournaments were staged.

However, the popularity of overseas holidays along with the closure of the railway line into Porthcawl means the park is now run on a much smaller scale.

7 MARCH

On 7 March 1946, Ray Milland became the first Welsh person to win an Oscar, for his portrayal of an alcoholic writer in *The Lost Weekend*.

Born in Neath on 3 January 1907, Ray Milland's screen career ran from 1929–85 and, at one time, he was the highest paid actor at Paramount Pictures. He initially took parts as an extra in many British productions before starring in *The Flying Scotsman*, which resulted in him getting a contract with MGM. He then moved to the United States where he signed to both Paramount and Universal, appearing in *Three Smart Girls* and *The Jungle Princess* with Dorothy Lamour, which made him an international star. After a further twenty years of acting success, he eventually moved into directing.

DID YOU KNOW?
Before taking up acting,
Ray Milland was a member of
the Household Cavalry of
the British Army.

---

8 MARCH

International Women's Day is celebrated annually on 8 March to commemorate the cultural, political, and historical achievements of women.

In 2016, a group of women highlighted the fact that there was no statue in Wales of a named Welsh woman.

They founded the Monumental Welsh Women campaign with the mission of 'celebrating female ambition and success by commemorating the achievements of great Welsh Women' and campaigned for the installation of statues of five Welsh women.

These were 'the most outstanding Welsh woman of the nineteenth century' Sarah Jane Rees (1839–1916) (find out more on 9 January); the award-winning writer and evolutionary theorist Elaine Morgan (1920–2013), whose book *The Descent of Woman* became an influential text in the women's liberation movement; Lady Rhondda (1883–1958), a suffragette and businesswoman who sat on the board of thirty-three companies and was chairman of seven; Britain's first Black head-teacher Betty Campbell (1935–2017) (find out more on 29 September) and Elizabeth Andrews (1882–1960), a suffragist, miner's wife and one of the most politically active Welsh women of the early twentieth century, campaigning for pit-head baths, better housing, maternity rights and childcare. She also founded one of the earliest nursery schools in Wales. She encouraged women to become politically engaged and became one of Britain's first female magistrates.

9 MARCH

On this day in 1950, Timothy Evans from Merthyr was executed by hanging. He was later granted a posthumous pardon and the case is now acknowledged as a major miscarriage of justice that was instrumental in bringing about the abolition of capital punishment in the United

Kingdom in 1965.

Evans was tried and convicted of murdering his wife and infant daughter at their residence in Notting Hill, London and sentenced to death. Three years later John Christie, a downstairs neighbour, was exposed as a serial killer. He confessed to murdering Mrs Evans and was subsequently found to have also murdered Evans's daughter.

10 MARCH

On 10 March 1945, around seventy (some estimate it could actually have been as many as eighty-four) German prisoners tunnelled out of Island Farm Prisoner of War (POW) Camp on the outskirts of Bridgend. This was the biggest escape attempt made by German POWs in Great Britain during the Second World War.

At around 10 p.m., the prisoners – each equipped with a map, a homemade compass and forged identity papers – made their move. A few got as far as Birmingham in a stolen car and another group got to Southampton. Officials claimed that all were recaptured – although some claim at least three evaded authorities. Three weeks after the escape all the remaining prisoners at the camp were transferred elsewhere.

The camp was later renamed Special Camp XI and was destined to receive senior German officers, including a number of Hitler's closest advisers, whilst they awaited trial at Nuremberg.

11 MARCH

The Welsh Presbyterian Church on Princes Rd, Liverpool, was formally opened on 11 March 1868. Because of its tall steeple, the church was often referred to as the Welsh Cathedral, or Toxteth Cathedral. At the time, it was both the largest Welsh church in the world and the highest building in Liverpool.

Liverpool is often called the unofficial capital of north Wales and the building of the church highlighted the strong cultural links between the two areas. The city's name is widely considered to be derived from the Welsh *Lle'r pwll* (the place of the pool) and Welsh surnames, such as Jones, Hughes, Williams and Owens, are common in the city,

Liverpool's city centre's Pall Mall was known as Little Wales. The 'Welsh Streets' in Liverpool are named after Welsh towns, valleys and villages. One of the stands at Everton F.C.'s Goodison Park is named the Gwladys Street Stand. The stand was constructed by Welsh builders for Welsh immigrants. It is estimated that, by 1850, over 20,000 Welsh builders were working within the city.

By 1813, around ten per cent of Liverpool's residents were Welsh, many drawn there from north Wales in search of work at the port. There was such an active Welsh community in the city that the National Eisteddfod of Wales was held there five times between 1840 and 1929.

12 MARCH

The Welsh Rugby Union (WRU) was founded on 12 March 1881. It was originally called the Welsh Football Union (WFU).

Rugby was first introduced to Wales in the middle of the nineteenth century at Lampeter College. In September 1875, the South Wales Football Club was created in Brecon, to be later superseded in 1878 by the South Wales Football Union. Following Wales's first international match, against England on 19 February 1881, eleven clubs met in the Castle Hotel, Neath on 12 March 1881 to form the WFU, which changed its name to the WRU in 1934. The eleven founder clubs were Bangor, Brecon, Cardiff, Lampeter, Llandeilo, Llandovery, Llanelli, Newport, Merthyr, Pontypool and Swansea.

13 MARCH

13 March is National Sheep Day.

Wales's mountains and highlands, combined with its mild, wet climate produces naturally green pastures that are ideal for grazing animals such as sheep. Consequently there are more than eleven million sheep in Wales and sheep farming accounts for approximately twenty per cent of Wales's agriculture.

Evidence of sheep farming goes back to the Iron Age where dark-fleeced native sheep were raised mainly for wool and only butchered for meat when they were mature. The Romans probably introduced white sheep, which they interbred with native species producing the different types of Welsh Mountain sheep. Large scale sheep-farming – again primarily for wool – was established by the Cistercian monks, following their arrival in medieval Wales in the twelfth century. By 1660, Wales's woollen industry had become a major contributor to the country's economy, accounting for sixty per cent of its exports. Welsh mutton was also popular, particularly as an ingredient in cawl.

This process of manufacturing wool remained largely unchanged until the mid-eighteenth century: wool carding, spinning and weaving were all routinely done at home, mostly by women. The nineteenth century saw the process mechanised and the wool trade started to be reorganised. It was the invention of the power loom in 1850, together with advances in the fulling process that made the industry more successful than ever and hundreds of small factories appeared in rural areas between 1860 and 1900.

However, recent years have seen sheep farming in Wales become less profitable, mostly due to it being so labour intensive and cheaper competition from overseas.

DID YOU KNOW?

The first ever recorded sheepdog trial in the UK was held by Mr R. J. Lloyd-Price at Garth Coch, about a mile from Bala on 9 October 1873.

14 MARCH

Pi Day is celebrated on 14 March.

Pi is the ratio of a circle's circumference to its diameter. The first three digits of the pi calculation 3.14 equate to the American date format 3/14, hence 'Pi Day' being on 14 March.

The earliest use of the Greek letter π to represent Pi was in 1706, by William Jones, who was born at Llanfihangel Tre'r Beirdd on Anglesey in 1675. Jones was a contemporary and close friend of both Sir Isaac Newton and Sir Edmund Halley. He became a Fellow of the Royal Society in November 1711 and would later become its Vice President.

15 MARCH

Monmouth's thirteenth-century stone-gated bridge is Britain's only preserved bridge of this design. On 15 March 2004, a second bridge was opened over the River Monnow, allowing the old bridge to become pedestrianised.

DID YOU KNOW?

Monmouth is an English contraction of 'Monnow-mouth'. The Welsh name for the town is Trefynwy, meaning 'town on the Monnow' – Monnow being an anglicised version of the Welsh 'Mynwy' which may translate as 'fast-flowing'.

The town was originally known in Welsh as Abermynwy (mouth of the Monnow) but had been replaced by Trefynwy by the 1600s.

16 MARCH

The Royal Welch Fusiliers were founded on 16 March 1689. They were originally formed to oppose James II in the Williamite War in Ireland, fighting at the Battles of the Boyne and Aughrim. It was one of the oldest regiments in the regular army, hence the archaic spelling of the word Welch. Soldiers of this regiment were distinguishable by the five overlapping black silk ribbons on the back of the uniform – a legacy of the time when soldiers wore pigtails. The regiment merged with the Royal Regiment of Wales on 1 March 2006, forming the Royal Welsh Regiment.

17 MARCH

St Patrick's Day is 17 March. St Patrick is generally associated with Ireland – but was he actually Welsh? Well maybe.

It is believed that St Patrick was born c.387 and died 17 March c.460. At that time, the Anglo-Saxons referred to the indigenous Britons in areas not under their control as 'Welsh', which comes from the old Germanic word *waelisc*, meaning 'foreigner' or 'not one of us'. So when we describe St Patrick as Welsh, it means he may have come from an area including Strathclyde, Northumbria, modern day Wales or even Cornwall and parts of Devon.

We do know he was born in the Romano-British town of Banna Venta Bernia, but we do not know this town's location. Many suggest it was Banwen in the Upper Dulais Valley, but there are also convincing suggestions for the Severn Valley, St Davids, Ravenglass (in Cumbria) and Strathclyde.

18 MARCH

On 18 March 1536, Henry VIII commenced the Dissolution of the Monasteries. The process occurred between 1536 and 1541, when Henry disbanded the monasteries, convents, friaries and priories of England, Wales and Ireland, and religious relics, colourful icons and pilgrimages were all banned. Most were closed immediately, but some – such as Strata Florida, Neath and Whitland Abbeys – paid fines in order to remain open. However, by 1540, they were all closed. The buildings were stripped and their lands sold off, mainly to the landed gentry to increase their estates. Some schools, such as King Henry VIII Grammar School, Abergavenny and Christ College, Brecon were founded from property seized from monasteries.

Most Welsh Catholics at the time seem to have reluctantly accepted these changes, but those who resisted were fined and those who protested openly faced execution. Sir John Prys of Brecon was the author of *Yny lhyvyr hwnn*, the first printed book in Welsh in 1547 and a notary public (public officer for matters usually concerned with foreign business) to King Henry VIII. He was also one of Thomas Cromwell's agents who conducted the major visitation of the monasteries in 1535, prior to their dissolution.

19 MARCH

Llyfrgell Genedlaethol Cymru, the National Library of Wales, was established in Aberystwyth by Royal Charter on 19 March 1907. The library is regarded as one of the greatest in the world and has the right of legal deposit, which is the right to obtain a copy of every printed work published in Britain and Ireland without cost. It has also digitised many of its most important manuscripts and books, which are freely available on the library's website.

20 MARCH

On this day in 1345, a Saturn-Jupiter-Mars conjunction occurred. At the time, such conjunctions were imbued with huge significance, and the medical faculty at the University of Paris suggested that this particular one caused 'a deadly corruption of the air around us'. Consequently, it was believed this conjunction was responsible for the Black Death.

The Black Death – also known as The Plague – was one of the most devastating pandemics in human history. Estimates of the number of victims range between 75 million and 200 million across Eurasia and North Africa. It is believed that the pathogen responsible was the *Yersinia pestis* bacterium. It's thought to have started in China or central Asia before travelling along the trade route called the Silk Road, reaching the Crimea by 1346. From there, it was carried into the Mediterranean and Europe via the fleas carried by black rats on merchant ships.

The Black Death struck Bristol in the summer of 1348 and arrived in Wales later that year, killing an estimated thirty per cent of the country's population. Further outbreaks of the plague occurred in 1360 and 1369 though these were not so virulent. It took 150 years for Europe's population to recover.

21 MARCH

Born on 21 March 1802 near Abergavenny, Augusta Hall, Baroness Llanover, was a patron of the arts in Wales.

Because of her interest in the Celts, local bard Thomas Price (Carnhuanawc) taught Baroness Llanover to speak Welsh. She adopted the bardic name 'Gwenynen Gwent', 'the bee of Gwent'. She was a patron of the Welsh Manuscripts Society, funded a Welsh dictionary, helped found *Y Gymraes* (meaning *The Welsh Woman*), which was the first Welsh-language periodical for women, and campaigned for church services to be conducted in Welsh. She was also instrumental in the adoption of the national costume of Wales.

22 MARCH

World Water Day is observed on 22 March.

Wales has mountainous terrain and abundant rainfall which means water is a plentiful resource. As a consequence, the highly controversial practice of drowning rural Welsh valleys to provide English cities with water, often by compulsory purchase and without compensation, was adopted.

In the 1880s, Lake Vyrnwy in Montgomeryshire became the first reservoir in Wales and the biggest man-made lake in the world at the time (this title is now held by Lake Kariba in Zimbabwe). It was built to supply water to Liverpool and Merseyside and its creation required flooding the head of the Vyrnwy Valley and submerging the village of Llanwddyn.

In 1904, the Elan Valley reservoir was opened to supply water to the city of Birmingham. A dam in the valley and neighbouring Claerwen reservoir opened in 1952. The area, which provides seventy-five tonnes of water per day, was leased by the Midlands for 999 years at a cost of five pence a year. (Find out more about these on 21 July.)

In 1907, Llyn Alwen near Betws-y-Coed was constructed by the Wirral Water Board to provide nine million tonnes of water per day to Birkenhead. Welsh MPs prevented the Corporation of Warrington drowning the Ceiriog Valley near Wrexham in 1923.

The village of Capel Celyn, in the Afon Tryweryn Valley, was drowned during the construction of the Llyn Celyn reservoir in Gwynedd in 1965. The reservoir supplies water to Liverpool.

In 1967, Llyn Clywedog near Llanidloes was built to supply water to Birmingham and the English Midlands, following an Act of Parliament ordering its creation, despite strong local opposition.

23 MARCH

The 23 March marks the United Nations' World Meteorological Day.

Sir David Brunt (1886–1965) from Staylittle, near Llanidloes, is regarded as being the 'Father of Meteorology'. Brunt first got involved in the practicalities of weather forecasting during military service in the First World War. Whilst serving with the Royal Engineers he did some important work around about the irresponsible use of poison gas; no one at the time knew how winds could disperse chemical weapons. After the war, he joined the Met Office – at the time, the use of aircraft was rapidly increasing and the need for detailed weather forecasting was paramount. Brunt excelled at the collection and analysis of the vast amount of highly complicated data used to measure the temperature, pressure and wind strength in the atmosphere. He served as President of the Royal Meteorological Society from 1942–4.

Another leading Welsh meteorologist was Sir Oliver Graham Sutton (1903–77), from Cwmcarn, Monmouthshire, who also researched air pollution. Sutton was engaged in the organisation of research into and the development of chemical weapons during the Second World War and was heavily involved in the Porton Down programme. He later became Director General of the Meteorological Office and was responsible for the early development of weather forecasting using the first electronic computers and satellites. These were made available at first by telephone in 1955 and then later adapted to the radio and television service.

24 MARCH

In an event later dramatised in the film *The Great Escape*, Allied prisoners of war, including Ken Rees from Wrexham, began breaking out of the German camp Stalag Luft III on the night of 24 March 1944.

Rees flew Wellington bombers during the war, before being shot down in flames over Norway in 1942 and taken prisoner. He eventually found himself held captive in the Luftwaffe-run camp. The prisoners considered it to be their duty to escape and decided to dig their way out.

As Rees was Welsh, it was – incorrectly – assumed that

he must have some experience of mining. After many months of tunnelling, the diggers broke through to the surface to discover that they were some distance short of the woods they expected emerge into, hampering progress. Seventy-six men were able to clamber out of the tunnel via a ladder, guided by Rees at the entrance. As Rees was about to ascend the ladder himself there was a gunshot. The Germans had been alerted. Rees was forced to crawl back to the prison camp. He was the last of the remaining prisoners to make it back before the trap door was closed and the Germans raided the hut. Of the seventy-six who did manage to escape, only three reached Britain. The other seventy-three were recaptured and fifty were shot.

After being liberated, Rees returned to north Wales with his wife, where he wrote a book about his life, *Lie in the Dark and Listen*. When he died in 2014, aged ninety-three, he was the last remaining British survivor of the Great Escape team.

25 MARCH

On 25 March 1807, the Mumbles to Swansea Railroad became the first fee-paying railroad in the world. At the beginning of the nineteenth century, there was no road link between Swansea and Oystermouth and the railway's original purpose was to move coal, iron ore and limestone between the Swansea Canal and Swansea Harbour. Then in 1807, approval was given to carry passengers along the line as well.

The line is renowned for having the most means of being

powered of any railway in the world. It has been horse-drawn, sail-powered, steam-powered and more recently, powered by electricity, petrol and diesel.

26 MARCH

The Pinnacle Club, the UK's only national rock-climbing club for women, was officially inaugurated at a meeting in the Pen y Gwryd Inn, at the foot of Snowdon, on 26 March 1921. The idea for the club was first conceived by Emily Kelly – known as Pat – a climbing enthusiast from Manchester and a founding member of the club. Pat tragically died the following year from head injuries she sustained from climbing Tryfan, in the Ogwen Valley, Snowdonia. The club's accommodation hut in Nant Gwynant is named for her. These days, the club organises regular climbing trips in the UK and abroad, especially in the Himalayas and the Alps, and many of its members have achieved many Alpine first-female ascents.

SOME MEMBERS' KEY ACHIEVEMENTS

1921 Founding members Dorothy Pilley, Lilian Bray and Annie 'Paddy' Wells ascend the 3,367-metre Egginergrat, making them likely to be the first all-female ascent of a peak in the Alps.

1928 Lilian Bray and sisters Sarah 'Biddy' and Emily 'Trilby' Wells make the first all-female traverse of the Cuillin Ridge on Skye.

1941 Nea Morris makes the first ascent of a grade VS 4b climb in the Llanberis Park, which is now named after her.

1953 Gwen Moffat becomes the first British woman to qualify as a mountain guide.

1984 Jill Lawrence makes the first female ascent of a renowned grade 5 climb in the Llanberis Pass, the first woman to lead a climb of that difficulty.

27 MARCH

On 27 March 1963, Dr Richard Beeching published his controversial report, 'The Reshaping of British Railways'.

In June 1961, Beeching became the first chairman of the British Railways Board. He was tasked with returning the rail industry to profitability following decades of declining passenger numbers. Beeching concluded that, due to the increased competition from car travel and the rapidly expanding road network, the only answer was a drastic reduction in the number of railway lines. Over 2,300 stations throughout Britain were closed and 70,000 jobs were lost.

Two hundred of those stations were in Wales, while line closures meant that it was no longer possible to travel from north to south Wales without going into England.

Beeching's plans were extremely unpopular. However, he

argued that the railway system had originally been built by competing businesses, which had led to many inefficiencies and this resulted in there being too many loss-making lines. Critics claimed that his action was an oversimplified solution to a complex problem. They also maintained that, by closing local routes and forcing people to travel by car, they would be more likely to complete their journey by car rather than parking and catching a mainline train.

The estimated savings of the closure programme was £7 million, substantially less than the £30 million Beeching anticipated.

28 MARCH

The last Luftwaffe air raid on Cardiff during the Second World War took place on the night of 28 March 1944.

Wales was believed to be too far west to be subject to German air raids. However, the docks and industrial works of Cardiff and Swansea made them obvious targets. Over the course of the war, 33,000 houses were damaged and over 500 were completely demolished in Cardiff, with 355 civilians killed. Swansea suffered the most intense attack in Wales: a three-night-long raid in February 1941 destroyed half the town's centre – 11,084 houses were damaged and 282 had to be demolished, with 227 people killed.

Other targets included Pembroke Dock with its aircraft station, Caernarfonshire – near the flight path targeting Liverpool – and Cwmparc in the Rhondda (find out more on 29 April).

29 MARCH

The first same-sex marriages in England and Wales took place on 29 March 2014.

The Civil Partnership Act of 2004 had granted civil partnerships to same-sex couples in the United Kingdom. The Marriage (Same Sex Couples) Act 2013 allowed same-sex couples to get married and also allowed for civil partnerships to be converted into marriage. It also enabled transgender people to change their legal gender without having to end their existing marriage.

Three same-sex marriages took place in Wales on that first day. These included Lisa and Claire, who married in Caerphilly at 10 a.m. and Federico Podeschi and Darren Williams, who were also married at 10 a.m. in Swansea's Civic Centre and had their marriage blessed by Archbishop Terry Flynn of Cardiff.

30 MARCH

During the reign of Mary I (1553–8), around 280 Protestants in Britain were burned at the stake for refusing to convert to Catholicism and 800 fled the country. Two high-profile executions took place in Wales on 30 March 1555.

Rawlins White was burned to death in Cardiff. He was a fisherman who had become a devout Protestant. Despite not being able to read and write, he had learnt large sections of the Bible and preached openly in Cardiff. When Mary became queen he refused to stop preaching, was arrested by the Bishop of Llandaff and sentenced to death. White was determined to die bravely, but broke down when he saw his wife and children weeping. However, he regained his composure and then helped arrange the wood and hay for the fire, so his death would be quick. As the flames consumed him, he commanded the large crowd not to listen to a priest who was speaking the words of the liturgy, and asked the Lord to receive his soul.

Robert Ferrar, Bishop of St David's, was burned at the stake at Carmarthen. Ferrar had pursued overzealous policies and reforms while at St David's, which brought him into conflict with his canons. In 1551, they brought fifty-six charges against him, including heresy and abusing his authority; he was sent to prison in 1553 after Mary came to the throne. Ferrar had married in 1548 and Mary refused to recognise the legality of this union. In 1554, he lost his bishopric for the crimes of heresy and his marriage. When he refused to repent, he was sentenced to death by burning.

31 MARCH

On 31 March 1406, Owain Glyndŵr composed the famous Pennal Letter to the French King, Charles VI, setting out his plans for an independent Wales. Pennal is a village on the north bank of the River Dyfi near Machynlleth. In the letter, Glyndŵr asked for French help in his uprising against English rule and called for recognition of Wales as an independent nation. He also stated his aims for establishing an independent Welsh church and university.

Glyndŵr had been a loyal soldier for Richard II of England, but, in 1399, when Henry IV did not support him in a dispute with Reginald de Grey, Lord of Ruthin, over land that de Grey had stolen from him, Glyndŵr rose up. Thousands of Welsh people, angered by unjust English rule, rose up with him, including Welsh students at Oxford University and Welsh workers in England. Ruthin was attacked and the castles at Harlech and Aberystwyth were taken. Glyndŵr raised his standard outside Ruthin and was proclaimed Prince of Wales.

Henry retaliated with burning and looting across north Wales, forcing Glyndŵr into the hills. Then in 1401, Glyndŵr's supporters took Conwy Castle and he took the fight into mid and south Wales, securing a significant victory at Pilleth near Knighton in June 1402, where he also captured the English leader Edmund Mortimer who then became Glyndŵr's ally.

By the end of 1403, Glyndŵr was in control of most of Wales and in 1404 he called a parliament at Machynlleth where he drew up treaties with France and Spain. The following year, Glyndŵr made plans with Mortimer and Thomas Percy, Earl of Northumberland to partition the Kingdom of England and Wales. Mortimer would take south and west England, Percy would take the Midlands and north England with Glyndŵr taking Wales and the Marches. In 1406, Glyndŵr sent his renowned letter to France.

The uprising had now turned into all-out war, with the English launching attack after attack, which the Welsh defended by using hit-and-run guerrilla tactics. However, by 1415 the uprising was exhausted and Glyndŵr was forced into hiding. He was offered and refused a royal pardon, but he was never betrayed and died a free man.

1 APRIL

On 1 April 1977, Richard Booth, a local second-hand book-shop owner, declared Hay-on-Wye to be an 'independent kingdom' with himself as its king and his horse as prime minister. The publicity stunt subsequently made the town a favourite destination for second-hand book lovers. It now hosts a literary festival each year, which was described by Bill Clinton as 'The Woodstock of the mind'. Held around the Whitsun Bank Holiday, the Hay Festival has expanded in recent years to include musical performances and film previews. A children's festival, 'Hay Fever', runs alongside the main festival.

2 APRIL

The Falklands War began on 2 April 1982, when Argentina invaded and occupied the Falkland Islands, followed by the invasion of South Georgia the next day.

The Falklands War resulted from a dispute between Argentina and the United Kingdom over the sovereignty of both these territories as well as the South Sandwich Islands. The British government dispatched a naval task force to retake the islands. The resulting conflict ended with the Argentine surrender on 14 June 1982. During the conflict, 649 Argentine military personnel, 255 British military personnel and 3 Falkland Islanders died.

There were a number of Welsh casualties, including Lieutenant Colonel H. Jones, whose mother was Welsh. The commanding officer of 2nd Battalion, Parachute Regiment, he was killed at the head of his battalion while charging into the well-prepared Argentine positions. He was posthumously awarded the Victoria Cross.

During the build-up to an offensive against the Islands' capital, Stanley, an uncoordinated attack was made on the disembarkation point of Bluff Cove. This led to confusion that left the Welsh Guards on the landing ships RFA *Sir Galahad* and RFA *Sir Tristan* as sitting targets in Port Pleasant. They were without defence escorts for almost two days and were targeted by Argentine air assaults that killed 32 of them and left 150 suffering burns and other injuries. Among them was Simon Weston, who endured over seventy major reconstruction operations and surgical procedures due to his severe burn injuries.

3 APRIL

Outlaw Jesse James was shot dead by Bob Ford on this day in 1882. Despite being born in Missouri, both he and his brother Frank considered themselves to be of Welsh descent – it's believed their great-grandfather was William James, a Baptist minister from Little Newcastle in Pembrokeshire.

The James brothers' career in crime began in revenge for an attack on the family farm by Union soldiers during the American Civil War. The brothers robbed banks, stagecoaches and trains owned by Northern establishments. Despite being a feared band of outlaws with a huge bounty offered for their capture, they remained popular in Missouri because of their active support of the Confederate cause.

During the early 1870s, the James brothers joined with the Younger brothers to form what came to be known as the James-Younger Gang and robbed banks, stagecoaches, and trains with near impunity. However, in 1876 a bank robbery in Northfield, Minnesota, went badly wrong, and only Jesse and Frank managed to escape. The brothers attempted to settle down but, by 1879, Jesse had become restless and returned to crime, forming a new gang. The reward for their capture was increased to $10,000, a sum too large to ignore and one of the new gang, Bob Ford, conspired with the governor of Missouri to hunt Jesse down and collect the reward. Ford shot Jesse dead, in the back of the head.

4 APRIL

Charles Dickens came to Wales on two occasions to give readings. The first was at the Music Hall in Swansea on 4 April 1867 and the second was at Newport on 21 January 1869. As with all of Dickens's readings there were huge crowds on both occasions; those who could not obtain tickets for the performances peered in through the windows and doors and there was a healthy black market, with tickets changing hands at rates well above the normal purchase price. The *Cambrian News* reported that Dickens was frequently interrupted by loud applause and that 'A richer treat has seldom, if ever, been enjoyed in Swansea.'

One of Dickens's most moving pieces was a journalistic account of the shipwreck and loss of the *Royal Charter* off the beach of Porth Alerth on the northeast coast of Anglesey on 26 October 1859. Over 450 men, women and children perished in the waves and it remains the highest death toll of any shipwreck off the Welsh coast. Dickens wrote the article for *The Uncommercial Traveller*, and he interviewed and reported on the activities of the rector of St Gallgo Church at Moelfre, Stephen Hughes. Hughes not only gathered up and buried many of the bodies from the wreck, he also wrote over 1,000 letters of condolence to the grieving relatives and friends of the deceased. Dickens remained on Anglesey for several days, staying at the Bull Hotel in Beaumaris, before returning home to write.

5 APRIL

The United Kingdom Census held on 5 April 1891 was the first to record the languages spoken in Wales by everyone over the age of three.

It showed here to be 1,685,615 Welsh speakers – 54.4 per cent of the population. By 1911 this had reduced to 43.5 per cent and to 18.5 per cent in 1991. The survival of the Welsh language is seen by many as having been a major contributing factor in the survival of Wales as a nation and its declining usage as worrying.

There are, however, encouraging signs such as the percentage of children aged 5–15 who can speak Welsh doubling since 1981, and areas with traditionally low numbers of speakers, such as Cardiff and Rhondda Cynon Taf, also showing increases. In 2010, the percentage of people reporting to be able to speak Welsh was 25.2 per cent and in 2018 this had risen to 29.9 per cent. (Find out more about the Welsh language on 26 September.)

DID YOU KNOW?

In 1547, William Salesbury produced *A dictionary in Englyshe and Welshe*, which some believe could be the first book printed in Welsh. Salesbury was also the principal translator of the first Welsh version of the New Testament – find out more on 7 October.

6 APRIL

The Snowdon Mountain Railway, which runs from Llanberis to the summit of Snowdon, opened on this day in 1896. The journey takes an hour to reach the summit and an hour to descend again with an average speed of five miles an hour.

A railway to the summit was first proposed in 1869, when Llanberis was linked to Caernarfon by the London & North Western Railway. It railway cost £63,800 (the equivalent of approximately £9 million today) to build. Swiss engineers advised on its planning, as they had experience in building this type of railway.

Following its official opening, one of the locomotives ran out of control and fell down the mountain. A passenger died from loss of blood after jumping from the carriage.

On 12 June 2009, a new visitor centre at Snowdon's summit, 'Hafod Eryri', was officially opened by First Minister Rhodri Morgan.

DID YOU KNOW?

After the Second World War, the shortage of coal led to the railway attempting to burn old army boots as fuel.

7 APRIL

The 7 April marks the feast day of St Brynach.

It is thought that Brynach was born in Ireland c.500. He journeyed to Rome, Brittany and then Pembrokeshire where he evangelised through valleys of the rivers Cleddau, Gwaun and Nevern. He is particularly associated with Nevern, where he was given land by a local chieftain to establish a site for Christian worship. It is believed that Brynach was visited at Nevern by St David and that he would regularly pray at the summit of the nearby mountain, Carningli. An English translation of Carningli is 'mountain or rocky summit of the angels', because, when Brynach died (7 April c.580), it's said he was taken to heaven from the summit by angels.

In the twelfth century, the Normans erected St Brynach's Church on Brynach's holy site at Nevern. The original Norman tower still remains, but the remainder of the church was built from the fourteenth century onwards and it was fully restored in 1864.

The famous, four-metre-high carved stone cross of St Brynach stands in the churchyard, and is thought to date from the tenth or eleventh century. Tradition has it that the first cuckoo of the year in west Wales sings from the top of St Brynach's cross on his feast day. Among the avenue of ancient yew trees on the pathway to church, there is one that bleeds red sap from a broken branch. A local legend has it that the yew will bleed until the Norman castle on the hill behind the church is once again occupied by a Welshman.

8 APRIL

Griffith Jones (1684–1761) died on this day in 1761. He was a key figure in a revolutionary educational movement that had a lasting impact on literacy in Wales.

Jones was an Anglican vicar who, as curate at Laugharne and minister at Llanddowror in Carmarthenshire, became concerned that the majority of his parishioners were illiterate. There was no compulsory education at the time. Jones became involved with the SPCK, the Society for the Promotion of Christian Knowledge, setting up circulating schools in barns, storehouses and church porches, where people were taught to read. The language of instruction was Welsh and the texts were mainly religious – predominantly the Bible.

Jones had many wealthy and influential supporters. By his death in 1761 more than 3,500 schools had been established, which helped more than 200,000 people learn to read. The system attracted interest all over Britain and beyond. In 1764, Catherine II of Russia commissioned a report on schools, with the intention of establishing a similar system.

Jones is also regarded as one of the earliest proponents of Methodist philosophy in Wales. He was an inspiring preacher who would often preach in the open air, despite the disapproval of bishops, who considered such evangelism to be 'irregular'.

9 APRIL

On 9 April 1738, Robert Jenkins from Llanelli had one of his ears cut off by Spanish coast guards. The incident was the catalyst for a conflict between Britain and Spain that lasted from 1739 to 1748.

Robert Jenkins, captain of a British merchant ship, was returning home from the West Indies when his ship was boarded by the Spanish who suspected him of smuggling. The Spanish commander bound Jenkins to the mast and cut off one of his ears. He then told him to tell his king that he would get the same.

On his return, Jenkins exhibited his severed ear in Parliament where there was already a simmering resentment towards the Spanish, who had reneged on an agreement for Britain to sell slaves in Spanish America. Jenkins's return was the spark that ignited all-out conflict – it became known as the War of Jenkins' Ear. This war then merged into the much larger War of the Austrian Succession (1740–48) during which most of the states in Europe became involved. In particular, France and Britain, who were fighting each other for control of the American and Asian Colonies.

10 APRIL

On this day in c.430, the 'Alleluia' battle occurred near Mold.

Prior to the Roman occupation of Britain, the native Iron Age Celtic people were polytheistic. Under Roman rule, Celtic societies underwent a gradual Christianisation and the area later known as Wales became one of the strongholds of the Celtic church.

It is estimated that in the year AD 429, Pope Celestine I sent the Bishop of Auxerre, Germanus, to Britain to combat the growing threat of Pelagianism (the belief that mortal will is capable of choosing good over evil without divine aid) and from the polytheistic beliefs of the Anglo-Saxons, Picts and Scots, who had begun to invade Britain following the Romans' withdrawal.

Germanus rallied the Britons to prepare for battle at the River Alyn, near Mold. He positioned troops at strategic points in the narrow gorge. As the invaders approached, the cry of 'Alleluia' was raised, which echoed throughout the valley and the Anglo-Saxons and the Picts fled in disarray, without a blow being struck. The valley is known as the Field of Germanus to this day.

11 APRIL

Llywelyn ap Iorwerth (1179–1240), also known as Llywelyn *Fawr* (Llywelyn the Great), died on this day 1240. Llywelyn was one of Wales's greatest rulers, combining the use of necessary force with diplomacy. He united Wales without oppression, and without provoking an English invasion.

12 APRIL

Sir William Lower (1570–12 April 1615) was a pioneer in astronomy who is credited with making Wales's first telescopic observations of the solar system.

Cornishman William Lower was living at Trefenty near Laugharne in Carmarthenshire after marrying his wife. In 1607, he observed and made measurements of Halley's Comet, which were subsequently used to calculate the comet's orbit.

The first telescope was invented in 1608 and, in the following year, Galileo improved its design to observe the solar system. At this time in Britain, a friend of Lower, Thomas Harriot was one of the leading scientists and had also constructed his own telescope. In 1610, Lower, assisted by local man John Prydderch from Nant-yr-Hebog, Sarnau near Bancyfelin, then built an observatory on high ground near Trefenty and acquired a telescope from Harriot. He then began recording their astronomical observations. Among these was a record of the irregular nature of the Moon's surface (later identified as craters) which was similar to an observation published by Galileo a few weeks later.

13 APRIL

Released on 13 April 1949, *The Last Days of Dolwyn* marked the first film appearance of Richard Burton. The film, directed by Emlyn Williams, depicts a Welshman returning home to his native village from London with orders to buy the land so that it can be flooded to provide water for Liverpool. The story echoes real events around the creation of Lake Vyrnwy (find out more on 22 March).

Burton went on to become an acclaimed actor of stage and screen, appearing in over forty films and earning seven Oscar nominations.

Richard Burton was born Richard Walter Jenkins Jr in Pontrhydyfen, near Port Talbot, in 1925. He was the son of a coal miner, the twelfth child, whose mother died when he was two years old. Richard was raised by his elder sister Cecilia and her husband in Port Talbot. Later, a local teacher, Philip Burton, became his guardian and encouraged him into acting and the theatre and Richard adopted Burton as his surname.

Richard Burton met Elizabeth Taylor on the set of *Cleopatra* (1963), and although they were both married to others at the time, they began a tempestuous relationship – which would include a divorce, remarriage and a second divorce. They also made eleven films together.

Burton died from a brain haemorrhage in 1984, aged fifty-eight. He was buried in Céligny with a copy of Dylan Thomas's poems.

14 APRIL

The act of union between Wales and England received the royal assent of Henry VIII on 14 April 1536. The act divided Wales into thirteen counties and established the modern borders of Wales. Despite being Welsh-speaking, much of the border territory was annexed to England. Consequences of the act included:

- All administration in Wales was to be carried out in English and no one using Welsh 'shall have or enjoy any manner of office'.

- Wales elected members to the English Parliament; the first members took their seats in the Tudor Parliament in 1542.

- The Court of Great Sessions was introduced, a system particular to Wales. They met twice a year in each county, administering English law in the English language. Of its 217 judges in its 288 years of existence only 30 were Welshmen.

- Every county appointed a Sheriff and nine offices of Justice of the Peace.

- The Welsh law of *cyfran*, which meant that all sons inherited equally, was abolished in favour of the English law of primogeniture, inheritance by the eldest son only.

It has been argued that the act's main intention was not to achieve political union but to gain control over the Marches. The Welsh gentry welcomed the changes, recognising that they would be granted equality under the law with English citizens. However, the cultural impact can be seen in Wales to this day.

15 APRIL

The RMS *Titanic* sank in the North Atlantic on 15 April 1912 during her maiden voyage from Southampton to New York. Out of the 2,224 passengers and crew on board, 1,502 tragically died.

Artie Moore, an amateur wireless enthusiast from Blackwood, near Caerphilly, was probably the first person to hear the *Titanic*'s distress signals. In the early hours of 15 April 1912, he received a faint Morse Code signal on his homemade radio from a distance of 3,000 miles. Moore relayed the news to the police, who refused to believe his explanation that he could pick up a 'message in the air' and it was two days before the news officially reached the UK. As a result of this incident, Artie was offered a scholarship to the British School of Telegraphy in London, where he came to the attention of Guglielmo Marconi (the 'Father of Wireless'), and he went on to join the Marconi Company.

Described by survivors as 'the real hero of the *Titanic*', Harold Godfrey Lowe of Llanrhos in Caernarfonshire was the Fifth Officer of the vessel and the only officer who returned to the ship to save drowning passengers. He also rescued a sinking lifeboat and towed another boat to safety. On his return to Barmouth, 1,300 people attended a reception held in his honour and he was presented with a commemorative gold watch.

DID YOU KNOW?
The main beer served on board the Titanic was Wrexham Lager.

16 APRIL

Owen Thomas Jones (16 April 1878–5 May 1967) was a geologist who dedicated his working life to the study of Welsh geology. He was part of the geological survey team that mapped the rocks of Pembrokeshire and worked with H. H. Thomas, the first geologist to propose that the source of the bluestones of Stonehenge was the Preseli Mountains. Recent research has confirmed that he was right and Preseli stones were indeed used in Stonehenge's building. One theory is that they were transported via raft, up the Bristol Channel and the River Avon and then overland to Stonehenge in Wiltshire, around 3000 BC to 1600 BC.

17 APRIL

The Brecon Beacons National Park was established on 17 April 1957. It encompasses 519 square miles and covers The Brecon Beacons, Fforest Fawr, The Black Mountains to the east as well as the Black Mountain to the west.

The western half, Fforest Fawr Geopark, became Wales's first designated geopark in 2005 after it gained membership of a European and global network of geoparks. In 2013, the sky above the National Park became the first area in Wales – and only the fifth in the world – to be granted the status of an international dark sky reserve.

DID YOU KNOW?
The highest peak in the Brecon Beacons is Pen y Fan at 2,907 feet.

18 APRIL

On 18 April 2013, the Pontfadog Oak was blown down by storm force winds.

The sessile oak, which was estimated to be over 1,200 years old, was situated on Cilcochwyn farm in Pontfadog, near Chirk and with a girth of over fifty-three feet (sixteen metres) was Wales's largest as well as oldest known oak tree. It was reputedly the meeting point of Owain Gwynedd's army prior to the Battle of Crogen in 1165 where the English army of Henry II was defeated and forced into a humiliating retreat.

The sessile oak (*Quercus petraea*) is regarded as the national tree of Wales. In the UK, it is most commonly found in the upland areas of Wales and the north and west of England. It is distinguished from the more common English oak (*Quercus robur*) by being taller and narrower in shape and in that its acorns are attached directly to the twigs and not held on stalks. Traditionally, during the autumn, livestock were encouraged to graze on acorns under these trees to fatten them. The sessile oak's timber was traditionally used for ship building and for making barrels and casks. It is also used for high quality furniture and in cabinetmaking.

19 APRIL

On 19 April 1866, Welsh settlers in Patagonia made their first recorded contact with the Tehuelche people of the southern Pampas regions of Argentina and Chile. The Teheulche were a hunter-gatherer nomadic people who had inhabited the area for the previous 1,400 years. They spent the winters in the lowlands hunting whale and catching fish and, during the remainder of the year, they migrated to the higher grounds where they hunted game.

The Welsh settlers had been made aware of the Tehuelche by their founder Michael D. Jones who had emphasised the need to treat them as the rightful owners of the land. The indigenous people made contact with the Welsh after their first year of hardship and struggle. Initially, there was suspicion between the two groups. However, a mutual respect developed between them which resulted in good relations. It was the Tehuelche who helped the early Welsh settlers of Y Wladfa, the Welsh settlement in the Chubut province of Patagonia, to survive their harsh early years. The Tehuelche taught the settlers how to ride the wild horses and how to hunt for guanaco (similar to the llama) and rhea (similar to the ostrich) using boleadores (a leather corded weapon holding three stone balls which would wrap around the animal's legs and bring it down). Over time, trade developed between the Welsh and the Tehuelche, with the Tehuelche trading animal skins and feathers in exchange for bread, sugar, tea and tobacco. (Find out more on 28 May.)

20 APRIL

Richard de Clare, second Earl of Pembroke – and known as Strongbow – died on this day in 1176. He was an Anglo-Norman lord, notable for leading the Norman invasion of Ireland and later becoming Lord of Leinster and Justiciar of Ireland.

In 1167 Diarmait Mac Murchada was deposed as King of Leinster and, to recover his kingdom, he travelled to Wales and solicited the help of Strongbow in exchange for the hand of Aoife, Mac Murchada's eldest daughter, and the succession to throne of Leinster.

Strongbow's army, which included Welsh archers, landed near Bannow, County Wexford on 1 May 1169. They were massively outnumbered but were able to kill 500 of their opponents and take seventy prisoners, as well as the Viking towns of Wexford, Waterford and Dublin.

Diarmait died in May 1171, making Strongbow the new king of Leinster. Henry II of England was concerned about Strongbow's growing power in Ireland and later that year he arrived with an army and forced Strongbow to supply a hundred knights for the service of the crown in return for control of his land.

That same year, Strongbow married Aoife in Waterford. He died in 1176.

DID YOU KNOW?

Alice of Abergavenny was the lover of a Norman Marcher Lord, who took her with him during Strongbow's invasion of Ireland in 1170. He was killed in action and, in revenge, Alice took an axe and beheaded all seventy of the Irish prisoners that had been taken during the battle, before throwing their bodies over a cliff.

21 APRIL

On 21 April 2017, Cardiff-born Geraint Thomas became the first British cyclist to win the Tour of the Alps. The following year, he also became the first British-born rider to win the Tour de France, and in 2022, aged thirty-six, he became the first British cyclist and the second oldest person ever to win the Tour de Suisse. He has also won three World Championships (2007, 2008 and 2012), two Olympic gold medals (2008 and 2012) and the BBC Sports Personality of the Year Award (2018).

DID YOU KNOW?

Geraint Thomas attended Whitchurch High School in Cardiff, where he was a contemporary of Wales football captain and Champions League winner Gareth Bale, and Wales and Lions rugby test winning captain Sam Warburton.

22 APRIL

On 22 April 1912, Denys Corbett Wilson made the first manned flight across the Irish Sea, from Goodwick, Pembrokeshire to Crane near Enniscorthy, County Wexford, in a time of one hour forty minutes.

Wales has been the site of many aviation achievements. On 22 July 1817, Windham Sadler became the first person to succeed in crossing the Irish Sea by hot air balloon, when he

flew from Dublin to near Holyhead. Amelia Earhart became the first woman to fly across the Atlantic Ocean when she landed in Burry Port on 18 June 1928, and on 22 July 1933, Amy Johnson and her husband Jim Mollison (the 'Flying Sweethearts') took off from Pendine Sands in Carmarthenshire, in their attempt to fly across the Atlantic non-stop.

23 APRIL

On 23 April 1927, Cardiff City won the FA Cup at Wembley Stadium against Arsenal. It was the first and only time to date that the FA Cup has not been won by an English club. This was also the first cup final to be broadcast live on BBC Radio, and the first time the FA Cup anthem 'Abide With Me' was sung.

Cardiff City were founded in 1899 as Riverside AFC and renamed Cardiff City in 1908. They purchased their own ground in 1910 with the financial help of Lord Ninian Stuart of the Bute family and after whom the ground 'Ninian Park' was named. The ground was on a former council rubbish dump on Sloper Road and it initially posed a hazard to players. Scotland international Peter McWilliam gashed his leg on a piece of glass and never played again. Players were even paid extra for turning up on the morning of a match to clear the pitch of broken glass and other objects.

The first match was a 2–1 defeat against the reigning Football League champions Aston Villa. Ninian Park also hosted many memorable international fixtures, including the Welsh victory over Israel in 1958, which saw Wales qualify for the World Cup finals.

24 APRIL

On 24 (some accounts say 25 April) 1649, John Poyer, a Parliamentarian soldier who switched his allegiance to the Royalists, was executed for treason.

Initially a prosperous merchant, mayor and governor of Pembroke Castle, Poyer raised a force on behalf of Parliament, defending the castle against the Royalists. When, in 1647, he was commanded to disband his army and surrender Pembroke Castle, he refused, claiming that he was owed money. He consequently joined a Royalist rebellion, which lost at the Battle of St Fagans. Poyer, along with fellow rebels Major General Rowland Laugharne and Colonel Rice Powell, the governor of Tenby Castle, fled to Pembrokeshire. Powell surrendered at Tenby. Poyer and Laugharne were besieged at Pembroke Castle by Oliver Cromwell, who had marched into Wales to personally deal with the rebellion. The siege ended when Cromwell discovered and cut off the castle's water supply.

Poyer, Laugharne and Powell were taken to London where they were court-martialled and sentenced to death. However, it was later decided that only one of the men would be executed and that they would draw lots to decide on who would face the firing squad. When the prisoners refused to participate, a young child drew the lots instead and presented slips of paper to each man. Laugharne and Powell's read 'Life given by God'. Poyer's, however, was blank and he was subsequently executed at Covent Garden.

25 APRIL

On 25 April 2021, eighty-three-year-old Anthony Hopkins became the oldest person to be awarded the Best Actor Academy Award, for his performance in *The Father*. This was the second time Hopkins had received the Oscar for Best Actor, the first being for *The Silence of the Lambs* in 1991.

Hopkins was born in Margam, Port Talbot on 31 December 1937. His schooldays were unproductive as he found that he would rather immerse himself in art – he enjoyed painting, drawing and playing the piano – rather than attend to his studies. His life path altered at age fifteen, following a brief encounter with Richard Burton, who encouraged him to become an actor. He enrolled at the Royal Welsh College of Music & Drama in Cardiff. Later, after two years of national service, he moved to London and was invited by Laurence Oliver to study at the Royal Academy of Dramatic Art. From that moment on, he was to enjoy a successful career in cinema, theatre and television, with his remarkable acting style reaching the four corners of the world. To learn scripts, Hopkins reads them out loud 250 times. He also learns a new poem every week to exercise his memory.

In 1998, Hopkins gave £1 million to the National Trust to help them buy a large piece of land on Snowdon and save it from private development.

26 APRIL

On 26 April 1986, a violent explosion blew the 1,000-tonne concrete and steel lid off one of the reactors at the Chernobyl nuclear power station. The resulting fire took rescue workers more than a week to put out, during which time dangerous levels of radioactive material were released into the environment.

The true scale of the disaster was not revealed for over a month, and by then the radioactive dust had moved over much of Europe. In Britain, upland hill farms of north Wales, Cumbria, Scotland and Northern Ireland were most affected as rain caused the dust to fall to the ground and contaminate the grass. Initially, the British government said there was no risk, but by late June was it was announced that a considerable number of sheep had dangerous amounts of radiation in their bodies and restrictions were put on animal movement. Before farmers could sell livestock, their radiation levels had to be below a certain level. These restrictions were lifted by the Food Standards Agency in 2012.

27 APRIL

David Lewis (born c.1520) from Abergavenny died on this day in 1584. He was a lawyer and personal advisor to Queen Elizabeth I, MP for Monmouthshire and a Judge of the High Court of Admiralty. He was also one of the founding members of Jesus College, Oxford and became its first principal in 1571.

A NOTABLE BENEFACTOR

Edwin Stevens (1905–1995),
from Panteg, Monmouthshire was
the inventor of the world's first
wearable electronic hearing aid,
as used by Winston Churchill.
He was a major benefactor
of Jesus College, where he studied
from 1927–9.

28 APRIL

Rhys ap Gruffydd (The Lord Rhys), ruler of the kingdom
of Deheubarth from 1155 to 1197, died on 28 April 1197.

From 1158 to 1163, Rhys battled with King Henry II over
lands that had once belonged to Rhys, with Henry even
imprisoning Rhys in 1163, though he was later released.
The following year, Rhys and Owain Gwynedd united in
an uprising. Henry invaded Wales again, but torrential rain
forced his army to retreat and Rhys won back most of his
lands. Henry had Rhys's son blinded, and in reprisal Rhys
burned down Cardigan Castle. Owain Gwynedd died in
1170, leaving Rhys as the acknowledged leader of all the
Welsh princes. In 1171, Henry wished to make peace with
Rhys. Rhys was to pay a tribute of 300 horses and 4,000
head of cattle but his possession of all the lands he had tak-
en from Norman lords was confirmed. The following year,
the two men met at Laugharne, where Henry appointed

him Justiciar for South Wales. From then on Rhys and Henry maintained good relations.

However, after Henry was succeeded by Richard I in 1189, Rhys considered that he was no longer bound by the agreement with Henry and attacked the Norman lordships in Pembroke, Haverfordwest and Gower. He launched a further, final campaign against the Normans in 1196, but died the following year.

When he died, Rhys had been the dominant ruling prince in Wales for more than forty years. He rebuilt Cardigan Castle, which was the earliest recorded native-built stone castle in Wales, as well as castles at Carreg Cennen near Llandeilo and Aberdyfi. He founded the religious houses of Talley Abbey and Llanllyr Nunnery and was the patron of the abbeys of Whitland and Strata Florida. He was buried in St David's Cathedral, Cardiff.

DID YOU KNOW?

In 1176, Rhys held a festival of poetry and song at his court at Cardigan which is generally regarded as the first recorded Eisteddfod.

29 APRIL

On 29 April 1941, the village of Cwmparc in the Rhondda Valley was bombed by the Luftwaffe, which killed twenty-seven people.

It is believed that anti-aircraft fire had forced the German pilots to divert from their planned target of Swansea and they had dropped their bombs randomly. Among the fatalities were three evacuee children, two boys and one girl, from the Jameson family of East Ham, London. They were killed when the house where they were staying, 14 Treharne Street, was hit. Another evacuee boy from New Malden, Surrey was also killed, as well as a local nurse, a police constable and a home guard.

30 APRIL

David Thompson (1770–1857) has been described as one of the greatest land explorers and geographers in history.

Born in London to Welsh parents on 30 April 1770, Thompson was only two years old when his father died. This resulted in financial hardship for his mother and he was placed under the guardianship of the school of the Grey Coat Hospital, for the disadvantaged of Westminster. He trained in navigation and surveying and, aged fourteen, was apprenticed to the Hudson's Bay Company who transferred him to Canada. In 1797 he joined their rival, the North West Company, where he worked surveying large areas of previously uncharted territory. His maps of western North America formed the basis of all later maps, contributing significantly to our understanding of the culture and history of North America. Thompson was the first white man to explore the whole length of the Columbia River, enduring incredible hardship and danger. He was respected by the Native Americans, who knew him as Koo-Koo-Sint ('you who look at the stars') because of his constant use of his sextant in map-making. Horrified by the maimings and killings he attributed directly to the trading of alcohol with the indigenous peoples, he took a firm stand against the highly profitable practice.

1 MAY

The beginning of summer, fairest season;
noisy are the birds, green the woods,
the ploughs are in the furrow, the ox at work,
green the sea, the lands are many-coloured.

This is a twelfth-century poem, celebrating Calan Haf and welcoming the new season. In Wales, *Calan Haf* or *Calan Mai* is a time for celebration and festivities as it signifies the beginning of summer, and was also traditionally when herds were turned out to pasture and when the *twmpath chwarae* (village green) was opened. Wales has a wealth of May Day customs and traditions, including:

- Beltane is one of many traditions dating to the time of the Druids. Fires are lit for Beli Mawr, the Celtic god of fire and sun, purification, science, fertility, crops and success.

- 'Spirit nights', or *ysprydnos*, took place on May Eve. It was a night when the world of the supernatural was considered to be closest to the real world.

- Villagers would gather hawthorn branches and flowers to decorate the outside of their houses to celebrate the new growth and fertility of the new season, but it was believed to be unlucky to bring them into the house.

- The maypole played a central role in Welsh May Day tradition. In south Wales, it was called *codi'r fedwen* (raising the birch). The maypole was brightly painted and the dancers would wrap ribbons around it, then it would be raised and the dancing would begin. In north Wales it was called *y gangen haf* (the summer branch), and was often decorated with silver watches and spoons. Young men dressed in white and decorated with ribbons would sing and dance around it as it was carried by another man called the *Cadi*.

2 MAY

On 2 May 1230, William de Braose (c.1197–1230) was publicly hanged on the orders of Llywelyn ap Iorwerth, after it was suspected that he had committed adultery with Llywelyn's wife Joan (Princess of Wales and Lady of Snowdon).

Born in Brecon, William de Braose was one of the most powerful barons in the Welsh Marches and held many lordships including Abergavenny and Builth. The native Welsh detested him and called him *Gwilym Ddu* (Black William).

At this time, through a series of military campaigns, astute political manoeuvrings and marriage alliances with several of the Marcher families, Llywelyn ap Iorwerth had emerged as the dominant ruler in Wales. Llywelyn captured and ransomed de Braose in 1228 and they later became allies when de Braose's daughter, Isabella, married Llywelyn's only legitimate son, Dafydd ap Llywelyn.

During Easter 1230, William paid a visit to Llywelyn at his royal court in Abergwyngregyn and was discovered in Llywelyn's bed chamber with Joan. Consequently Joan was placed under house arrest for twelve months and de Braose was hanged on 2 May. The execution jeopardised Llywelyn's good relations with the royal government and precipitated the outbreak of war in Wales in 1231. However, in 1234, Llywelyn made peace with King Henry III of England and their good relations were maintained until Llywelyn's death in 1240.

3 MAY

The General Strike of 1926 was called for by the Trades Union Congress (TUC), at one minute to midnight on 3 May 1926.

For the previous two days, a million coal miners – many of them in Wales – had been locked out of their mines over a pay dispute that would have resulted in their wages being decreased by thirteen per cent and their daily working hours increased from seven to eight. In solidarity, large numbers of people from other industries refused to work. On the first full day of action there were over 1.5 million people on strike.

The strike crippled the transport network and the roads became choked with cars. Food deliveries were held up and printing presses ground to a virtual halt. Police charged rioting strikers with batons and fights broke out.

The government reacted aggressively with the armed forces quickly brought in to escort food lorries. Volunteers got some buses and trains running, thousands of special policemen were recruited and a warship was sent to Newcastle. The government tried to exert greater control over the media by producing its own newspaper, the *British Gazette*. They used the fledgling BBC to reinforce its message, and Prime Minister Stanley Baldwin appealed to the people in a series of personal radio broadcasts to the nation.

The TUC had been involved in secret talks with the mine owners and, after nine days, called the strike off without a single concession being made to the miners' cause. Taken by surprise, the miners struggled on alone, but by the end of November most had drifted back to work.

4 MAY

Star Wars Day is celebrated on 4 May. The date was chosen as a play on the popular *Star Wars* catchphrase 'May the Force be with you'. Wales's connections to the films include:

- Richard Marquand, director of *Return of the Jedi*, was born in Cardiff.

- The full-scale model of the Millennium Falcon was built in Pembroke Dock by Marcon Fabrications.

- The Church of Jediism, a religion based on the philosophical and spiritual ideas of the Jedi as depicted in *Star Wars*, was founded in Anglesey in 2007 by Daniel M. Jones. The organisation has over 20,000 members across the globe and was the most selected 'alternative faith' in a 2012 census of England and Wales.

- Welsh actors in the films include Andy Secombe, who voiced the computer-generated slave owner Watto in *The Phantom Menace* and *Attack of the Clones*; Spencer Wilding, who played Darth Vader in *Rogue One: A Star Wars Story* and Mark Lewis Jones, who portrayed Captain Canady in *The Last Jedi*.

5 MAY

On this day in 1986, the castles and town walls of Caernarfon and Conwy, and the castles of Harlech and Beaumaris were granted World Heritage Status. They were chosen as they were considered to be among the 'finest examples of late thirteenth-century and early fourteenth-century military architecture in Europe'. The castles were built by Edward I of England following his defeat of Llywelyn ap Gruffydd in 1282 and the subsequent subjugation of Wales, to enhance his grip over the country.

6 MAY

The 6 May 1999 marked the first elections for the National Assembly of Wales (known as the Senedd since 2020). On 12 May 1999 the office of First Minister of Wales (originally known as the First Secretary for Wales) was formed as the leader of the Welsh Assembly.

The Senedd is a devolved assembly with the authority to make legislation in Wales. Initially it assumed most of the powers of the Welsh Office and Secretary of State for Wales, but following a referendum on 3 March 2011 it was able to legislate in many more areas without having to consult with the UK Parliament and was devolved further powers in 2017.

7 MAY

On 7 May 1915, during the First World War, the luxury passenger liner RMS *Lusitania* was sunk by an Imperial German Navy U-boat on her homeward voyage across the

Atlantic from New York to Liverpool. She sank within twenty minutes, and 1,198 of the 1,959 passengers aboard were killed. Arthur Rowland Jones from Prestatyn, the liner's first officer, was commended for his life-saving efforts in organising the lifeboats and picking up survivors from the sea.

A number of those lost in the sinking of the *Lusitania* had connections to Wales. These included George Davies, the conductor of the Royal Gwent Singers who were returning from touring in the United States, and who had performed 'Star Spangled Banner' and 'Wales, my Wales' as the ship was leaving New York (the other members of the group all survived).

Others with Welsh connections who perished in the sinking included David Alfred Thomas, First Viscount Rhondda, the politican and coal-mining entrepeneur, his secretary Arnold Leslie, and his daughter and prominent suffragette Lady Margaret Mackworth; Henry Adams from Tenby, the director of the Mazawattee Tea Company; Owen Ladd, a watchmaker originally from Eglwyswrw near Cardigan who had become a prominent figure within the Welsh community in Winnipeg, Canada; Henry St Giles Humphreys from Brigend, the brother of Welsh rugby international Noel Humphreys; Constance Brown from Henllan, Denbighshire; and Frederick Davies, a printer from Newport, Monmouthshire.

8 MAY

The death of David Fitzgerald, Bishop of St Davids, on 8 May 1176 led Gerald of Wales to conduct a passionate although ultimately unsuccessful campaign for Wales to have its own Archbishop.

Gerald of Wales (c.1146 – c.1223), was born at Manorbier Castle in Pembrokeshire. His father, William de Barry, was one of the most powerful Anglo-Norman barons in Wales and his mother, Angharad, was a first cousin of Rhys ap Gruffydd (Lord Rhys), native Welsh ruler of the kingdom of Deheubarth.

Gerald received his early education from his uncle David Fitzgerald, after which he went to study at the University of Paris. On his return in 1172, he was tasked by the Archbishop of Canterbury with collecting church taxes on wool and cheese for the diocese of St Davids and was subsequently Archdeacon of Brecon, an office he held until he retired.

After his uncle David Fitzgerald's death in 1176, Gerald expected to succeed him as the Bishop of St Davids, but King Henry II refused his nomination. Disappointed, Gerald went to Paris where he spent three years as a very successful lecturer.

In 1198, he was offered the Bishoprics of Bangor and Llandaff in Wales and Ferns and Leighlin in Ireland but refused them as he was still determined to become Bishop of St Davids. However, once again the King and the Archbishop of Canterbury objected to his appointment. Gerald saw this as a struggle for the recognition of St Davids as independent of Canterbury.

The conflict lasted for five years and Gerald went to Rome three times to put forward the case for St Davids to Pope Innocent III, to no avail.

9 MAY

'That's the way to do it!'

On 9 May 1662, the diarist Samuel Pepys noted seeing a Punch and Judy puppet show in Covent Garden, London. It is Mr Punch's first recorded appearance and is now recognised as his birthday in the UK.

Llandudno, Conwy, may not be the site of the first recorded Punch and Judy show but it is home to Britain's longest-running one. It was founded by Richard Codman in 1860. Richard, a travelling showman from Norwich, found himself stranded in Llandudno in 1860 when his horse died. To make a living, he collected driftwood from the beach and hand carved the Punch and Judy puppets to put on a show. The show is now in the care of the fifth generation of the Codman family and the puppets are still the original ones carved by Richard.

10 MAY

The 10 May marks the anniversary of two mining disasters in Wales.

On 10 May 1837, twenty-one men and boys were killed when the Plas yr Argoed colliery near Mold, Flintshire flooded. Among the victims were the father and two brothers of the novelist Daniel Owen, who is generally regarded as the foremost Welsh-language novelist of the nineteenth century.

On 10 May 1852 tragedy fell on the village of Pontyberem, Carmarthenshire when the Gwendraeth colliery flooded, killing all twenty-six men and boys on the night shift. It is said that it took eighteen months to recover the bodies.

11 MAY

On this day in 1963 Welshman Greville Wynne, an MI5 agent, was found guilty of spying for the West by a Moscow tribunal.

Wynne, from Ystrad Mynach, had acted as a go-between, passing on information about Soviet rockets provided for him by an informant during secret meetings in London, Paris and Moscow. Wynne was sentenced to three years in prison and five in a labour camp. The informant and his co-accused, forty-three-year-old Soviet official, Oleg Penkovsky, was given the death sentence and executed by firing squad one week after the trial. Their trials came at the height of the Cold War when relations between the superpowers were particularly strained.

Seventeen months into his sentence Wynne was exchanged for Soviet spy Gordon Lonsdale. On his release, Wynne was in poor health. He had lost a lot of weight and doctors said his time in prison had left him 'emotionally and mentally exhausted'.

Wynne went on to write about his time as a spy in a book entitled *The Man from Odessa*, which was one of the early examples of a book being published about secret work that the government never expected to be made public.

12 MAY

On 12 May 2012, Only Boys Aloud, the Welsh choir made up of boys aged fourteen to nineteen, finished third in *Britain's Got Talent*, singing their version of iconic Welsh hymn '*Calon Lân*' which subsequently became number one in the iTunes classical singles chart. The winner of the competition was the dancing dog act Ashleigh and Pudsey.

Only Boys Aloud was founded in 2010 by Tim Rhys-Evans, former musical director of Welsh National Youth Opera. In forming the choir, Rhys-Evans said that he hoped to 'inject some new blood into the Welsh tradition of choir singing' and 'to use it as a way of getting teenage boys doing something positive'. They first appeared publicly at the opening of the National Eisteddfod in Ebbw Vale in 2010.

13 MAY

On 13 May 1897, radio pioneer Guglielmo Marconi made history when he successfully transmitted a radio signal from the island of Flat Holm near Cardiff and Barry to Lavernock Point in the Vale of Glamorgan. It was the first time that a radio signal had been transmitted across open sea.

This was not Wales's only connection to Marconi's work. William Henry Preece, from Caernarfon, the chief engineer for Britain's General Post Office, admired Marconi and organised financial assistance from the Post Office that helped develop his work. This ultimately resulted in Marconi successfully transmitting from Cornwall to Newfoundland, Canada in 1901. Later Marconi set up a powerful radio station at Waunfawr, near Preece's hometown of Caernarfon.

14 MAY

William Marshal, first Earl of Pembroke, died on 14 May 1219. He was regarded by many to be the 'best knight that ever lived' and one of the most powerful men in Europe. He served four kings: Henry II, Richard the Lionheart, John and Henry III. By the time he died, people throughout Europe referred to him simply as 'the Marshal'.

William Marshal played an important role in the political and military history of Wales and the Marches. He was a benefactor of the abbeys of Tintern and Pembroke, the priory at Pill near Milford Haven and he granted the town of Haverfordwest its charter. In 1213, he also became King John's representative in south Wales and commander of the Marcher barons' struggle with Llywelyn ap Iorwerth.

15 MAY

On 15 May 1962, Emlyn Hooson won the Montgomeryshire by-election brought about by the death of Clement Davies.

In the run-up to the by-election, a rock at the roadside near Eisteddfa Gurig on the A44, midway between Llanidloes and Aberystwyth, was painted with the graffiti 'Elis' by supporters of Plaid Cymru candidate Islwyn Ffowc Elis. This was altered to 'Elvis' by pranksters and despite several attempts to remove it, kept reappearing.

Today it has become known as the Elvis Rock and is a popular landmark, even appearing on maps.

16 MAY

Dr Rice Williams of Aberystwyth (1757–1842), who died on 16 May 1842, was claimed to be the last of the Physicians of Myddfai. Williams was coroner for north Wales and responsible for the building of the Marine Baths on the Aberystwyth seafront.

A BRIEF HISTORY OF THE PHYSICIANS OF MYDDFAI:

Rhiwallon Feddyg was the physician to Lord Rhys, ruler of the kingdom of Deheubarth from 1155 to 1197, and his son Rhys Gryg. According to legend, Rhiwallon's mother was the 'Lady of the Lake' at Llyn y Fan Fach in the Brecon Beacons and from her he acquired herbal knowledge for use as medicine. In recognition of his service, Rhiwallon and his sons Cadwgan, Griffith and Einon were given land in the village of Myddfai near Llandovery. From here, knowledge of their treatments and herbal remedies spread throughout the country and their fame grew. Rhiwallon's descendants continued to practise medicine. Written sometime between 1375 and 1425, the medieval manuscript the *Red Book of Hergest* contains the family's instructions for over 500 of their preparations, using over 200 different herbs.

17 MAY

The 17 May is Twm Siôn Cati day.

Born Thomas Jones in Tregaron c.1530, Twm was the illegitimate son of Catherine Jones and the local squire. He was raised Protestant, so when the Catholic Mary I became queen, he went into hiding and initially earned his living by robbing the rich of west and mid Wales.

One tale tells how, when a farmer was looking for him for stealing one of his bullocks, Twm disguised himself as a beggar and directed the farmer into his house where he assured him the thief was. He even offered to mind his horse whilst he went in. Twm then galloped off on the horse to the farmer's house where he convinced the farmer's wife that her husband was in serious trouble and that he needed money. Suitably convinced, the farmer's wife gave Twm the money, and he then rode off on the horse to London.

Twm is also remembered for the sympathetic way he treated his many victims. There are reports that he would fire arrows to pin people to their saddle rather than killing them.

It is said that his arch-enemy was the Sheriff of Carmarthen, from whom he hid in a cave on Dinas Hill, near to village of Rhandirmwyn. However as the law officers started to close in on him, he fled to Geneva and only returned when the Protestant Elizabeth I ascended to the throne and gave him an official pardon.

Later in life, Twm changed his ways and married Joan, the heiress of Ystradffin and became a respected Justice of the Peace.

18 MAY

The first peace conference in The Hague was held on 18 May 1899. Now, this is the day each year that the people of Wales share a 'Message of Peace and Goodwill' with young people around the world.

The first message was sent in 1922 by Reverend Gwilym Davies, a pacifist who was instrumental in establishing the Welsh Union of the League of Nations. Today the message is broadcast in many different languages and reaches all corners of the world. Sir Ifan ab Owen Edwards, founder of the Urdd Gobaith Cymru (the Welsh League of Youth), decided that the Urdd should support the campaign and it is now given the responsibility of composing the message. (Find out more on 26 May.)

19 MAY

On this day in 1935, T. E. Lawrence (also known as Lawrence of Arabia) was fatally injured in a motorbike crash in Dorset.

Born in Tremadog, Carmarthenshire, Thomas Edward Lawrence gained fame as a leader of an Arab revolt against the Ottoman Empire during the First World War. Lawrence embraced Arabic culture in an attempt to empathise with his Arab partners and it was this ability that made him such a successful military leader.

Winston Churchill said of Lawrence, 'I deem him one of the greatest beings alive in our time… We shall never see his like again. His name will live in history. It will live in the annals of war… It will live in the legends of Arabia.'

20 MAY

On 20 May 2009, William Windsor (Billy), the goat of the 1st Battalion of the Royal Welsh, retired due to old age. Soldiers from the battalion lined the route from his pen to the trailer as he left the camp for the last time. He had served since 2001.

Billy was not regarded as a mascot but as a serving lance corporal. His duty was to march at the head of the battalion on ceremonial occasions. However, he was demoted to fusilier for a three-month period in 2006 after inappropriate behaviour during the Queen's Official Birthday Celebrations, when he failed to keep in step and tried to headbutt a drummer.

His replacement, William Windsor II, began as a fusilier whilst being trained for military life. He received a ration of two cigarettes per day, which he ate but he was not permitted Guinness until he was older.

The tradition of the goat possibly originated in 1775 when a wild goat walked onto the battlefield during the Battle of Bunker Hill in the American Revolutionary War.

21 MAY

'Myfanwy', arguably Wales's most famous love song, was first performed on 21 May 1875, at the opening concert of the Aberystwyth University Musical Society. The occasion was the thirty-fourth birthday of the song's composer, Joseph Parry, who, at the time, was Professor of Music at Aberystwyth University.

Joseph Parry was born in Merthyr Tydfil, one of eight

siblings of a musically talented family. At age nine, he began working in a local coal mine to help financially support his family. At twelve, he joined his father working at the Cyfarthfa Ironworks. Parry and his family emigrated to Pennsylvania in 1854, where he worked at the iron works in Danville. His interest in music resulted in him joining local choirs and becoming the organist for the Mahoning Presbyterian Church in Danville. He attended music classes which gave him the ability to compose his own music and, after winning at the Eisteddfod at Utica in 1861, he entered and was successful at the National Eisteddfod of Wales at Llandudno in 1864.

Parry subsequently travelled throughout Wales giving concerts of his own works and moved to London in 1868, where he studied at the Royal Academy of Music. During this time he became a particular favourite of Queen Victoria. Later Parry became the first Welshman to receive both Bachelor's and Doctor's degrees in music from Cambridge University. In 1874, Parry was appointed as Aberystwyth University's first Professor of Music and in 1888, took up a similar position at Cardiff University.

22 MAY

The Roman road Sarn Helen is named after St Elen whose feast day is celebrated today.

St Elen is thought to have been the daughter of the British King Octavius and the wife of Magnus Maximus (Macsen), Emperor in Britain, Gaul and Spain. She is said to have introduced into Wales the Celtic form of monasticism from Gaul. Elen's story is told in 'The Dream of Macsen Wledig', in the *Mabinogion*. Elen is also remembered for having Macsen build roads across the country so that the soldiers could more easily defend it from attackers. She is a patron of the churches of Llanelan on the Gower and at Penisa'r-waun near Caernarfon.

Maximus and Elen's daughter, Sevira, is recorded on the Pillar of Eliseg (an early medieval inscribed stone near Llangollen), which says she was married to Vortigern, King of the Britons. This gave Maximus the role of founding father of the royal dynasties of Powys and Gwent, whose kings would later use the authority of Magnus Maximus as the basis of their inherited political legitimacy. (Find out more on 28 August.)

23 MAY

On 23 May 2022, the yellow John Ystumllyn rose, symbolising friendship, community and tolerance was planted in the rose garden at Buckingham Palace. It is believed to be the first rose named after an ethnic minority Briton.

In c.1746, eight-year-old Ystumllyn was abducted in west Africa and taken into the household of the Wynn family of Ystumllyn in Criccieth, North Wales. As his true birth name was not known, he was christened John Ystumllyn. Ystumllyn soon became fluent and literate in both Welsh and English and as he showed a particular interest and aptitude for horticulture, he worked as the estate's gardener.

Ystumllyn married a local housemaid, Margaret Gruffydd in 1768, and they were both employed at the Ynysgain

Fawr estate, Criccieth. Ystumllyn later returned to the employment of the Wynn family who gave him a cottage and large garden at Y Nhyra Isa.

Ystumllyn was by all accounts, a 'very honest man, with no malice, and was respected by the gentry and the common people alike'. He died of jaundice in 1786 and was buried in St Cynhaearn's Church, Ynyscynhaearn. He was survived by Margaret and five of their children.

The John Ystumllyn rose was created after Zehra Zaidi, founder of We Too Built Britain, approached Harkness Roses following Black Lives Matter protests in summer 2020. Having grown up as a Black person in Carmarthen, Zaidi identified with Ystumllyn's experience and she chose his story because it promotes a more inclusive portrait of gardening, recognising Britain's colonial past and how many British plants have been brought over from the Empire.

24 MAY

The first Eurovision Song Contest was held in Lugano, Switzerland on 24 May 1956. Nicky Stevens is the only contestant from Wales to have won the contest.

25 MAY

On 25 May 1999, the last pit pony in south Wales, Robbie, worked his final shift underground at Pant y Gaseg, Pontypool.

In 1913 there were 70,000 ponies working underground in Britain's coal mines. Small ponies no more than twelve

WELSH EUROVISION CONTRIBUTIONS

Artist	From	Song	Year	Place
Mary Hopkin	Pontardawe	Knock, Knock Who's There?	1970	2
Nicky Stevens (*performing with Brotherhood of Man*)	Carmarthen	Save Your Kisses for Me	1976	1
Emma (*Emma Louise Booth*)	Bridgend	Give a Little Love Back to the World	1990	6
Elaine Morgan (*representing France with the band Dan Ar Braz & L'Héritage des Celtes*)	Cardiff	Diwanit Bugale (Breton-language song)	1996	19
Jessica Garlick	Kidwelly	Come Back	2002	3
James Fox	Bargoed	Hold On To Our Love	2004	16
Jon Lilygreen (*representing Cyprus with The Islanders*)	Newport	Life Looks Better in Spring	2010	21
Bonnie Tyler	Skewen	Believe in Me	2013	19
Joe Woolford (*performing with 'Joe and Jake'*)	Ruthin	You're Not Alone	2016	24
Lucie Jones	Pentrych	Never Give Up on You	2017	15

hands high were needed, with Shetlands commonly used. The ponies were stabled underground, coming to the surface only during the colliery's annual holiday. They would work an eight-hour shift, during which they might haul thirty tons of coal.

The ponies were gradually replaced by mechanised haulage and by 1984 only fifty-five ponies were still in use.

26 MAY

The first Urdd National Eisteddfod was held on this day in 1929 at Corwen in north Wales. It is one of the biggest youth festivals in Europe and is hosted by a different area of Wales each year, with over 15,000 young people competing during the week in a variety of events including dancing, singing and drama. The competitors are the winners of local and regional rounds held earlier in the spring. The pavilion, seating 1,800 people, is the focal point of the event, but the Eisteddfod field, the *maes*, has stalls, live music and sporting events. It is one of the most popular cultural events in Wales, attracting 100,000 visitors each year.

Sir Ifan ab Owen Edwards established Urdd Gobaith Cymry in 1922, with the aim of protecting the Welsh language. Sir Ifan's father, O. M. Edwards, was Wales's first Chief Inspector for Education and, in 1892, established a monthly magazine *Cymru'r Plant* (Children's Wales), which encouraged awareness amongst the Welsh people of their country's culture and traditions. He twice unsuccessfully attempted to establish a youth movement for the young people of Wales, and so, following O. M. Edwards's death in 1920 when Sir Ifan became the editor for *Cymru'r Plant* he was inspired to fulfil his father's dream. He appealed to the youth of Wales to join Urdd Gobaith Cymru Fach and received such a positive response that the first local Urdd branch was established in Treuddyn, Flintshire by 1922.

27 MAY

The 27 May marks the feast day of St Melangell, patron saint of hares and rabbits.

Prince Brochwel Ysgithrog was hunting near Pennant in AD 604 when his hounds chased a hare into a thicket. Here they found a beautiful maiden at prayer. The hare sheltered under the hem of her garment, and the dogs fled. The prince discovered that the lady was Melangell, a king's daughter who had fled Ireland to escape a forced marriage. He gave her the valley as a place of sanctuary. Melangell remained there in the valley, where she founded a nunnery.

28 MAY

On 28 May 1865 the clipper ship *Mimosa* carrying 153 Welsh emigrants and bound for Patagonia in Argentina finally set sail from Liverpool after being delayed for three days due to a bad storm. Their aim was to establish Y Wladfa, a Welsh colony in the Chubut River valley in a bid to preserve the Welsh language and culture.

The notion of a Welsh colony in South America had been proposed by Professor Michael D. Jones, a non-conformist preacher based in Bala. He had spent several years in the United States, where Welsh settlers had adapted to a new lifestyle very quickly. He advocated establishing a Welsh-speaking colony far from the influence of the English language in Patagonia. The destination was chosen not only for its isolated position but the Argentines had also offered a hundred square miles of land along the Chubut River.

Pushing their meagre belongings and food in wheelbarrows, the settlers walked forty miles across the desert to the proposed site for the colony. Here, where the river Camwy (known to Argentinians as the Rio Chubut) cuts through the desert from the nearby Andes, the permanent settlement of Rawson was established. At first, though, the colony looked as if it were doomed to failure.

Unfortunately, the settlers found that Patagonia was not the fertile land they had been promised. They had been led to believe that it was similar to the fertile lowlands of Wales. In fact, it was a windswept pampas, with no water and very few sources of food. To make things more difficult, whilst the settlers on the *Mimosa* included miners, carpenters, brick makers, cobblers and tailors, there were very few farmers. This proved to be a serious disadvantage, as the terrain was dry and dusty and it was difficult to grow crops. Also, there were no woodlands to provide building materials or shelter. Some of the settlers' first homes were simply dug out from the soft rock of the cliffs in the bay.

Life for the settlers was made even more difficult by arguments over land ownership, bad harvests and floods, and there was no direct route to the ocean to import necessities. Without the help of the indigenous Tehuelche people, the settlement may not have survived the early food shortages. (Find out more on 19 April.)

Simple irrigation of the Chubut River was successful, and over the next several years, new settlers arrived from both Wales and Pennsylvania. By the end of 1874, the settlement had a population of 270, with a patchwork of farms beginning to emerge. In 1875, the Welsh settlers were granted official title to the land by the Argentine Government, and this encouraged many more people to join the colony, with more than 500 arriving from Wales. There were further migrations from Wales between 1880–87, and 1904–12. The settlers had seemingly achieved their utopia with Welsh-speaking chapels, schools and local government.

29 MAY

On 29 May 1953 Edmund Hillary and Sherpa Tenzing Norgay were the first to conquer the summit of Everest. However, it could easily have been a Welshman, Charles Evans, planting a flag on the highest mountain in the world. Evans, who was raised in Wales and was a fluent Welsh speaker, was a senior member of the 1953 expeditional team and had been nominated as the one to make the final ascent. He was only 300 metres short of the summit when he had trouble with his oxygen equipment and had to return to Everest base camp, leaving Hillary and Tenzing to take the glory. The first Welshman to reach the summit was ultimately Caradog 'Craig' Jones from Pontrhydfendigaid, near Tregaron, on 23 May 1995, and the first Welsh woman was Tori James from Pembrokeshire, on 24 May 2007. At twenty-five she also became the youngest British woman to achieve the feat.

(The mountain's Tibetan name is *Chomolungma,* meaning 'Mother Goddess of the World' and its Sanskrit name *Sagarmatha* means 'Peak of Heaven'.) But Mount Everest's English name actually comes from a Welshman; in 1865 the Royal Geographical Society named it after Colonel Sir George Everest from Crickhowell, who was the Surveyor General of India from 1830–43.

30 MAY

On this day in 1929, Lady Megan Arfon Lloyd George (1902–1966) became Wales's first female MP when she won Anglesey for the Liberals.

As the daughter of the former Prime Minister David Lloyd George, and the dominant figure in Welsh politics, Megan Lloyd George's selection to fight the then safe Liberal seat of Anglesey in 1929 was a matter of some controversy. Megan's brother Gwilym was already an MP and it seemed to some that David Lloyd George was intent on creating his own dynastic power base. Suggestions of nepotism faded as Megan began a parliamentary career that, despite a lengthy interruption in the 1950s, would span thirty years. Although the declining fortunes of the Liberals would keep her out of high office – the last Liberal government was that of her father – she nevertheless became Deputy Leader of the party and a prominent political personality in her own right. Welsh issues were high on her agenda, with her campaigns leading to significant concessions to Welsh interests both in parliament and in the apparatus of government.

Defeated on Anglesey by Cledwyn Hughes in 1951, she defected to the Labour cause soon afterwards – one of the several prominent figures to do so. She returned to Parliament in 1957 after winning Carmarthen for Labour and remained an MP until her death nine years later.

31 MAY

Robert Edwards (1716–c.1788) was a Welsh buccaneer given seventy-seven acres of then largely unsettled land in Manhattan, US for his services in disrupting Spanish sea lanes. On 1 June 1778 Edwards leased the land for ninety-nine years to John and George Cruger on the agreement that the land and all improvements thereon were to revert to the descendants of Edwards and his siblings when the lease expired on 31 May 1877. Apparently, this never happened, and the land ended up in the hands of Trinity Church, of which the Crugers were wardens.

Subsequently, all attempts by Edward's heirs to file a claim to the land have proved fruitless, with the case eventually being defeated by the state's statute of limitations.

1 JUNE

On 1 June 1831, the symbolic socialist red flag was raised for the first time in Wales at the Merthyr Rising.

The Merthyr Rising started as a popular rebellion against unjust working and living conditions, but quickly rose into armed insurrection, which has been described by historian John Davies as 'the most ferocious and bloody event in the history of industrialised Britain'. The Great Depression of 1829 led to massive unemployment and, when Merthyr ironmaster William Crawshay lowered his employee's wages, the panic in the town led to a series of local demonstrations. One, led by Thomas Llewelyn, a Cyfartha miner, resulted in prisoners being released. Another marched from Hirwaun on Merthyr,

raiding property and shops to return previously confiscated goods to their owners.

In an attempt to restore order, Scots Highlanders from the Brecon Barracks were sent in and opened fire on a large crowd that had assembled outside the Castle Inn. Over two dozen of the crowd were killed and hundreds wounded. However the Highlanders were forced to retreat and the following day the Swansea Yeomanry were sent in, but they were ambushed and disarmed. It took a week for order to be restored and the resulting punishment was severe, with Richard Lewis (known as Dic Penderyn) being hanged at Cardiff Gaol on the charge of wounding a soldier. (Find out more on 13 August.)

2 JUNE

On 2 June 1982, Pope John Paul II became the first reigning Pope to visit Wales.

The pontiff celebrated Mass in Pontcanna Fields for over 100,000 people and his message in Welsh of '*Bendith Duw arnoch*' ('the blessing of God be on you') was received with enthusiastic applause from the crowd. Earlier in the day he had been awarded the freedom of Cardiff. After the Mass, he addressed a gathering of over 33,000 young people at Ninian Park, the home of Cardiff City F.C. at the time, where he called on the young people of Britain to launch a crusade of prayer.

3 JUNE

The first women's suffrage meeting in Wales was held at the Temperance Hall in Merthyr Tydfil on 3 June 1870. Suffrage is defined as the right to vote in political elections without restriction due to gender, race, religion, social status, education level or wealth. Notable campaigners for women's suffrage with Welsh connections include:

- **Rose Mary Crawshay**, who married into Merthyr's great iron dynasty, was a fervent supporter of the early feminist movement and signee of the first women's suffrage petition in 1866.

- **Millicent Mackenzie** was professor of education at Cardiff University and a founder member of the Cardiff branch of the suffragette movement. In 1918 she was the first woman to stand for Parliament in Wales.

- **Elizabeth Andrews**, from Penderyn near Hirwaun. (Find out more on 8 March.)

- **Margaret Haig Mackworth**, Viscountess Rhondda, secretary of the WSPU's Newport branch, who attempted to destroy a postbox with a bomb, which resulted in her serving a period of time in prison, only being released after going on a hunger strike.

· **Rachel Barrett**, from Carmarthen, who was national organiser for the WSPU and put in charge of the *Suffragette* newspaper.

· **Megan Lloyd George,** the daughter of prime minister David Lloyd George, who became Wales's first female MP in 1929. (Find out more about Megan on 30 May.)

4 JUNE

On this day in 1039, Gruffydd ap Llywelyn, King of Gwynedd and Powys, defeated a Mercian army at Rhyd y Groes near Welshpool.

Gruffydd ap Llywelyn (c.1007–1063 or 1064) was the son of Llywelyn ap Seisyll, King of Gwynedd and Deheubarth, who claimed descendance from Hywel Dda. Gruffydd is known as 'the only Welsh king ever to rule over the entire territory of Wales'. This was a claim he himself made after a victory over an English army near Glasbury in 1056, and one the English also recognised.

According to an ancient story, Gruffydd had been a lazy youth, but one New Year's Eve he was watching a cook boiling pieces of beef in a cauldron. The cook was complaining that there was one piece of meat that kept coming to the top of the cauldron, however often it was thrust down. Gruffydd took this as a lesson for himself, and thus began his rise to power.

5 JUNE

On 5 June 2022, Wales qualified for the 2022 men's FIFA World Cup tournament in Qatar by defeating Ukraine 1–0 in a play-off final in Cardiff.

It is, to date, only the second time the Wales national football team has reached the World Cup Finals. The other occasion was the 1958 finals held in Sweden where Wales went on to cause a shock by progressing to the quarter-finals after beating Hungary 2–1. Critically, Wales were without their best player for the quarter-final – the 'Gentle Giant' John Charles, who was injured, and they were defeated 1–0 by the eventual champions, Brazil. The winning goal was the first World Cup goal scored by the great Pele. (Find out more about this historic goal on 2 February.)

6 JUNE

Ann Thomas (the 'Maid of Cefn Ydfa') who died pining for her true love, was buried on 6 June 1727 in St Cynwyd's Church, Llangynwyd, near Maesteg.

Ann was born in 1704, a cousin of philosopher Richard Price. Her father died in 1706 and she was placed in the wardship of her uncle, Rhys Price of Tynton Farm, Llangenior. Anthony Maddocks from Cwmrisga was the solicitor and advisor for the Prices of Tynton and persuaded the family that Ann should marry his son, also called Anthony.

According to folklore, Ann had, however, already fallen in love with the poet and thatcher Wil Hopcyn. When this was discovered, she was forbidden to see him.

Ann and Wil continued sending secret love letters to

each other but these were uncovered by Ann's mother, who confiscated her writing materials. Unable to be with Ann, Hopcyn left the area and Ann was forced to marry Anthony Maddocks against her wishes. She is said to have pined so badly for her lost love that she fell seriously ill. The story goes that, on her death bed, she requested to see Hopcyn for the last time who arrived in time for Ann to die in his arms. In reality, it's quite possible than Ann actually died either during childbirth, or from an illness like smallpox or typhoid rather than of a broken heart.

7 JUNE

Gwenllian ferch Llywelyn (1282–1337), the only child of Llywelyn ap Gruffydd, Prince of Wales, died on 7 June 1337 in Sempringham Priory, Lincolnshire.

Gwenllian's mother, Eleanor de Montfort, had died during her birth or soon after and a few months later, her father was killed in battle against Edward I's English army so Gwenllian's uncle, Dafydd ap Gruffydd, assumed her guardianship in 1283. North Wales was encircled by the English army and Dafydd was captured and executed at Shrewsbury.

Gwenllian was taken by Edward I and sent to the Gilbertine Priory at Sempringham, to prevent her from marrying and having sons who might lay claim to the Principality of Wales. Sempringham was chosen because of its remote location and was run by the Gilbertines, an order of nuns that were hidden from view behind high walls. Having been taken from her native land so young, Gwenllian never learned any Welsh and she signed her name 'Wentliane' or 'Wencilian', but her royal rank was acknowledged at least once by Edward when he asked the Pope for money for Sempringham Priory stating that 'herein is kept the daughter of the Prince of Wales, whom we have to maintain'.

There is a memorial stone of Welsh blue slate to her memory in Sempringham and there is also a plaque at the summit of Snowdon.

8 JUNE

The Viking attack on the monastery at Lindisfarne on 8 June 793 is generally considered to mark the beginning of the Viking Age in Britain.

Through a courageous defence and a series of alliances with both the Vikings and the Anglo-Saxons, it would appear that the Welsh kingdoms managed to hold on to a considerable amount of autonomy and were not colonised to the degree that eastern England and Ireland were after the arrival of the Vikings.

Rhodri ap Merfyn (otherwise known as Rhodri Mawr or Rhodri the Great) ruler of Gwynedd (844–78) was instrumental in repelling Viking raids and won a significant victory in 856 in which the Danish King Gorm was killed.

In 893, forces from Gwent, Glywysing and Gwynedd fought with those from Mercia and Wessex to defeat a Danish army at the Battle of Buttington (thought to be near Welshpool). However, in 895 the Danes launched raids into Brycheiniog, Gwent, Gwynllwg, Morgannwg and Buellt. Then, in 899, the Norse of Dublin embarked on a series of raids into Anglesey during which Merfyn ap Rhodri, King of Powys, was killed.

In around 909, Hywel Dda became King of Seisyllwg (modern day Ceredigion and parts of Carmarthenshire). As a result of his policy of maintaining good relations with the English kings, there were no significant Viking raids in Wales during his reign. Following Hywel's death in 950, Viking raids became more numerous, especially on religious centres. In 987, Vikings seized 2,000 men from Anglesey and sold them as slaves and in 989, Maredudd ab Owain of Deheubarth was obliged to pay a tribute to the Vikings – likely in the form of gold, cattle or slaves.

Gruffydd ap Cynan, King of Gwynedd (1081–1137) was of Norse ancestry, as his mother Ragnhilda was the daughter of Olaf Sigtryggsson, king of the Norse settlement in Dublin. In 1081, Gruffydd was assisted by the Norse from Waterford in taking the throne of Gwynedd and in 1098, Magnus Barefoot, King of Norway, supported Gruffydd in driving a Norman force from Anglesey.

Place names of Norse origin in Wales include:

· **Anglesey:** from the Nordic *Önguls ey*, meaning the island of Öngul.

· **Worms Head** (on Gower Peninsula): from *orm*, meaning dragon.

· **Great Orme** (near Llandudno): from *orms-höfuthl*, meaning snake's head.

- **Stack Rock** (in Pembrokeshire): from *stakk*, meaning pillar-shaped.

- **Swansea:** from *Sweyns ey*, meaning Sweyn's island.

- The names of the islands of Skokholm, Grassholm and Skomer are also of Norse origin.

9 JUNE

Milford Haven was founded on 9 June 1790.

The town is named after the natural harbour of Milford Haven, where the shelter it offers was used by the Vikings. It was described by Shakespeare in *Cymbeline* as 'blessed Milford'. It was used as a staging point for the invasions of Ireland by Henry II in 1171, and Oliver Cromwell in 1649, as well as a landing point for the French reinforcements for the Glyndŵr Rising in 1405 and by Henry VII in 1485 prior to his march through Wales to take the English crown.

Following its founding, Milford Haven was a whaling centre, but by 1800 it was developed by the Royal Navy as a dockyard. When the dockyard was transferred to Pembroke in 1814, Milford Haven then became a commercial dock, and a successful fishing port and boat building centre. By the start of the twentieth century, Milford was the sixth largest fishing port in the UK.

During the Second World War Milford Haven was a base for approximately 1,000 American military personnel and played a significant role in preparations for D-Day. In 1960, Esso opened an oil refinery near the town, which was followed by other big oil companies. By 1974, Milford's oil trade was three times that of all of the other Welsh ports combined and by the early 1980s, Esso's refinery was the second largest in the UK. However in 1996 the area was affected by a substantial oil spill when the oil tanker *Sea Empress* ran aground.

10 JUNE

The Heyope hoard was found during ploughing on Cwmjenkin Farm, Heyope, near Beguildy in Powys on 10 June 1955. The hoard comprised of three gold ribbon torcs crushed into a ball and is the only known find of Middle Bronze Age (1400–1275 BC) in Wales. This find and a subsequent similar discovery in Somerset suggested a deliberate re-combining of these gold ornaments before they were returned to the ground. Gold ornaments were status symbols designed to demonstrate wealth and power and their hoarding and burial is possibly symbolic and linked to the death of the people who wore them. Alternatively, the symbolism of creating a ball of gold objects could be related to worship of the sun.

11 JUNE

On 11 June 1916, an abandoned distillery in Frongoch, near Bala, became an internment camp for 1,863 Irish prisoners following the Irish Republican Easter Rising.

Previously, the site had held German prisoners of war who were relocated to accommodate the junior officers and rank-and-file members of the Irish Republican movement, notably including Michael Collins and Arthur Griffith. British authorities had previously executed fifteen of the leaders of the rising, with the surviving leaders being sent to high-security prisons. The camp however, became a breeding ground for the revolution in Ireland, with Collins, for example, giving impromptu lessons in guerrilla tactics. Indeed, Frongoch transformed the rebel army into the driving force behind the subsequent Irish War of Independence.

Prisoners were permitted to exercise with route marches across the Welsh countryside and to organise fancy dress competitions, seasonal games at Halloween and sporting challenge matches. A typical example was the athletics day, in which Collins won the hundred yard race in 10.8 seconds.

The region of Wales in which the Irish prisoners found themselves ironically bore many similarities to Ireland. The local population had also suffered from evictions and enforced emigration, and soon after, established a Land Commission modelled on the Irish Land League, even inviting its instigator, Michael Davitt, to address a meeting at Blaenau Ffestiniog.

12 JUNE

The Welsh National War Memorial, located in Cathays Park, Cardiff, was unveiled on 12 June 1929.

The memorial consists of a circular colonnade enveloping bronze figures of an airman, a soldier and a sailor, each raising a wreath to a central elevated figure of a winged messenger of victory who holds a sword aloft. It was designed by J. Ninian Comper and now commemorates the servicemen who died during the two World Wars.

13 JUNE

A courageous but ultimately tragic attempt to reach the North Pole in a tiny ship built in a Welsh dockyard came to an untimely end on 13 June 1881.

In 1861, *The Pandora* was launched from Pembroke Dockyard and used for a series of voyages to the Arctic in 1875 and 1876. Then in 1877, she was sold to the rich and eccentric New York newspaper magnate James Gordon Bennett Jr, who renamed her *Jeanette*. In 1879, he sent her on a trip to the North Pole through the Bering Strait, under the command of Lt. Commander George De Long. Disaster struck when she became caught in the ice and, for eighteen months, drifted northwards closer and closer to the pole. During this time they did however discover and claim the islands of Jeanette, Henrietta and Bennett for the United States.

On the morning of 13 June 1881, the pressure of the ice began to crush the ship's hull, which split and the ship disappeared under the ice. De Long and his men had to trek over the ice to the Siberian coast, pulling their supplies in the long boats they had rescued from the *Jeannette*. It was a hard and brutal journey and, just as they thought they had reached open water, they ran into a storm. One of the boats capsized and eight crewmen were drowned. The other two boats were separated in the gale. In De Long's boat, sick in body and despairing in their hearts, most of the men died one after the other – De Long amongst them. Only two of the sailors managed to eventually reach safety. In the third boat, eleven men survived the elements to make it home.

DID YOU KNOW?

The expression 'Gordon Bennett' was probably coined after James Gordon Bennett Jr who had something of a reputation for being an outrageous playboy and causing surprise.

---

14 JUNE

Nine days of race riots in Newport ended when Welsh Regiment troops were sent in on 14 June 1919. The riots started in the docklands where a majority of Caribbean and some African people worked as sailors, sea merchants and manual labourers. A Black man allegedly accosted a white girl and a soldier intervened, knocking the Black man to the ground. During the ensuing disturbances – which involved violence using revolvers, pokers and sticks – a Chinese laundry, refreshment houses and lodging houses were wrecked. The *South Wales Argus* reported that 'White mobs wrecked so many properties that the town looked as if it had suffered an air raid.'

The rioting culminated the next day, with thousands involved in an affray that was only quelled by a police baton charge. There was extensive damage to property, but no serious injuries. The riots resulted in thirty arrests of which twenty-seven were Black people. Given the violence from both sides this was indicative of the racism of the authorities at the time and it has subsequently been concluded that non-whites received far harsher retribution.

This was one of several riots that were sparked by racial tensions in British ports that spring, and was associated with the demobilisation of the armed forces after the First World War into a society suffering from economic crisis.

15 JUNE

On 15 June 1910, Robert Falcon Scott's expedition to the North Pole began when the *Terra Nova* sailed from Cardiff. It departed in front of a huge crowd, flying the flag and coat of arms of the city.

The *Terra Nova* Expedition, also known as the British Antarctic Expedition, aimed to be the first to reach the geographical South Pole. However when they reached the pole on 17 January 1912, they found that the Norwegian team led by Roald Amundsen had beaten them to it.

All of Scott's party perished on the return journey and

a memorial lighthouse, erected in 1915, still exists on Cardiff's Roath Park Lake. (Find out more about the expedition and Wales's connection to it on 17 February.)

16 JUNE

Nelson Mandela received the Freedom of the City of Cardiff on 16 June 1998.

Mandela's visit to Wales attracted a huge public interest: tickets to the freedom ceremony at Cardiff Castle were in high demand, and cheering crowds greeted him throughout the day. During a walkabout prior to the ceremony, he took time out to sing with a group of local schoolchildren. Accepting the honour, Mr Mandela acknowledged the magnificent support that the people of South Africa had received from the Welsh during their struggle against apartheid and described the people of Wales as their friends.

17 JUNE

The Ukrainian city of Donetsk was founded by a Welshman who died on this day in 1889.

Born in Merthyr Tydfil, John Hughes (1814–17 June 1889) followed in his father's footsteps to become an engineer. He worked in Ebbw Vale and Newport, where he patented inventions in armaments and armour plating. He later moved to London, where he became a director of the Millwall Engineering and Shipbuilding Company who specialised in iron cladding for the British Admiralty's wooden warships.

When the company received an order from the Russian Empire in 1870 to plate a naval fortress at Kronstadt on the Baltic Sea, Hughes went out with eight shiploads of equipment and specialist ironworkers and miners, mostly from south Wales, to build a rail producing factory and metallurgical plant. The settlement that grew in the shadow of Hughes's factory was named after him and hence, the town of Hughesovka (now called Donetsk) was born. The town grew rapidly and Hughes provided schools, a hospital, tea rooms, bath houses, a fire brigade and an Anglican church dedicated to St David and St George.

Following Hughes's death in 1889, the company was taken over by his four sons. They rapidly expanded the works, especially with the need for artillery shells at the outbreak of the First World War in 1914. The Bolshevik Revolution of 1917 led to the departure of almost all the company's foreign employees, but the works prospered under Communist rule.

18 JUNE

The Battle of Waterloo occurred on this day in 1815.

During the battle, the 23rd Royal Welch Fusiliers were positioned on the crest behind Hougoumont, where they were ravaged by cannonballs and harassed by regular cavalry attacks the whole day, knowing that they formed the cornerstone of the front line and that they must hold at all costs. Out of an initial force of 641, the 23rd lost eighteen men, with eighty-six wounded.

Sir Thomas Picton from Poyston, near Haverfordwest

was the highest ranking victim of the battle on the Allied side. It's reported that he fought the battle wearing his civilian clothes and a top hat, as his luggage had not arrived in time. Opinion on Picton was at the time divided and it remains so now. He was seen as a military hero, a roisterer, a duellist and a fornicator. He also gained notoriety as the 'blood-soaked governor' of Trinidad from 1797–1803 and was described by Wellington as 'a rough, foul-mouthed devil as ever lived'. In one of the greatest scandals of the age, he was recalled to London and found guilty of the brutal execution, torture and mutilation of slaves. However, a retrial found Picton's behaviour, although deplorable, was legal, which allowed him to continue his military career.

Public monuments were erected to Picton's memory in St Paul's Cathedral and Carmarthen. However, in 2021, Carmarthenshire Council announced that information boards were going to be placed near Picton's monument in Carmarthen to give a fuller picture of his controversial career.

19 JUNE

On 19 June 916, Æthelflæd, Lady of the Mercians raided Brycheiniog to avenge the death of Ecgberht, a Mercian monk. She captured the Queen of Brycheiniog along with thirty-three others from the royal *llys* (royal court) on a *crannog* (man-made island) in Llangorse Lake near Brecon.

Æthelflæd was the eldest daughter of Alfred the Great, King of Wessex, and ruled Mercia from 911 to her death on 12 June 918. The Queen of Brycheiniog at the time was probably the wife or mother of King Tewdwr ab Elisedd.

Prior to Æthelflæd's raid, the threat of raids from Viking and neighbouring Welsh kingdoms had forced Brycheiniog to seek the help of Alfred the Great. However, the effect of the assault seems to have persuaded the kings of Brycheiniog to accept the overlordship of the newly formed kingdom of Deheubarth under the rule of Hywel Dda. Following the Norman Conquest of England in 1066, native Welsh resistance suffered a devastating blow with the defeat and death of the King of Deheubarth, Rhys ap Tewdwr in 1093. Rhys's death marked the beginning of significant Norman expansion into south Wales. Brycheiniog was seized by the Norman lord Bernard de Neufmarche who converted it into the Lordship of Brecknock.

DID YOU KNOW?

Llangorse Lake is the largest natural lake in south Wales and in Welsh mythology is the home of the Afanc – a lake monster described as taking the form of a giant beaver or a large crocodile, which devoured anyone or anything that entered its waters. One legend tells of the wild thrashings of the Afanc causing flooding. Another tells of a maiden trying to tame the Afanc and letting it sleep in her lap, whilst other villagers attempt to capture it. However, the Afanc awakes and crushes the maiden.

20 JUNE

The Kidwelly and Llanelli Canal and Tramroad Company came into being through an Act of Parliament on 20 June 1812. The Kidwelly and Llanelli Canal was an extension to Kymer's Canal in Kidwelly, Carmarthenshire, Wales's first major canal of significant length at approximately three miles.

Thomas Kymer had started mining coal in the Gwendraeth Valley in 1760 and in 1766 he was granted approval by the government to construct a canal and tramroad from his coal mine at Pwll y Llygod to a dock that he built at Ythyn Frenig, close to Kidwelly. The Act also allowed him to divert the course of the Gwendraeth Fawr River to avoid the Kidwelly to Llanelli turnpike road that crossed the river at Pont Spwdwr.

However, navigation into the dock became dangerously affected by silting and so it was decided to extend the canal to Llanelli via Pembrey through the creation of the Kidwelly and Llanelli Canal and Tramroad Company.

There are two notable features on Kymer's canal: a stone tramroad bridge over the Gwendraeth River, and the low arched Glastony aqueduct.

21 JUNE

The summer solstice is the first day of astronomical summer and the longest day of the year – people in the northern hemisphere generally celebrate it between the 20 and 22 June.

In ancient times, solstices and equinoxes were important

in helping people to maintain calendars and grow crops. The solstice has constituted a special moment of the annual cycle of the year since Neolithic times and over the centuries has been marked by festivals and celebrations.

In Wales, the solstice is called *Gŵyl Ifan Ganol Haf* (St John's of Midsummer). Historically it was marked by great agricultural fairs, which included dancing, merriment and the lighting of bonfires.

Welsh tradition says that gathering St John's wort on the night before the summer solstice would bring good luck and imbue it with extra healing powers. Mistletoe was particularly important to the Celtic Druids, as it was believed to cure all ills. On Midsummer Eve, it is reported that they would cut it with a golden scythe and catch it in a cloth before it touched the ground. A sprig of mistletoe gathered on Midsummer Eve and placed under the pillow was said to bring prophetic dreams. Branches from birch trees were used to decorate maypoles and town squares.

DID YOU KNOW?

Dating to around 2000 BC, there is open burial chamber at Bryn Celli Ddu on Anglesey. The chamber is so perfectly aligned that for only twenty minutes each year, as the sun rises on the summer solstice, a beam of sunlight aligns exactly with the opening to the chamber and shines shafts of light down the tomb's passageway and into the chamber.

22 JUNE

On this day in 1402 the Battle of Bryn Glas, which was part of the Glyndŵr Rising, occurred at Pilleth near Knighton. It was Owain Glyndŵr's greatest victory, with the vastly outnumbered and poorly armed Welsh army defeating a far superior English one.

The battle resulted in the collapse of English governance in Wales. For the English, it was a national humiliation on such a scale that within days, news had reached Rome and it led to the destabilisation of English politics for several years afterwards.

By 1401, Glyndŵr's uprising had been on the verge of collapse. Henry IV had toured north Wales, hanging suspected rebels and pillaging settlements. The two-tier society where Englishmen held privileges above Welshmen was re-emerging. However, in early 1402, Glyndŵr galvanised his support, the rebellion was reinvigorated and he had taken Ruthin and held Lord Grey, Henry's trusted counsellor, for ransom. In riposte, Henry raised an army of 2,000 men from Herefordshire and appointed Edmund Mortimer as commander. On June 22, 1402, when Glyndŵr was near Knighton the two armies confronted each other.

Although heavily outnumbered, Glyndŵr gambled on dividing his army. Knowing that the majority, including his archers, held the higher ground, he hid a small detachment in a valley to the left. As Mortimer's army advanced up the slope, they came into range of the Welsh archers and before they could return fire they were showered with arrows. Then two crucial events turned the battle: firstly the concealed Welsh troops joined in the conflict and then some Welsh archers, who had infiltrated Mortimer's force, turned and fired into the English ranks.

The English army was routed and 600 of them were killed. It is said that after the battle, Welsh women camp followers dismembered many of the English victims in reprisal for their acts of brutality and rape in the preceding campaigns. Sir Edmund Mortimer was taken prisoner. When Henry IV made no effort to pay a ransom for him, he switched his allegiance to Glyndŵr and married his daughter, Caitrin.

23 JUNE

On 23 June 2012, Christine James became both the first woman and the first Welsh learner to be appointed Archdruid of the National Eisteddfod of Wales. Brought up in an English-speaking household in Tonypandy, Ms James learnt Welsh at school in Porth and Aberystwyth University. The Archdruid presides over the most important ceremonies at the National Eisteddfod including Chairing of the Bard, Crowning of the Bard and The Award of the Prose Medal.

24 JUNE

On 24 June 1277, King Edward I began his first campaign against the Welsh following Llywelyn ap Gruffydd's refusal to pay him homage.

A timeline of the First War of Welsh Independence:

1267 Llywelyn ap Gruffydd and Henry III of England agreed to The Treaty of Montgomery in which Henry III agreed to recognise Llewelyn as Prince of Wales. He also accepted that the title should descend to Llewelyn's heirs and all other Welsh rulers had to pay homage to Llewelyn, while Llewelyn agreed to pay homage to the English monarch in exchange for his support.

1272 Edward I became King of England.

1274 After failing in an assassination attempt on Llywelyn, Gruffydd ap Gwenwynwyn of Powys and Llywelyn's younger brother Dafydd ap Gruffydd defected to the English.

1275 Edward demanded that Llywelyn come to Chester to pay homage to him. Llywelyn refused.

1275 Llywelyn was married by proxy to Eleanor, which antagonised Edward further as she was the daughter of Simon de Montfort, the leader of a rebellion against the crown during the reign of Edward's father, Henry III.

1276 Edward declared war on Llywelyn and when Eleanor sailed from France to meet Llewelyn, Edward hired pirates to seize her ship and imprisoned her at Windsor Castle.

1277 On 24 June, Llywelyn refused to pay homage to Edward.

1277 In July, Edward launched a punitive expedition into Wales with a force of 15,500. English armies were successfully deployed from Carmarthen in Deheubarth, from Chester in Powys Fadog and also from Builth, Brycheiniog and Gwrtheyrnion. Overwhelmed by the magnitude of the invading force, Llywelyn, realising that his position was hopeless, surrendered. In November 1277, Llywelyn was forced to accept The Treaty of Aberconwy.

According to the terms of the Treaty, the concessions granted by the earlier Treaty of Montgomery were effectively removed and Llywelyn had to undergo the humiliation of swearing oaths of fealty, pay Edward a fine of £50,000 and lose the fealty of the other Welsh rulers. He was left with only Uwch Conwy (the lands west of the river Conwy) but allowed to still use the title of Prince of Wales. Once signed, Edward began building the castles of Flint, Rhuddlan, Aberystwyth and Builth.

25 JUNE

The Battle of Little Bighorn is a well-known story. Less well-known is that one of the men of the 7th Cavalry, who fought to the death alongside Lieutenant Colonel George Armstrong Custer of the US Army on 25 June 1876, was a farmer's son from Pembrokeshire.

Sergeant William B. James was from Pencnwc Farm, in Dinas Cross, near Newport. Following the death of his father and two sisters, William went to America to look for a new start in 1872. He ultimately became a soldier and rose rapidly up the ranks to sergeant in only three years, a promotion that normally took twelve years at the time. In a sad twist of fate, records show he had just one year left on his contract in the army and had saved $80 to secure a brighter future when he was killed.

Little Bighorn was the US Army's worst defeat during the Plains Wars of 1854–79. By the 1860s, settlers and the US government had either forced most Native Americans onto reservations or killed them, and warriors from the Lakota Sioux and Cheyenne Nations were attempting to resist this happening to them. In 1874 the US Government broke a treaty that recognised the South Dakota Black Hills as part of the Great Sioux Reservation, and Custer led an excursion of miners to search for gold there. Custer's task also involved relocating all the Native Americans in the area to the reservations.

Thousands of Sioux, Cheyenne and Lakota Indians rebelled and gathered at Little Bighorn River to resist this, under the warriors Sitting Bull and Crazy Horse. Three army columns, including Custer's 7th Cavalry, were dispatched to Montana to return the resisting Native Americans to the reservations.

After spotting a Sioux village and a group of forty warriors along the Rosebud River, Custer attacked. But he had grossly underestimated the number of warriors in the village and was soon massively outnumbered. Custer and all of his 210 men were killed.

Outraged at the death of a famed Civil War hero, the nation demanded retribution. Within a year, the US Army had either forced all resisting Native Americans to relocate or killed them.

26 JUNE

Cardiff's Millennium Stadium (known as the Principality Stadium since 2016) was opened on 26 June 1999. Initially built to host the 1999 men's Rugby World Cup, it replaced the National Stadium of Wales, which had stood on the same site, and had increased capacity, had better access to the grounds and gave better visibility to the playing area.

- The first major event to be held was an international rugby match on 26 June 1999 when Wales beat South Africa by 29–19, the first time they had ever beaten the Springboks.

- It has a seating capacity of 73,931 (up from the 53,000 the National Stadium of Wales could hold, which would have reduced to 47,500 if converted to an all-seater stadium). Additional seating can be added and the current record attendance is 74,576, at the Wales rugby team's 30–15 victory over Scotland in 2008.

- It is the second largest stadium in the world with a fully retractable roof. However, by capacity it is the largest rugby stadium in the world with this feature.

- It cost £121 million to construct.

- In each of the stadium's bars, so-called 'joy machines' can pour twelve pints every twenty seconds.

- The stadium has a resident hawk named 'Dad' who is employed to drive seagulls and pigeons out of the stadium.

27 JUNE

Y Mabinogi (the English title is *Otherworld*) was released on 27 June 2003, and starred Matthew Rhys, Daniel Evans and Jenny Livsey. The Welsh film is mainly animation but also contains live action sequences which are based on *The Mabinogion* – a Welsh language collection of eleven short stories drawing on Celtic myths, folklore and tradition. The stories appear in two fourteenth-century manuscripts, the *White Book of Rhydderch* and the *Red Book of Hergest* and refer to tales commonly thought to be dated to the late eleventh and twelfth centuries.

The works were brought to a much wider audience in 1838 when Lady Charlotte Guest published an English Language translation of the works. Lady Charlotte was originally from Lincolnshire and moved to Wales when she married John Josiah Guest, the owner of the Dowlais Iron Company. She learnt Welsh and immersed herself in all matters concerning the language and culture of Wales.

28 JUNE

The 'Riot Act' (an act of the British Parliament which authorised local authorities to disperse any group of more than twelve people deemed to be unlawful) was read at Mochdre in the Vale of Clwyd on 28 June 1887, during the Tithe War.

Tithe payments entitled the Church to a tenth of people's annual income and were usually paid in the form of produce, such as crops, wool and milk. Then, in 1836, the payment became required in cash with tithe maps being drawn up of the Welsh landscape to show how much landowners should pay. These measures caused much contention, as most farmers at the time were Nonconformists (Protestant Christians who did not conform to the governance of the Church of England) and also contributed to the upkeep of their own local churches. Being required to contribute to Anglican Churches as well provoked bitterness and anger.

These tensions were further aggravated by the agricultural depression which began in the 1870s and resulted in many people refusing to pay the tithe. In the 1880s, the authorities responded by enforcing the sale of land and property to collect the money, which led to confrontations between the farmers and the authorities, particularly in Denbighshire, where the Welsh National Land League was established, based on the model of the Irish Land League.

There were violent protests in Llangwm, Llanefydd and Mochdre, where eighty-four people were injured, including thirty-five police officers and the following year troops were deployed to maintain order. However, the Tithe War only came to an end when, in 1891, the Tithe Bill was introduced, stating that paying the tithe was the landlord's, rather than the tenant's, responsibility.

29 JUNE

Today is the feast day of St Gelert. It is believed that Gelert was a missionary, evangelising in Llangeler (Carmarthenshire), Beddgelert (Snowdonia) and the surrounding Gelert Valley. At some stage, Gelert lived as a hermit in a cave near what is now known as the Holy Well of St Celer near Llandysul, and pilgrims would travel there to be healed by him. Eventually a chapel, Capel Mair, was erected over the well, of which the ruins still remain.

However, local Welsh legend more often identifies Gelert as the favourite hunting wolfhound of Llywelyn the Great. One morning, unusually Gelert did not greet Llywelyn for his morning ride, so reluctantly Llywelyn left without him. On his return, Llywelyn was delighted to be greeted excitedly by his faithful hound but noticed that the dog was covered in blood. Llywelyn hurried in to look for his baby son: there was blood all over the room and baby's cradle was overturned and empty. Unable to find his child, Llywelyn assumed that Gelert had killed him.

Llywelyn drew his sword and struck Gelert a fearsome, fatal blow. Immediately after, a baby's cry was heard from under a pile of bedding that had fallen from the cradle. Llewelyn's son was alive and lying next to the body of a large wolf that Gelert had slain. Llywelyn was so devastated that he had killed his loyal friend, it is said that he never smiled again.

This story, however, was fabricated in the eighteenth century by David Pritchard, the owner of the Goat Pub in Beddgelert. Pritchard even made an inscribed burial mound for Gelert in an attempt to attract tourists to the village. Although, in reality, the village of Beddgelert is not named after Gelert the wolfhound, but the early Christian saint, tourists still come to see the last resting place of Llywelyn's faithful dog.

30 JUNE

On 30 June 1940, during the Second World War, a community of 219 people were evicted from their homes in the upland area of Breconshire known as Epynt, to make available approximately 60,000 acres of land for a military training range.

The community – comprising farms, smallholdings, a school, a chapel and a public house (the Drover's Arms) –

initially thought that they would be allowed back to their homes after the war. However, this was not the case and the range still functions as the Sennybridge Training Area. The Drover's Arms building is used as a military billet.

DID YOU KNOW?

A type of herding, droving is the practice of walking livestock over long distances. The Drover's Arms, originally called Tynmynydd ('house in the mountain'), was located on an important droving route, from west and mid Wales to Brecon and England and was made more identifiable for the drovers in the remote mountainous terrain by the planting of a group of trees in the otherwise mainly treeless environment.

1 JULY

On 1 July 1847, the infamous 'Blue Books' – a series of reports on the state of education in Wales – were presented to the Government.

A public enquiry was carried out as a result of pressure from Welshman William Williams, the MP for Coventry, who was concerned about the state of education in Wales. The enquiry was carried out by three Englishmen. Because none of them spoke Welsh, they relied on information of witnesses, mostly Anglican clergymen at a time when Wales was mostly Nonconformist.

The report concluded that schools in Wales were extremely inadequate. It noted that teachers were teaching in English with English textbooks in areas where children only spoke Welsh and so Welsh-speaking children had to rely on the Nonconformist Sunday Schools to acquire literacy. They concluded that the causes behind these findings were that the Welsh were ignorant, lazy and immoral as a result of the use of Welsh and Nonconformity.

There was a furious reaction in Wales, where the books were referred to as 'Brad y Llyfrau Gleision' – 'The Treachery of the Blue Books'. The response to the reports are thought to have been instrumental in the birth of the modern Welsh self-government movement. Saunders Lewis suggested that they were 'the most important nineteenth century historical document we possess'.

2 JULY

On 2 July 1940, 800 people drowned when the *Arandora Star* was torpedoed off the Irish coast by a German U-boat. Among the 1,200 internees aboard were more than one hundred Welsh-Italians who had settled in Wales decades earlier but were now being deported to Newfoundland, Canada.

In early June 1940, Italy entered the Second World War as an ally of Germany. All Italian males in Britain, who were aged between eighteen and seventy years and had been in the country for less than twenty years, were arrested and forced to leave their homes or workplaces with immediate effect. They were to be indefinitely interned under orders from the British War Cabinet. Subsequent reports from the Red Cross and other organisations reveal that these internees were badly treated by the British authorities. They were imprisoned in inhumane conditions, without access to sufficient food, adequate sanitation or medical care. More than 700 were transported to Liverpool, where they were herded aboard the *Arandora Star*, a former cruise liner, along with some 450 German and Austrian internees and Prisoners of War.

The first Welsh national memorial to the victims of the *Arandora Star* was unveiled at a ceremony in Cardiff's Metropolitan Cathedral of St David in Charles Street, on 2 July 2010. The memorial is a collaboration between the Welsh-Italian artist Susanna Ciccotti from Swansea and the world-renowned stone carver from Ammanford, Ieuan Rees.

3 JULY

Robert of Rhuddlan, the hated Norman Lord of much of north-east Wales was killed by a volley of Welsh spears on 3 July 1093.

Robert was the cousin of Hugh d'Avranches (1047–1101), a Norman Marcher Lord appointed as Earl of Chester by William the Conqueror after the Norman Invasion of 1066.

The Marcher lords were given special powers to bring the border area between Wales and England under control. Robert was appointed Hugh's 'commander of troops' in 1072 and began a campaign of hostility against the Welsh; his savage ferocity against the natives gained him the moniker 'Lupus' (Wolf). He captured lands and built castles at Twthill near Rhuddlan and, later, Deganwy, to consolidate his advances, ultimately ruling most of northern Wales to the east of the River Conwy.

In 1081, Gruffydd ap Cynan, King of Gwynedd, was captured by Robert and imprisoned by Earl Hugh in Chester

Castle. Robert claimed Gruffydd's lands and built further castles at Bangor, Caernarfon and Aberlleiniog.

Robert's career was brought to a sudden and dramatic end at the beginning of a Welsh revolt in 1093. When advised of a Welsh raiding party near the Great Orme, he immediately rushed to confront them, supported only by his armour-bearer. He was killed and the raiders made their escape with his head attached, triumphantly, to the mast of one of their vessels. Subsequently, Gruffudd ap Cynan escaped from captivity and regained most of the lands taken by Robert. Despite attempts from the Normans to recover lost lands, he managed to consolidate his rule until his death in 1137.

4 JULY

Independence Day in the US commemorates the Declaration of Independence that was made on 4 July 1776. On this day, the Continental Congress announced that the thirteen American colonies, then at war with Great Britain, regarded themselves as independent states and therefore no longer a part of the British Empire.

According to the Welsh Society of Philadelphia, sixteen of the signatories of the Declaration of Independence were of Welsh descent, the largest ethnic group of signatories on the original document. The principal author was Thomas Jefferson, a Founding Father of the US, whose family originated from Snowdonia and were fluent Welsh speakers.

5 JULY

The National Health Service (NHS) was created on 5 July 1948 as an embodiment of the ideal that quality healthcare should be available to all, regardless of wealth or social status. For the first time in British history, the provision of doctors, nurses, dentists, pharmacists, opticians and hospitals was brought under the auspices of a single organisation that was free for all at the point of delivery, bringing good healthcare to every individual in the UK.

The then Health Secretary Aneurin Bevan (1897–1960) was the chief architect of the NHS. Born on 15 November 1897 in Tredegar, Bevan was raised in a working-class community where he witnessed the hardships caused by disease and poverty. In 1911, aged fourteen, he began working underground, for the Tredegar Iron and Coal Company. By nineteen, he had become a member of the Independent Labour Party and was active in the South Wales Miners' Federation. In 1919, he won a scholarship to study at the Central Labour College in London. Bevan became one of the leaders of the South Wales Miners during the General Strike in 1926, and in 1929 he was elected as Labour MP for Ebbw Vale. During the Second World War, Bevan emerged as one of the opposition leaders in the House of Commons, and following the Labour victory in the 1945 general election, was appointed as the Minister of Health in charge of setting up the NHS.

In 1951, Bevan became Minister of Labour but resigned from the government in protest at the introduction of prescription charges for spectacles and dental care. He led the 'Bevanites', the left wing of the Labour Party, for the next five years. Bevan was elected deputy leader of the Labour

Party in 1959, despite suffering from terminal cancer – he made his last speech at the end of that year, and passed away on 6 July 1960.

6 JULY

Glamorgan County Cricket Club (CCC) was formed on 6 July 1888 at a meeting in the Angel Hotel, Cardiff.

The first recorded cricket game in Wales took place in Pembroke in 1763, and the earliest known occurrence of the game in Glamorgan is found in a reference to a match at Swansea in 1780.

The club competed in the Minor Counties Championship for many years and then applied for first-class status after the First World War. It played its inaugural first-class match against Sussex CCC at Cardiff Arms Park on 18–20 May 1921, a match that Glamorgan won.

Glamorgan County Cricket Club is one of eighteen first-class county clubs playing cricket in England and Wales, and the only Welsh one. It has won the English County Championship three times (in 1948, 1969 and 1997) and has beaten all of the major test playing nations. Based in Cardiff, the club now plays most of its home games at Sophia Gardens, though matches are occasionally played at Swansea, Cresselly and Colwyn Bay.

DID YOU KNOW?

Glamorgan's all-time top run scorer is Alan Jones with 34,056 runs. The club's all-time top wicket-taker is Don Shepherd with 2,174 wickets.

7 JULY

Amgueddfa Werin Cymru, the National Museum of Wales at St Fagans was first opened on 7 July 1948.

Commonly known as St Fagans, the museum is situated in the grounds of a sixteenth-century manor house, St Fagans Castle, and showcases the history, culture and architecture of Wales and Welsh people. It is among the most popular open-air museums in Europe and as of 2022, was the long-standing most popular heritage attraction in Wales.

Since the museum's inauguration, more than forty original buildings from various historical periods have been reconstructed in the castle's hundred acres of parkland, including a farm, chapel, church, school and a Workmen's Institute.

Welsh breeds of livestock are raised in the farmyards and fields and ancient farmyard tasks are demonstrated every day, and traditional craftsmen demonstrate their skills in workshops. Visitors will also often hear Welsh being spoken by these craftsmen as well as interpreters and staff.

There are many galleries exhibiting artefacts from daily life, farming and costume from various periods in Welsh history. Throughout the year traditional festivals, including music and dance, are celebrated, providing insight and pleasure to generations of visitors who are interested in the language, culture and history of Wales.

8 JULY

On 8 July 1557, Ysgol Friars (Friars School) in Bangor was established thanks to a bequest in the will of Geoffrey Glyn. It is one of the oldest secondary schools in Wales.

Geoffrey Glyn was originally from Anglesey and had enjoyed a successful career in law in London. In 1538, following the Dissolution of the Monasteries, he acquired the grounds and building of the thirteenth-century friary belonging to the Dominican Order. The school was inaugurated and formally recognised in 1561 by Elizabeth I. It was originally known as 'The free grammar school of Geoffrey Glyn, Doctor of Laws', but because of its association with the Dominican Black Friars, the school was later renamed as Friars School. It existed within the boundaries of the old friary, near the banks of the River Adda for more than two hundred years.

The school was transferred to a different location, further from the river, in 1789 and was then moved in 1900 to Ffriddoedd Road. In 1971, in a drastic education authority reorganisation, three schools were amalgamated: Friars School, Bangor County School for Girls and Deiniol School. These combined to form a new comprehensive school, under the Friars name, but on three different sites. The entire three-part comprehensive school was relocated to a new permanent location, Eithinog, in 1999.

9 JULY

Mettoy introduced Corgi Toys model cars on 9 July 1956. The manufacturing base was at Fforestfach in south Wales.

Mettoy's first factory was in Northampton and had 600 employees within six years. Such was the success of the company that, by 1956, a new production plant was constructed at Fforestfach in Swansea to meet the manufacturing demand for the new range of Corgi Toys. Corgi Toys were the only ones at this time to feature plastic glazing, which gave the models more authenticity and aesthetic appeal, and gave rise to the advertising slogan 'the ones with windows'.

Designer Philip Ullman named them 'Corgi Toys' after the iconic Welsh breed of dog, to recognise the company's new home. The short and memorable name, together with the appealing 'Corgi dog' emblem, was intended to rival that of a similar company, Dinky Toys.

10 JULY

The 10 July 1940 marked the start of the Battle of Britain.

Following the British withdrawal from the European continent and the Nazis taking control in France, the German Airforce (Luftwaffe) launched a series of attacks on shipping convoys and ports on the south-east coast of England. Hitler's assumption was that this would expose Britain's vulnerability to invasion and compel Winston Churchill, the wartime Prime Minister, to agree to a peace settlement.

However, the Royal Air Force and the Fleet Air Arm's successful defence against these unremitting air raids is seen as a crucial turning point in the Second World War. Among those Churchill would call 'the few', who saved 'the many', were several Welsh pilots. These included Fred Rosier from Wrexham, Denis Crowley-Milling from St Asaph and Frederick 'Taffy' Higginson from Gorseinon near Swansea.

11 JULY

Cardiff-born Ernest Thompson Willows (11 July 1886–3 August 1926) was a pioneer aviator and aircraft designer who was the first person in the United Kingdom to hold a pilot's certificate for an airship. He also devised a technique of powering hot air balloons using moveable propellers, which meant that, for the first time, balloons could be steered.

Willows started designing his own aircraft at the age of nineteen. His first airship, the Willows No. 1, made its maiden flight over East Moors, Cardiff on 5 August 1905 and lasted for eighty-five minutes. Then, in 1910, he flew his airship from Cheltenham to Cardiff. This aircraft was followed by an improved version, Willows No. 2, which he landed outside Cardiff City Hall on 4 June 1910. This was remodelled as No. 3, which he named the 'City of Cardiff' before flying it from London to Paris in 1910.

Willows moved to Birmingham where he constructed his next airship, the Willows No. 4. It was piloted for the first time in 1912, before Willows sold the craft to the Admiralty for £1,050, where it became 'His Majesty's Naval Airship No. 2'. Willows used the profit from the sale to establish a gas balloon school at Welsh Harp in Hendon, London. He also built Willows No. 5 in 1913 – a four-seater craft built to take pleasure flights over London.

During the First World War, Willows built kite or barrage balloons to protect Cardiff. After the war he resumed his career but on 23 August 1926, he was killed in a balloon accident at Hoo Park, near Bedford, a tragedy that also claimed the lives of two passengers.

His achievements are commemorated in Cardiff, where a street, a public house in City Road and Willows High School are all named in his honour.

12 JULY

On 12 July 1916, during the First Battle of the Somme in the First World War, the 38th (Welsh) Division succeeded in clearing the Germans from Mametz Woods in northern France. They had initially been forced to retreat due to the intensity of German machine gun fire and were ordered to regroup and attack for a second time on 10 July. This turned out to be one of the most brutal battles of the First World War, and the success of the Welsh Division had come at a painfully high price with more than 1,000 soldiers killed and 3,000 wounded. In November 1916, Christopher Williams visited the scene of the Welsh losses at Mametz Wood and later produced his famous painting, 'The Welsh at Mametz Wood' at the request of David Lloyd George, who was Secretary of State for War at the time, and Prime Minister soon after.

13 JULY

The 13 July was the birthday of John Dee (1527–1608), a mathematician, astronomer, astrologer, geographer and consultant to Queen Elizabeth I who relied on him for guidance mainly relating to astrology.

Dee was proud of his Welsh descent. His grandfather, Bedo Ddu (Dee coming from *du*, the Welsh for black) was from Pilleth in Radnorshire and claimed descendance from Rhodri the Great, King of Gwynedd (844–c.877).

It seems Dee was an enthusiastic proponent of psychic arts, including alchemy and divination (in Tudor times there was no real distinction between magic and science). He graduated from college when he was seventeen, lectured at the University of Paris, almost completed his doctorate, and wrote books on mathematical subjects and volumes outlining improvements he had made to navigational science.

Dee was in good standing with the royals until Mary Tudor took the throne. At this time, Mary's half-sister, Elizabeth, was imprisoned under house arrest to prevent her from trying to become queen. Someone asked for Dee's help. He prepared a horoscope for Elizabeth that predicted the death of Queen Mary and that Elizabeth would be the Queen of England. Unfortunately, Mary had a spy in the house, who betrayed Dee. He was imprisoned on the charges of treason and for writing of the Queen's death. They even accused him of trying to bring it about with magic. After a long legal process, Dee managed to repudiate the charges.

On 17 November 1558, Dee's predictions came true. Mary died and Queen Elizabeth I took the throne, making Dee a private consultant and royal astrologer. He had many good years until Queen Elizabeth died in 1603 but Dee eventually retired to his home in Mortlake where he died old and impoverished.

14 JULY

On this day in 1966, Gwynfor Evans became Plaid Cymru's first MP when he won the Carmarthen by-election following the death of Labour's Megan Lloyd George. (Find out more about Lloyd George on 30 May.)

Evans was only a teenager when Plaid Cymru was founded in 1925 and he learnt Welsh as an adult. He was elected president of Plaid Cymru in 1945, a position he held for thirty-six years. In the 1950s, he led the campaign against the flooding of the Tryweryn Valley and of the Welsh-speaking Capel Celyn by the Liverpool Water Corporation. (Find out more about this on 31 July.)

A shy and introverted individual, Evans was an unlikely participant in the melee of Westminster, an institution he regarded as 'the very symbol of the complete subjugation of Wales, the most mighty manifestation of the Englishness which is killing our country'. He lost his seat in 1970, returned to Parliament in 1974, and lost it again in 1979, never to return.

In 1980, he announced that he would fast 'to the death' if the Conservative government failed to fulfil its pledge to establish a Welsh language television channel. Evans regarded the entire history of Wales since the sixteenth century as constituting a sustained and deliberate English attempt to eradicate the Welsh language and culture and believed that the government's intention of reneging on its promise was part of this historic vendetta. His threat was initially dismissed as empty rhetoric, but Evans was in poor health and government supporters were alarmed at the prospective repercussions of his perceived martyrdom – especially in a period of high unemployment and industrial closures in Wales. Weeks before his fast was due to begin, Margaret Thatcher capitulated, and the creation of S4C was assured. The decision was hailed by Evans as 'the biggest victory we have ever won for the Welsh language'.

15 JULY

One of the UK premieres of the science fiction action film *Jurassic Park* was held at the Lyric Theatre in Carmarthen on 15 July 1993.

The Lyric Theatre relied heavily on high-profile blockbuster films to survive financially, but had been let down by a distribution company on their promise to send a copy of *Jurassic Park*. The theatre's manager and founder – who was also a hairdresser and youth theatre leader – Liz Evans (1944–2004), sprung into action and organised a campaign to get the decision reversed. She approached Carmarthen's mayor, Richard Goodridge, and they decided to contact the film's director, Steven Spielberg. That night, Goodridge wrote to Spielberg, telling him how important the film was to the town and how angry and disappointed the local people were. Six days later, he received a reply from the managing director of United International Pictures, who not only agreed to send a copy of the film but also said that the Lyric Theatre had been chosen to premiere the film on the same evening as a star-studded London event.

The story has now been made into a film in its own right, *Save The Cinema* (2022).

16 JULY

On this day in 1976, Gwynfor Evans unveiled a plaque at Nant y Moch Dam to commemorate Owain Glyndŵr's victory over Henry IV against overwhelming odds during The Battle of Hyddgen in the summer of 1401. The battle was considered to be Glyndŵr's first victory in the field. It subsequently set the tone for the spread of his uprising against English rule in its early stages and turned him from a local rebel into a national leader.

Not much is known of the battle, but the probable site of the conflict is a remote area of the Pumlumon Mountain range. It is thought that Owain's force of just 120 men would have mostly been made up of archers mounted on hill ponies that would have been well suited for travelling across boggy or mountainous regions. The English-Flemish army meanwhile would have generally consisted of infantry with some light cavalrymen supporting them. Despite having decent equipment, many of the English-Flemish soldiers were lacking in military experience, and there was a general lack of discipline within their army.

On the plaque's unveiling, Gwynfor Evans made a powerful speech, declaring 'His spirit lives on like an unquenchable flame, a symbol of the determination of the Welsh to live as a free nation.'

17 JULY

On 17 July 1951 the Abbey Works steel plant at Margam, Port Talbot was opened. It is named after nearby Margam Abbey.

Steelmaking at the Port Talbot complex began with the Margam Iron and Steel Works, which was completed between 1923 and 1926 and closed in 1953. After the Second World War, a group of steelmakers from south Wales formed the Steel Company of Wales to erect a modern integrated steelmaking site and subsequently the new Abbey Works was planned in 1947, opened in 1951 and was operating at full strength by 1953.

By the 1960s, the steelworks were the largest in Europe and the largest single employer in Wales, with a labour force of 18,000. In 1967, the company was nationalised and became a part of British Steel. By 2000, following privatisation, the works was part of Corus and then in 2010 it was announced that Corus was to be rebranded to Tata Steel.

18 JULY

On 18 July 1947, the Indian Independence Act stipulated that British Rule in India would come to an end and that the Provence of British India was to be partitioned into the independent nations of India and Pakistan. The boundary demarcation line between the two countries, the Radcliffe Line, was named after the chairman of the boundary committee, Sir Cyril Radcliffe, from Llanychan, Denbighshire, who had no previous knowledge of India.

Incredibly, the process of dividing the 175,000 square

miles of territory and 88 million people was to be achieved within a month. The work was inevitably rushed and produced instances where the border was drawn leaving some parts of a village in India and some in Pakistan. There were even instances where the dividing line passed through a single house. Then the Indian and Pakistani representatives were given only two hours to study copies before its publication. By his own admission, Radcliffe's work was hampered by his lack of fitness for the Indian climate and his eagerness to depart India. He justified the inaccuracies by saying that no matter what he did, people would suffer. However, he destroyed all his papers before he left India.

Radcliffe had attempted to base the partition on religious demographics, but its implementation resulted in massive population exchanges between the two newly formed states in the months immediately following. It is estimated that 7.2 million Muslims went to Pakistan from India while a further 7.2 million Sikhs and Hindus moved to India from Pakistan. About 11.2 million people migrated at this time, the majority of the people moving into or out of Punjab. The newly formed governments were unequipped to deal with migrations of such magnitude, and massive violence and slaughter occurred on both sides of the border. It is estimated that 500,000 were killed. The violent nature of the partition created an atmosphere of mutual hostility and suspicion between India and Pakistan that plagues their relationship to this day.

After seeing the mayhem occurring on both sides of the boundary that was created by him, Radcliffe refused his salary of 40,000 rupees (then £3,000) but did accept a knighthood in 1948.

19 JULY

On 19 July 1984, the UK's largest recorded onshore earthquake struck the Llŷn Peninsula, measuring 5.4 on the Richter scale. The effects were felt throughout Wales and most of England, the biggest concentration of damage being in Liverpool, but the aftershocks were felt as far away as Dublin.

The Llŷn Peninsula is known locally as the 'Dragon's Tail' as it is so prone to earth tremors. It forms part of a band of seismic activity that spans the north-west of England, north Wales and Scotland. This could be the result of plate-tectonic activity under the Atlantic Ocean and could also reflect the fact that this area was covered in thick ice twenty millennia ago. Although the ice has melted, the release of its weight is still causing contractions in the earth's crust.

Some other notable Welsh earthquakes took place on the following dates:

11 September 1275: An earthquake of 6.0 affected an area stretching across south Wales and southern England.

19 July 1727: A quake in Swansea caused church bells to ring in Oxford.

9 November 1852: Located in Caernarfon, this earthquake was similar to the 1984 Llŷn Peninsula event, reaching 5.3 on the Richter scale.

27 June 1906: This earthquake in Swansea was one of the most damaging in twentieth century British history.

20 JULY

On 20 July 1969, Neil Armstrong became the first human to walk on the surface of the moon. Watching avidly from earth was George Abbey, Assistant Director of the Johnson Space Center, whose mother was from Laugharne, Carmarthenshire.

Abbey has close connections with Wales and with Laugharne in particular. At a 2013 lecture at Swansea University, he recalled 'There was a very strong Welsh feeling in our home because my mother spoke Welsh.' He described feeling a close relationship with Laugharne. Abbey's desire to remain loyal to his Welsh roots encouraged him to read and appreciate Dylan Thomas's work. His cousin, Dick Lewis – Laugharne's milkman – was a close friend of Dylan Thomas and his wife, Caitlin, and appeared in Thomas's works as 'Dick the Milk'. He was a pallbearer at the writer's funeral. Abbey arranged it so there a was a treasured photograph from Dylan Thomas's cottage on the space shuttle and asked the astronauts to take pictures of Wales for him if the weather was good.

In 1983 Abbey became Director of flight operations, putting America's first woman into space. By 1996, he had become overall Director of the Johnson Space Center, and the man most responsible for the International Space Station.

21 JULY

The Elan Valley Reservoirs were officially opened on 21 July 1904. The reservoirs are a chain of five man-made lakes created by the damming of the Elan and Claerwen Rivers within the Elan Valley in mid Wales, which also involved flooding a village and evicting more than a hundred people. While the reservoirs were being constructed, thousands of manual workers and their families lived in the purpose-built Elan Village.

The reservoirs were built because of the lack of clean water in the rapidly growing English city of Birmingham. Outbreaks of water-borne diseases resulted in the Birmingham Corporation Water Act of 1892, which allowed the acquisition of land by compulsory purchase for the purpose of creating an adequate water supply for the city. Among the reasons Elan Valley was chosen was its high rainfall, and because the valleys were narrow downstream, making it easier to build masonry dams. Birmingham is built on relatively high ground and reservoirs in the moorlands of mid Wales would allow the water to be supplied via aqueduct by gravity alone, without the cost of pumping. The local bedrock was suitable for retaining the water held in the reservoirs, and the sparse population, in what was a remote area, made securing ownership of over seventy square miles relatively easy.

However, only the affected landowners were given financial compensation, with tenant farmers and smallholders being evicted without payment. Those employed by the two large estates of Cwm Elan and Nantgwyllt also lost their income and homes.

In 1982, the Welsh Army of Workers claimed responsibility for a bomb explosion in 1982 at the Birmingham headquarters of the Severn Trent Water Authority. The action was part of a campaign to force local authorities from Birmingham and the West Midlands to pay for the water they receive from the Elan Valley reservoirs. No one was hurt by the bombing.

Birmingham City Council has not yet followed the lead of its Liverpool counterpart, who apologised for the flooding of Capel Celyn in Snowdonia (find out more on 31 July). They also refused to donate money towards a museum charting the impact of supplying water to the UK's second city. A spokeswoman for Birmingham City Council said: 'The city council is unable to make a direct donation because of the limited direct benefit to Birmingham people and, therefore, the restrictions on our legal powers.' However, it's felt that this attitude does not reflect the feelings of the majority of people in Birmingham.

22 JULY

Running from 22 July–5 August 1943, Exercise Jantzen was a major training exercise carried out by the British armed forces on the beaches at Amroth and Saundersfoot in preparation for the D-Day landings in Normandy the following year.

Ships at Port Talbot, Swansea and Tenby were loaded with troops and supplies before practising landing at the Pembrokeshire beaches. Residents were banned from the beaches during the exercise and police enforced a curfew.

According to locals, Prime Minister Winston Churchill was present during the exercise and drank tea at a local hostelry.

The D-Day landings would prove to be a key turning point in the Second World War, and the beginning of the liberation of Europe from Nazi control.

23 JULY

During the English Civil War (1642–51) Roger Mostyn from Mostyn Hall, Holywell, supported King Charles I. However, he bankrupted his estate in the service of the crown and had to live in impoverished seclusion for many years afterwards. In 1660, following the subsequent restoration of the English monarchy, Mostyn was rewarded by Charles II who made him a baronet. Subsequently, his finances improved through profits derived from lead and coal mines so much that, on 23 July 1684, he was reported as being one of the richest men in north Wales.

The Mostyn estate included the land on which the seaside resort of Llandudno would be established, and the Mostyn baronets' fortune was used to fund the town's foundation and development. When the Chester and Holyhead Railway opened the local line of the Dublin to London rail link in 1848, the potential of the area as a tourist destination was realised. The idea of developing the marshlands behind Llandudno Bay as a holiday resort was accepted by Lord Mostyn. Between 1857 and 1877, Lady Augusta Mostyn of Gloddaeth Hall became a major contributor to Llandudno being specifically developed as a holiday destination, under the supervision of the Mostyn estate's architect.

The railway line linking the main line to Llandudno was opened in 1858 and as early as 1861 it was being described as 'the Queen of the Welsh Watering Places'. Subsequent developments from the Mostyn estate include Lord Mostyn gifting 'Happy Valley' to the town in 1887, which consisted of extensive gardens and lawns, an open-air theatre and two miniature golf courses. Then in 1901, Llandudno's international art gallery – now known as Mostyn – opened in 1901, to house the art collection of Lady Augusta Mostyn.

The town is also now home to Wales's longest pier at 700 metres, and Britain's longest funicular railway, single-stage cabin lift and toboggan run.

24 JULY

The scientist and engineer Sir Barnes Neville Wallis theorised that a bomb small enough to be carried in an aircraft could collapse a dam wall. He was proven right on 24 July 1942, following a 'spectacularly successful' test on the Nant-y-Gro dam, near Rhayader.

The Nant-y-Gro dam's remoteness made it an ideal site for Barnes Wallis's highly secret experimental work. The dam had been built in the 1890s to provide water for the construction workers of the Elan Valley Reservoirs (for more on this, see 21 July) and had become redundant following the completion of the main dam.

It was part of a series of preparatory trials that resulted

in the famous 'bouncing bomb' raid on the Möhne and Edersee dams in Germany, code-named Operation Chastise – now more commonly known as the Dambusters Raid – during the night of 16 and into the morning of 17 May 1943. The resulting flooding of the Ruhr and Eder river valleys had a significant impact on Germany's coal and steel production and also served as a major morale boost in Britain. The raid was dramatised in the 1955 film *The Dam Busters*.

25 JULY

On 25 July 1277, Edward I of England began constructing castles at Aberystwyth and Flint.

Following Llywelyn ap Gruffydd's refusal to pay homage to him at Chester in 1275, Edward I declared Llywelyn a rebel. In 1277, Edward began invasions into south and mid Wales, which were met with considerable success. He then launched a major military expedition into Gwynedd from Chester, marching his forces up the Welsh side of the Dee estuary and establishing a base at Flint.

Realising his position was hopeless, Llywelyn negotiated a settlement that confined his authority to *Gwynedd Uwch Conwy* (west of the River Conwy) and Edward began the construction of castles to consolidate English control of the area. Flint was chosen because it was strategically positioned on the Dee estuary for easy access by sea and was only a day's march from Chester and Aberystwyth.

26 JULY

Held in Cardiff, the 1958 British Empire and Commonwealth Games came to an end on 26 July with the closing ceremony at Cardiff Arms Park.

The venue hosted much of the games, though Maindy Stadium was used for track cycling and the Wales Empire Pool was built especially for the aquatic events. Boxing events were held at the Sophia Gardens Pavilion, where Howard Winstone won a gold medal at bantamweight for Wales.

Cardiff had originally been scheduled to host the games in 1946, but the event was cancelled because of the Second World War.

DID YOU KNOW?

The 1958 games were the last in which South Africa participated until 1994, after the abolition of apartheid. There were objections and demonstrations against South Africa at the games in Cardiff because their team had been selected on the basis of race and colour rather than ability.

27 JULY

On 27 July 1946, the cause of an outbreak of typhoid in Aberystwyth was traced to a local ice cream producer whose power supply had failed, preventing them from heating up the cream properly before freezing it. Up to 210 people contracted the disease and four died.

The outbreak led to some adverse publicity for the town. One national newspaper carried the banner headline 'Typhoid Town' above a story covering the infection and, as a result, the number of visitors to Aberystwyth that summer and the following year was dramatically reduced.

28 JULY

On 28 July 2021, it was announced that the slate landscape of north-west Wales had been designated a UNESCO World Heritage site.

North Wales slate is regarded as high quality as it is not only very strong but also relatively light. It occurs mainly in three geological deposits: a strip running south-west from Conwy to near Criccieth, which was quarried in Penrhyn and Dinorwig; a strip running south-west from Betws-y-Coed to Porthmadog which was mined at Blaenau Ffestiniog; and a band running from Llangynnog to Aberdyfi, which was mainly quarried in the Corris area.

It is known that the Romans used slate from north Wales from AD 77 and that it was being exported from medieval times. The industry expanded rapidly from the mid-eighteenth century, reaching its peak between 1856 and 1900 when over 500,000 tonnes were produced each year to satisfy worldwide demand. The industry is also acknowledged for its export of technology and skilled workers to other quarrying countries, such as the United States and France. In particular, the method of transporting the slate from the quarry to navigable water by locomotive-worked, narrow-gauge railway was one that was copied worldwide.

DID YOU KNOW?

There are four UNESCO World Heritage sites in Wales. The others are the castles and town walls built by King Edward I in Gwynedd, Pontcysyllte Aqueduct and Canal, and the Blaenavon Industrial Landscape.

29 JULY

Regarded by many historians as one of the most powerful kings in early Anglo-Saxon England, King Offa was ruler of the Anglo-Saxon kingdom of Mercia from AD 757 until his death on 29 July 796.

Mercia was particularly aggressive in threatening the eastern borders of the Welsh kingdoms of Powys, Gwent and Gwynedd as they strove for control of the fertile river plains of the rivers Dee, Severn and Wye. Gwent had successfully repulsed the Mercians at the Battle of Pont y Saeson in AD 630 and a resurgent late seventh-century Powys also checked Mercian advancement. However, the threat was relentless and continued under the rule of Offa who attacked Powys in AD 760 at Hereford and is recorded as campaigning against the Welsh in AD 778, 784 and 796.

Offa is best known for his association with Offa's Dyke, the great earthen barrier that runs over approximately two-thirds of the Wales-England border, from near Llanfynydd in the north to Rushock Hill, near Kington in Hereford-shire. It is hard to ascertain exactly when the dyke was built, but in his biography of Alfred the Great, the Welsh monk Asser says it was Offa's work. It was designed to impress, overlook approaches from Wales and exclude the Welsh from what had formerly been theirs.

The Offa's Dyke Path walking trail opened in 1971. Starting at Sedbury Cliffs near Chepstow, its 177 miles criss-cross the current border between England and Wales, passing through eight counties and ending at the coastal town of Prestatyn on the shores of the Irish sea. It also links three designated Areas of Outstanding Natural Beauty – the Clwydian Hills, the Shropshire Hills and the Wye Valley.

30 JULY

David Morgan (c.1695–1746), from the Penygraig estate near Quakers Yard, was executed on 30 July 1746 for his involvement in the Jacobite rising of 1745.

Morgan, who attended Christ Church College, Oxford and was trained in the law, supported the Jacobian cause of restoring the line of James II to the throne of England. He was closely associated with the senior Welsh Jacobites,

Sir Watkin Williams-Wynn in north Wales and Sir John Philipps of Picton Castle in south Wales.

When Charles Edward Stuart (Bonnie Prince Charlie) launched an attempt to regain the British throne in 1745, Welsh Jacobites initially held the position that they would rise up only on the intervention of the French. Morgan, however, decided to join Charles's invasion of England at Preston where he obtained a captain's commission in the Jacobite army.

When the invasion reached Derby, the Jacobite Council of War felt they were overstretched. Unaware that London was in a state of panic and that King George II was ready to flee to the continent, they decided to retreat. Morgan did not support this decision and went on the run. He was captured shortly afterwards by the government, found guilty of treason and sentenced to be hanged, drawn and quartered. After the execution, Morgan's head was displayed on Temple Bar in London and his remains are thought to have been buried in the grounds attached to the Foundling Hospital, now St George's Gardens, in Bloomsbury.

31 JULY

On 31 July 1957, the Tryweryn Reservoir Bill became law, despite the fervent opposition of Welsh MPs. It gave Liverpool City Council permission to build a reservoir which would drown the Welsh-speaking village of Capel Celyn near Bala.

These events led to increased support for the Welsh nationalist party, Plaid Cymru, and gave impetus to the demand for Welsh devolution. The official opening of the reservoir in 1965 was disrupted by protesters who had cut microphone wires and whose chanting drowned out the speeches.

In October 2005, Liverpool City Council published a public apology for the incident.

1 AUGUST

The opening of the Irish Mail railway service from London to Holyhead, connecting with ferry services to Dublin, opened on 1 August 1848. The new line resulted in the name of the village station of Llanfair Pwllgwyngyll being changed to Llanfairpwllgwyngyllgogerychwyrndrobwll-llantysiliogogogoch.

The name change was made to appeal to tourists and the ploy has subsequently proved to be very successful, with over 200,000 visitors being attracted to the village every year. The village has the longest place name in Europe and the second longest place name in the world, and the village's internet domain name is also the world's longest. Its station has the longest railway station name in the world. The English translation of the name is 'The church of St Mary in the hollow of white hazel trees near the rapid whirlpool of St Tysilio's of the red cave'.

2 AUGUST

The life and work of nurse Betsi Cadwaladr (1789–1860) were commemorated on this day in 2012. There was an official service at Abney Park Cemetery, London – where Betsi is buried in a pauper's grave – which included the unveiling of a memorial stone and bench.

Betsi was born Elizabeth Cadwaladr in Llanycil, near Bala, one of sixteen children. She moved to Liverpool aged fourteen and then travelled widely before settling in London.

Betsi joined the military nursing service after learning of the conditions suffered by British soldiers wounded in the Crimean War (1853–6). Her first post was in a hospital run by Florence Nightingale but, after working there for many weeks, Betsi ran out of patience with Nightingale's incessant bureaucracy and red tape and made her way nearer to the frontline at Balaclava, in Crimea. Here Betsi became the unsung heroine of the Crimean War, saving countless lives as she worked tirelessly to improve the unhygienic conditions. Eventually she even gained the respect of Florence Nightingale. In 1855, one year before the war ended, Betsi contracted cholera and dysentery and was forced to return home. She died five years later.

Named in her honour, the Betsi Cadwaladr University Health Board is the largest health organisation in Wales. It provides health services for the six counties of north Wales, parts of mid Wales, Cheshire and Shropshire.

3 AUGUST

On 3 August 1958, at the *Cymanfa Ganu* (singing festival) on the evening before the opening of the National Eisteddfod in Ebbw Vale, Paul Robeson delivered an address to the people of Wales.

Robeson was a distinguished singer and actor and also a leading civil rights activist. He is regarded as one of the most respected African-Americans of the twentieth century. His association with Wales began in 1928 when, whilst starring in the musical *Show Boat* in London's West End, he met a group of south Wales miners who had walked to London to draw attention to the hardship and suffering being endured by thousands of unemployed miners and their families. Robeson subsequently visited and performed in south Wales many times between 1929 and 1939. Then in 1939, he starred in *The Proud Valley*, a film about a mining community in the Rhondda.

In 1957, Robeson participated in the Miners' Eisteddfod in Porthcawl by means of a transatlantic telephone link to a secret recording studio in New York. He was unable to travel because his passport had been withdrawn by the US Government because of his outspoken left-wing and anti-racist views. The south Wales miners added their voice and signatures to the international petitions that eventually forced the US Supreme Court to reinstate his passport in 1958. This enabled him to attend the 1958 Eisteddfod, where he sat alongside Aneurin Bevan.

4 AUGUST

On 4 August 1914, within minutes of the outbreak of the First World War, Newport police captured the German freighter *Belgia*, which was anchored in the Bristol Channel. The previous day, Germany had declared war on France and the freighter's captain, fearing he might be attacked by the French, had headed for what he thought would be safer waters.

This incident, during which twenty crew and seventy-five naval reservists were taken prisoner, is considered by many to be the first British action of the war against Germany. Interestingly, as part of her cargo, the *Belgia* was carrying animals for Hamburg Zoo, which included alligators, chameleons, racoons and rattlesnakes. These were apparently sold off as they were later seen on display at a fair in Abergavenny.

The *Belgia* herself was commandeered by the British merchant navy and renamed the *Huntstrick*. She remained in service until she was sunk off Morocco in 1917 by a German U-boat with the loss of fifteen lives.

5 AUGUST

Plaid Cymru (The Party of Wales) was established on 5 August 1925. Plaid Cymru's aims are to secure independence for Wales in Europe and to ensure economic prosperity, social justice and the health of the natural environment, based on decentralist socialism. It also aims to create a bilingual society by promoting the revival of the Welsh language, to promote Wales's contribution to the global community, and to attain membership of the United Nations.

The founder members were Lewis Valentine and the academic and dramatist Saunders Lewis, who was the party's first leader. They fought their first general election in Caernarfon, north Wales in 1929, fielded seven candidates in the 1950 general election and twenty-four in 1964. Then in a 1966 by-election, the party's then-leader Gwynfor Evans captured the seat of Caerfyrddin (Carmarthen), becoming the party's first MP in Westminster.

By 1970, Plaid Cymru would fight for every Welsh seat in parliamentary elections. Today the party also fields a candidate for every seat in Welsh Assembly elections. In the first election for the newly established Welsh Assembly in 1999, Plaid Cymru became the second largest party, forming the official opposition to Labour. This was a major breakthrough for Plaid Cymru, as they broke out of their traditional Welsh-speaking heartlands to capture seats in what was previously Labour's industrial heartland of south Wales. Then in 2007, following the Assembly Elections, Plaid Cymru, with fifteen seats, formed a government with the Labour Party, becoming a government party for the first time.

6 AUGUST

War ended in Europe with the surrender of Nazi Germany on 8 May 1945. However, the Japanese refused to agree to an unconditional surrender and war in the Pacific continued.

In agreement with the United Kingdom, the United

States dropped nuclear bombs on the cities of Hiroshima and Nagasaki on 6 and 9 of August respectively. It is estimated that the number of people killed by both explosions and the after-effects was between 129,000 and 226,000 – most of them civilians. This, combined with the Soviet Union's declaration of war on Japan, led to the Japanese surrender on 2 September 1945, effectively ending the Second World War.

The manufacture of the bomb dropped on Hiroshima involved capturing the radioactive isotope U235 by a very fine meshed membrane of nickel powder after it had been separated from uranium ore. The contract for the supply of this mesh was awarded to the Mond Nickel Works in Clydach, Swansea, which at the time was the only company in the world that was capable of producing it in sufficient volume.

7 AUGUST

On 7 August 1485, Henry Tudor (the future Henry VII) landed at Mill Bay, at the mouth of the Milford Haven waterway. He then marched through Wales, mustering support for his attempt to seize the throne of England from Richard III.

Henry's actions would result in the climax of The Wars of the Roses, a series of civil wars fought in the fifteenth century between two rival royal branches – the houses of Lancaster and York – for the control of the English throne. In 1471, Henry had been forced to flee to Brittany under the guardianship of his uncle Jasper when he unexpectedly became the main Lancastrian claimant to the throne. Henry and Jasper remained in exile for fourteen years before being encouraged to return during the controversial rule of Richard III.

On 1 August 1485, with the support of the French king, Henry sailed from Harfleur with a 4,000-strong invasion force, with the intention of overthrowing Richard and claiming the English throne for himself. After arriving in Wales, Henry made use of his Welsh ancestry by flying the Red Dragon banner of Cadwaladr as he marched through Haverfordwest, Cardigan, Aberystwyth, Machynlleth and Newtown. He attracted the support of the Welsh and enlisted fighters on the way, before finally engaging Richard at the Battle of Bosworth on 22 August 1485. Richard was defeated and killed and Henry was crowned King of England. He later married Richard's niece, Elizabeth of York, which resulted in the end of the divisive war between the families and the establishment of the royal House of Tudor.

8 AUGUST

The creation of Cornelius 'Corny' Rooster, the Kellogg's Corn Flakes mascot, could all have been down to a Welsh woman.

It is widely considered that cornflakes were invented by John Harvey Kellogg and his younger brother William Keith Kellogg on 8 August 1894. The brothers later fell out and William founded the Battle Creek Toasted Corn Flake Company in 1906, which later became Kellogg's.

It's said that on one of her overseas trips in 1922, the internationally acclaimed Welsh harpist Nansi Richards was invited to the home of William Kellogg. At the time, he was looking for marketing ideas for his cornflakes and apparently Nansi suggested a pun on the name Kellogg and the Welsh word *ceiliog*, meaning cockerel. William liked the idea and Cornelius Rooster was born, appearing on packs of Kellogg's Corn Flakes ever since.

9 AUGUST

On 9 August 1211, Marcher lord William de Braose, 4th Lord of Bramber, a major landholder in Wales, died in France after fleeing there from Wales the previous year disguised as a beggar.

William de Braose was a favourite of King John, who gave him the titles of Lord of Gower, Glamorgan, Brecknock, Abergavenny, Builth, Radnor and Kington. His wife Maud was put in charge of Hay Castle and is often referred to as the 'Lady of Hay'.

However in 1208, de Braose quarrelled with King John after Maud made accusations against the King regarding the murder of John's nephew, Arthur of Brittany. The King took all of their land and castles and the de Braoses were forced to flee to Ireland. He returned to Wales in 1210 after the King had him hunted in Ireland, and allied himself with Llywelyn ap Iorwerth in his rebellion against King John. However, he had to flee to France and Maud and her son were soon apprehended and imprisoned at Corfe Castle, Dorset, where they were starved to death.

DID YOU KNOW?

William de Braose was responsible for the 1175 Abergavenny Massacre, when three Welsh princes and other local leaders were lured to their deaths at a Christmas feast at Abergavenny Castle. He was subsequently called the 'Ogre of Abergavenny' by the Welsh.

10 AUGUST

On 10 August 2008, Nicole Cooke claimed Britain's first gold medal of the Beijing Olympics in the road race, becoming the first Welsh woman to win in an individual Olympic event and the first British woman to claim an Olympic Gold in any cycling discipline.

Born in Swansea in 1983 and raised in Wick, Vale of Glamorgan, Cooke began competitive cycling with Cardiff Ajax Cycling Club aged eleven. At sixteen, she was the youngest ever winner of the senior women's British National Road Race Championships and the youngest rider to win the senior women's title at the 2001 British National Cyclocross Championships. Her illustrious career has also seen her become the youngest winner of the Giro D'Italia at the age of twenty-one, and the women's Tour de France winner, twice. The former World Number One has also won four Junior World Championships, ten British Elite

Road Race Championships, the World Road Race Championships and Commonwealth Games Gold.

Cooke retired from cycling in 2013 and has since been an outspoken critic of drug use and campaigned for gender equality in sport. Her autobiography, *The Breakaway*, was named *The Sunday Times* Sports Book of the Year 2014, and the following year she graduated with an MBA from Cardiff University.

11 AUGUST

Raymond Davis-Hughes, a Welshman who broadcast propaganda for the Germans during the Second World War, was born on 11 August 1923.

Davis-Hughes (1923–99), from Mold, was an RAF airman whose plane was shot down over Germany during a bombing raid. He was in a POW camp when he was approached by the German authorities with an offer. Joseph Goebbels was the Third Reich's Propaganda Minister and he realised the importance and influence of mass media, and knew that a Welsh speaker could reach a new audience.

Hughes agreed to broadcast propaganda for the Germans in Welsh and went on to work with the traitor William Joyce, better known as Lord Haw-Haw, who broadcast propaganda programmes in English for the Nazis. After the war, Lord Haw-Haw was hanged for treason while Hughes was sentenced to five years hard labour, which was subsequently reduced to two years following an appeal for clemency.

12 AUGUST

On 12 August 1891, world-famous soprano Adelina Patti opened her private theatre at Craig-y-Nos Castle in the Swansea Valley.

Adelina Patti (1843–1919) was one of the most famous sopranos in history. The composer Giuseppe Verdi described her as being perhaps the finest singer who had ever lived. Patti's career was one of continuous success, inspiring frenzied acclaim and critical adulation. Her youthful good looks gave her an attractive stage presence, which considerably enhanced her celebrity status. At the peak of her career, Patti demanded to be paid, in gold, the equivalent of $5,000 a night, before she even deigned to perform.

When she retired from the stage, Patti settled in the Swansea Valley, where she bought Craig-y-Nos Castle. She commissioned a private theatre to be built, emulating in miniature the theatre at Bayreuth. The theatre remains intact to this day, and the stage is probably the only surviving example of original nineteenth-century 'backstage' equipment.

Patti also had a railway station built at Craig-y-Nos/Penwyllt on the Neath and Brecon Railway, and additionally, in 1918, she presented the Winter Garden building from her Craig-y-Nos estate to the city of Swansea. This was rebuilt near the Guildhall and renamed the 'Patti Pavilion'. The castle itself became a chest hospital in 1921, which remained in use until 1986 when it was sold and converted into a hotel.

13 AUGUST

On 13 August 1831, Dic Penderyn was hanged on the gallows in St Mary's Street, Cardiff, outside the city's gaol. His last words are reported to have been '*O Arglwydd, dyma gamwedd*' ('Oh Lord, here is iniquity').

Dic Penderyn was a Welsh labourer and coal miner, who was born Richard Lewis in Aberavon in 1808. His family moved to Merthyr Tydfil in 1819, where he and his father worked in the local mines. Richard was always known as Dic Penderyn after the village of Penderyn near Hirwaun, where he lodged.

On 3 June 1831, he was involved in the Merthyr Rising (find out more on 1 June). During the uprising, a mob ransacked the building where court records of debt were being stored. In a bid to restore order, a detachment from one of the Highland Regiments stationed at Brecon fired into the unarmed crowd, killing sixteen people. No soldiers were killed in the affray but one, Private Donald Black, was stabbed in the leg with a bayonet. Along with his cousin Lewis Lewis, Dic Penderyn was arrested for the attack even though neither man could be identified as carrying it out. It's thought that Dic had limited involvement in the rising, but both he and his cousin were convicted and sentenced to death, though Lewis later had his sentence commuted to transportation.

The people of Merthyr Tydfil were convinced that Dic Penderyn was not guilty and raised a petition demanding his release, which was signed by over 11,000 people. However, the Home Secretary Lord Melbourne, well known for his severity, refused to reduce the sentence and Dic Penderyn was hanged. Thousands grieved and lined the route as Dic's coffin was taken from Cardiff to Aberavon, where he was buried in St Mary's churchyard, Port Talbot.

Dic's death embittered relations between Welsh workers and the authorities and strengthened the Trade Union movement and Chartism in the run up to the Newport Rising in 1839. He became a working-class hero and a symbol for those who tried to fight and resist oppression.

14 AUGUST

Taking place from 1461 to 1468, the siege of Harlech Castle during the War of the Roses is famous as, arguably, the longest siege in British history and the inspiration for the song 'Men of Harlech'.

At the Battle of Towton in 1461, the Lancastrian King Henry VI was defeated and later deposed by the Yorkist King Edward IV. Henry's wife, Queen Margaret of Anjou fled to Harlech Castle which, due to its natural defences and the supply route by sea, became a refuge for the Lancastrians. Despite coming under frequent attack, for the next seven years it remained under Lancastrian control – the only place in England and Wales that was – for the last four years of the siege.

Harlech was eventually taken for the Yorkists by William Herbert, Earl of Pembroke and his brother Richard following a Lancastrian counter-attack by Jasper Tudor (uncle of the future Henry VII). Jasper, with the aid of Louis XI of France, had landed a force in Harlech and captured Denbigh, which provoked Edward IV into ordering William

Herbert to finally take Harlech. The campaign was brutal: Harlech was blockaded and placed under constant bombardment until the castle's garrison under its constable, Dafydd ap Ieuan, surrendered on 14 August 1468.

The song 'Men of Harlech' was first published in 1794 as a harp melody, based on a much earlier folk song by renowned Welsh harpist Edward Jones. The earliest known version with lyrics was published in 1862. The song gained international recognition when it was featured in the films *How Green Was My Valley* (1942) and *Zulu* (1964). It is also widely used as a regimental march for military regiments associated with Wales.

15 AUGUST

On 15 August 1620, the Pilgrim Fathers on board the *Mayflower* left Southampton to embark on their historic transatlantic voyage. The Pilgrim Fathers were Separatists who wanted to cut their ties with the Protestant Church of England because they believed that it had not rid itself of all Roman Catholic practices and, as such, was only partially reformed. Following persecution for their beliefs, they had initially fled to the Netherlands but later decided to go to America in order to obtain their religious freedom.

According to local legend, the *Mayflower* stopped to pick up water and supplies at the mainly Welsh colony of Cambriol at Renews in Newfoundland, Canada, before continuing on to Plymouth Rock. The colony was founded in 1617, by Sir William Vaughan from Carmarthenshire, in response to the poor economic conditions in Wales, but was ultimately unsuccessful and failed in the early 1630s, due to inadequate preparation, raids by pirates and a lack of cooperation from French fishermen.

Today Thanksgiving Day is celebrated in the United States on the fourth Thursday of November every year, to give thanks for the year's harvest. The celebration is generally thought to have its origins in the 1621 feast by the Pilgrim Fathers at Plymouth in modern day Massachusetts, to acknowledge their survival of the first year in the New World.

16 AUGUST

Sir Tasker Watkins (1918–2007) was awarded the Victoria Cross for extraordinary bravery on 16 August 1944 in Normandy during the Second World War. He had launched an assault on a German machine-gun post, where his actions as commanding officer saved the lives of at least half of his men.

After the war, Tasker Watkins studied law, acting as deputy to the attorney-general in the tribunal into the 1966 Aberfan disaster (find out more on 21 October). He received a knighthood in 1971, along with other honours including a GBE and Knight of St John.

Sir Tasker was an avid supporter of Welsh rugby. He became president of the Welsh Rugby Union (WRU) to general acclaim in 1993, and oversaw the game's change from amateur to professional in 1995, and the move from club to regional rugby in Wales. In 2006, he was made a Freeman of the City and County of Cardiff, joining a select group that includes Pope John Paul II, Winston Churchill, David Lloyd George and Nelson Mandela.

Such was his modesty that he disliked speaking of his heroism during the war, however, Graham Henry, the former Wales rugby coach, displayed Watkins's citation from his being awarded his Victoria Cross in the Welsh changing room before international matches to inspire the team. Former WRU chairman David Pickering said of Sir Tasker: 'He was one of the greatest ever Welshman, who will be remembered as one of our nation's heroes; a man who was an inspiration to so many people.'

17 AUGUST

The Monty Python film *The Life of Brian* was released on 17 August 1979. The film was directed by Colwyn Bay-born Terry Jones and featured Sue Jones-Davies from Dinas Cross, Pembrokeshire as Judith Iscariot.

The film tells of the life of Brian Cohen, who was born next door on the same day as Jesus Christ and is mistaken as being the Messiah. The film was controversial at the time, with some religious groups accusing it of being blasphemous. Thirty-nine local authorities in the UK banned it, as did some countries, such as Ireland and Norway. However, the film makers used this notoriety to their advantage with advertising slogans such as 'So funny it was banned in Norway!'

The film's ban was not lifted in Aberystwyth until 2009, when Sue Jones-Davies was elected mayor of the town.

18 AUGUST

On 18 August 1802, during a tour of Wales, Vice Admiral Nelson, accompanied by Lady Emma Hamilton and her husband Sir William, arrived in Monmouth.

During the two-day stay, Nelson recognised the importance of the area's woodland in providing timber for the British Navy's ships and approved the Naval Temple on The Kymin Hill, which had been built to commemorate his victory at the Battle of the Nile in 1798.

The touring party then attended a dinner held in Nelson's honour at the Beaufort Arms Inn where he said that he was much taken by the fact that a tribute such as the Naval Temple should be made by a small Welsh town that had no real seafaring connections, noting that it was 'the only monument of its kind erected to the Royal Navy in the Kingdom'. During the tour, Nelson also visited Swansea, Milford Haven, Cyfarthfa Ironworks, Tenby, Haverfordwest, Llandovery, Chepstow and Carmarthen, being welcomed with enthusiasm wherever he went.

The Monmouth Museum, formerly the Nelson Museum, is home to one of the largest collections of Nelson material in Britain. It was bequeathed to the town by Lady Llangattock, mother of the motoring pioneer Charles Rolls (of Rolls-Royce fame) who was also a native of Monmouth.

19 AUGUST

The 19 August is National Potato Day.

The humble potato is thought to have been first cultivated in the area between the south of Peru and the northeast of Bolivia over three thousand years ago, though scientists believe they may have grown wild in the region as long as 13,000 years ago. The vegetable was first introduced to Europe by the Spanish conquistadors, who first encountered potatoes during their campaigns of conquest in South America in the sixteenth century. In 1589, Sir Walter Raleigh is reputed to have been the first to bring the potato to Ireland. By 1776 it was reported that potato cultivation was widespread at Milford Haven.

Pembrokeshire potatoes were a particularly popular brand from the 1920s, when Pembrokeshire Earlies began to be grown on a large scale. They are harvested from the beginning of May until the end of July, after which they are called main crop potatoes. Pembrokeshire has a mild climate, which minimises the risk of frosts damaging newly emerged potato crops, and enables potatoes to be grown and harvested earlier than in most areas in the UK. There are also particular skills associated with growing Pembrokeshire Earlies. For example, stones are left in the soil to aid warming and hand picking is necessary to minimise damage during the first two weeks of the harvest when the potatoes are very soft. As the season progresses, the potatoes harden sufficiently to allow careful machine harvesting.

It remains a brand that is in strong demand and is used by many top chefs.

20 AUGUST

The fast-growing coniferous evergreen tree, the Leylandii (Leyland cypress), originated on the Leighton Estate east of Welshpool.

On 20 August 1846, the Leighton Estate was gifted to John Naylor as a wedding present from his uncle, the Liverpool banker Christopher Leyland, who was one of Britain's richest men. Naylor invested significantly in rebuilding the house and commissioned the well-known landscape architect Edward Kemp to design the gardens, which included two North American species of conifers in close proximity to each other, namely the Monterey cypress and the Nootka cypress. These two trees cross-pollinated to produce the hybrid Leylandii, which gets its fast speed of growth from the Monterey cypress and its hardiness from the Nootka cypress.

21 AUGUST

21 August marks World Senior Citizen Day.

The longest living Welsh man was John Evans (19 August 1877–10 June 1990) of Fforestfach, Swansea, who lived to the age of 112 years and 295 days.

The longest living Welsh woman was Jeanetta Thomas (2 December 1869–5 January 1982) of Llantrisant, who lived to the age of 112 years and 34 days.

22 AUGUST

On 22 August 1832, a pledge of abstinence from all strong drink was drawn up by the leading temperance campaigner

Joseph Livesey of Preston, Lancashire.

In the early part of the nineteenth century, the consumption of beer and spirits in Wales had reached dangerous levels, particularly in the newly created industrial regions. Beer was considered a good and necessary beverage for hard-working men as water quality was poor, and was severely limited in places like Merthyr and Swansea. This caused serious concern to the employers who saw the detrimental effects of drink on their workforce, and to the wives who saw hard-earned money being spent on alcohol. Consequently, the first half of the nineteenth century saw a rapid increase in temperance societies.

Joseph Livesey opened the first temperance hotel in England in 1833 and the British Association for the Promotion of Temperance was established in 1835. The movement spread quickly and, by the end of 1835, there were twenty-five temperance societies in Wales. Initially they advocated moderation, but it soon became clear that total abstinence was required when it was discovered that some members of the Ebbw Vale Temperance Society, who allowed its members to drink two pints of beer a day, were saving up their allowance for the weekend. The first teetotal society in Wales was created as early as 1835.

A high point for the movement came in 1881, following a successful campaign for Sunday closing of public houses in Wales. After the First World War, it began to decline in popularity and influence as it quickly became clear that alcohol was only one of many causes of poverty.

23 AUGUST

On 23 August 55 BC, Julius Caesar, accompanied by two Roman legions, set sail from the northern coast of modern day France to begin a planned invasion of Britain. They landed near Dover on or around 26 August. This invasion attempt failed, but it paved the way for further expeditions, which resulted in a successful invasion under the rule of Emperor Claudius in AD 43.

At this time, the inhabitants of the area later referred to as Britain were the Brythons, who spoke Brythonic, from which modern-day Welsh is derived. They lived in extended family units in round houses, and their dwellings were grouped together on high ground, forming enclosed hillforts. The extended family units connected with others in the locality to form tribes.

There were a number of tribes in what was later called Wales. The Silures lived on the high ground and valleys of the area that now covers the Brecon Beacons and the Valleys of South Wales, and there are remains of Silurian hillforts at Llanmelin and Sudbrook, roundhouses at Gwehelog and Thornwell (Chepstow) and evidence of lowland occupation at Goldcliff. The territory of the Ordovice tribe covered most of what is today mid Wales and parts of north and west Wales, while the Demetae – whose name is derived from the warrior god Demotos, which literally means the god of mead or drunkenness – lived in Pembrokeshire and much of Carmarthenshire.

The Gangani tribe is connected with an Irish tribe, the Concani, who occupied the region now known as Leinster. Part of this tribe migrated to the Llŷn Peninsula, where their stone-built forts, such as Tre'r Ceiri still survive. A second body of the Concani tribe migrated further east, becoming known as the Deceangli. They lived mainly in the area between the Clwyd and Dee rivers (in what is now Flintshire, Denbighshire, Anglesey and part of Cheshire) There is a chain of their hill forts running through the Clwydian mountain range including sites such as Moel Hiraddug and Dinas Dinorwig which overlooks Menai Strait.

24 AUGUST

Wales's leading cancer charity, Tenovus, was founded following an industrial accident. On 24 August 1943, Cardiff-based haulage contractor Eddie Price was unloading heavy machinery when one of the lathes fell on him, pinning him to the ground. He subsequently spent three months in Cardiff Royal Infirmary, where he was visited regularly by eight friends, all businessmen. They were joined by a Mr D. R. Edwards, the head of Prudential Insurance, who had traced Mr Price to thank him. Mr Price had rescued Mr Edwards by bringing him petrol after his car had broken down.

The men were determined to find a distraction for their injured and bored friend. They bought a radio for the hospital and headsets for the patients so that they could listen to it without disturbing others. They even managed to broadcast Cardiff City football games from Ninian Park to the hospital.

Inspired by this act of friendship, the men decided to

continue their philanthropy under the name Tenovus – ten of us.

Between them they had contacts and they used them, and they started to be approached by other people who needed help. They began fundraising activities. On the first Tuesday of the month, they would invite Cardiff dignitaries to a fundraising dinner at the Angel Hotel, where they would raise up to £10,000. Their achievements ranged from small to grand: they bought a washing machine for a widow with seven children and they raised money to build the Sunshine House for Blind Babies just outside Cardiff. Then towards the end of the Second World War, they were asked to raise £26,000 for a rest home for injured soldiers in Burma (Myanmar) who could not return home. They also funded research that led to pregnant people being advised to take folic acid to prevent spina bifida in babies.

Since the 1960s, Tenovus have concentrated their efforts on cancer research and support, and are now recognised for their pioneering work.

25 AUGUST

On 25 August 1945, the children who had been evacuated from English cities to the comparative safety of Wales returned home.

Evacuation had begun in September 1939 – an operation nicknamed 'Pied Piper' – when approximately 110,000 children were sent to Wales. Also included in the evacuation were mothers of young babies, pregnant women and disabled people. In some cases, teachers were evacuated and stayed in the same village as their pupils.

The child evacuees were all given a gas mask and food for the journey and had a label stating the child's name, home address, school and destination pinned to their clothing. Most of the children adapted well to country life, staying in touch with their host family after the end of war.

26 AUGUST

On 26 August 1981, the 'Women for Life on Earth' group began a 110-mile protest walk from Cardiff City Hall to the American airbase at RAF Greenham Common in Berkshire. Their aim was to raise awareness of the British government's decision to allow cruise missiles to be based at the site.

On arrival, some of the women chained themselves to the railings in an attempt to get an interview with the base's commander. When a response was not forthcoming, some pitched tents, determined to stay until their protest was recognised: the Greenham Common Women's Peace Camp was born. The following year, it was decided that the protest should involve women only, to draw attention to the male-dominated political decision-making of the time. The camp soon attracted the media's attention, bringing its aims to a worldwide audience. This caused annoyance to the authorities and over the years the site saw many clashes between demonstrators and the police.

The last missiles left the site in 1991, but the peace camp remained until the base was closed in 2000. The land was then returned to the public.

27 AUGUST

The story of Katheryn of Berain (c.1534/5–27 August 1591) and her many husbands and supposed lovers has become one of the great romances of north Wales.

Katheryn was the heiress to the Berain Estate in Denbighshire and the Penymynydd Estate in Anglesey. Her maternal grandfather, Sir Roland de Velville, was thought to be an illegitimate son of King Henry VII of England by 'a Breton lady'. She married four times to high-profile Welshmen, becoming part of the most well-off and influential families of north Wales. Katheryn's descendants went on to form some of the country's richest families, earning her the title *Mam Cymru* – the Mother of Wales.

28 AUGUST

Western Roman Emperor Magnus Maximus was executed on this day in AD 388.

Magnus Maximus became part of the Welsh legend of St Elen as Macsen Wledig in the *Mabinogion* (find out more about the *Mabinogion* on 22 May). Born in modern day Portugal c.335, he first came to Britain in 368 as a junior officer during the quelling of the Great Conspiracy, when the Roman garrison on Hadrian's Wall rebelled. He was assigned again to Britain in 380 as a general in the Roman Army. He was stationed in Wales, probably in Caernarfon, and defeated an incursion of the Picts and Scots in 381.

As Roman control over the Western Empire began to break down in the late fourth century, Maximus was chosen by his men as Emperor of Britain and Gaul. Then in 383,

he declared himself Western Emperor. As Emperor he stripped western and northern Britain of troops and senior administrators to consolidate his bid for imperial power.

That same year, Maximus took advantage of the increasing dissent against Roman Emperor Gratian by invading Gaul with a large army. He attempted to preserve the security of Britain by organising the peaceful settlement of the Irish Déisi tribe in Dyfed. Sources suggest that he conscripted the Cunedda and the Votadini tribes from Yr Hen Ogledd (southern Scotland) to deal with the aggressive Irish Uí Liatháin tribe in north Wales.

For a time, Maximus was recognised as Western Emperor by Theodosius the Eastern Emperor. However, in 388, Theodosius campaigned against Maximus and defeated him in the Battle of the Save in modern day Croatia, thus forcing Maximus to retreat to Aquileia, Italy (at the head of the Adriatic) where he surrendered. Although he pleaded for mercy, Maximus was executed.

There is nothing to suggest that any Roman effort was made to regain control of the west or north of Wales after 383 and that year is considered the definitive end of the Roman era in the country.

29 AUGUST

Gwyl Ieuan y Moch or The Beheading of John the Baptist is a holy day that commemorates the martyrdom of St John the Baptist. The Welsh name translates as St John of the Swine as historically, 29 August was the day pigs were turned out into the woods to forage through the winter.

30 AUGUST

On 30 August 1682, the first group of Welsh settlers set sail for the New World, in the area later known as Pennsylvania, including Thomas Wynne from Ysceifiog in Flintshire, the personal physician of William Penn.

The period following the restoration of Charles II to the English throne in 1660 saw the implementation of religious intolerances that inhibited the rights of several groups, including Quakers, to worship in their chosen fashion. Large numbers of people, in some cases whole communities, elected to leave Wales to escape persecution.

In the Court of Great Sessions in Bala, threats were made against Quakers' lives, impelling the society of Welsh Quakers to acquire land from William Penn. This was known as The Welsh Tract, comprising an area of approximately 40,000 acres in and around what is now known as Pennsylvania. By 1700, the Welsh accounted for about one-third of the colony's estimated population of twenty thousand.

During the 1790s, immigrants from the village of Llanbrynmair in Montgomeryshire established the Welsh colony of Cambria – now Cambria County, Pennsylvania

– on land purchased by Baptist minister Morgan John Rhys. In Cambria, Welsh culture and Welsh religion were embedded in a community with a distinct Welsh identity. Many towns in the area still carry Welsh names, including Radnor, Haverford Township, Lower Merion, Upper Merion and Bala Cynwyd.

Pennsylvania still has the largest number of Welsh-Americans, with approximately 200,000 concentrated in the state's western and north-eastern regions.

31 AUGUST

Korea's first Protestant martyr, Robert Jermain Thomas, was beaten to death on 31 August 1866.

Born in Rhayader in 1839, Thomas moved to Llanover when his father became its chapel minister. After leaving college he joined the Protestant evangelical London Mission Society, now part of the Council for World Mission, who sent him to China.

During this trip, Thomas became keen to work in Korea. However, Korea was closed to foreigners and had recently executed approximately 8,000 Christian converts. Undeterred, Thomas first visited Korea in 1865, attempting to learn about the people and their language. The following year, he joined an American trading ship headed for Korea as an interpreter. As the ship sailed up the Taedong River, Thomas threw gospel tracts onto the riverbank.

The Koreans declared the ship as a non-friendly and, when it ran aground near Pyongyang, a battle commenced, which lasted for two days. Eventually the Koreans set fire to the ship, which resulted in eighteen of the crew being either shot or burnt to death. Thomas and another crew member jumped to shore, where they were beaten to death by angry civilians.

However, local people had picked up the Bibles that Thomas had thrown overboard and these are thought to have contributed to a revival of Christianity in Korea fifty years later. In 1931, the Thomas Memorial Church was built by Korean Christians on the riverbank where Thomas was killed. Although it was destroyed in 1946, it is now the site of a Christian university.

1 SEPTEMBER

In September 2022, Wales became the first nation in the UK to make the teaching of Black, Asian and Minority Ethnic histories and experiences a mandatory element in the school curriculum.

The development of the new curriculum follows years of work by teachers and other education professionals.

Jeremy Miles, the Minister for Education and Welsh Language said: 'It is vitally important that our education system equips our young people to understand and respect their own and each other's histories, cultures and traditions.'

2 SEPTEMBER

On 2 September 1800, construction started on the Penrhyn Quarry Railway.

In 1765, Richard Pennant married Anne Susannah Warburton, heiress to half of the Penrhyn estate. Richard Pennant leased, and later bought, the other half of the estate. Anne Susannah was also heir to a number of plantations in Jamaica. Together they owned 8,000 acres of sugar plantations and over 600 slaves on the island. Richard Pennant was an outspoken supporter of slavery.

He used his great wealth, amassed on the proceeds of enslaved labour in Jamaica, to industrialise and rapidly expand the Bethesda slate quarries and capture international markets; build Port Penrhyn; and link his quarries to the port. In 1798, the one-mile long Llandegai Tramway was built to connect Lord Penrhyn's slate quarries at Bethesda to a local flint mill that ground clay and chert into flints. Encouraged by its success, the Pennants started construction of the Penrhyn Quarry Railway on 2 September 1800, and it opened the following June. It connected the quarry to the sea at Porth Penrhyn and was one of the earliest overground narrow-gauge railways in the world. However, by 1874 the railroad was no longer able to keep up with the quarry's output and a steam locomotive was introduced. It was closed in 1962.

The Penrhyn slate mine was also the site of a long industrial dispute. (Find out more on 22 November.)

3 SEPTEMBER

The last hanging at Cardiff jail occurred on 3 September 1952.

Mahmood Hussein Mattan was a Somali merchant seaman who was wrongly convicted of the murder of Lily Volpert in the docklands of Cardiff in 1952, mainly on the evidence of a single prosecution witness and despite a lack of other evidence.

In 1996, Mattan's family were given permission to have his body exhumed and moved from a felon's grave at the prison to be buried in consecrated ground in a Cardiff cemetery. Soon after, his case was the first to be referred to the newly formed Criminal Cases Review Commission and in 1998 the Court of Appeal quashed his conviction, finding the judgement to be 'demonstrably flawed'. His wife and three children were awarded compensation.

South Wales police issued an apology to Mattan's family in 2022. The chief constable, Jeremy Vaughan, said, 'This is a case very much of its time – racism, bias and prejudice would have been prevalent throughout society, including the criminal justice system. There is no doubt that Mahmood Mattan was the victim of a miscarriage of justice as a result of a flawed prosecution, of which policing was clearly a part.'

In 2021, Nadifa Mohamed became the first British Somali novelist to be shortlisted for the Booker Prize with her novel, *The Fortune Men*, a retelling of Mattan's life and story. The novel also won the 2022 English-Language Wales Book of the Year Award.

4 SEPTEMBER

The first Pride Cymru festival (then known as Mardi Gras) was held in Cardiff on 4 September 1999, with more than 2,000 people in attendance. The event was planned as a celebration, and to highlight equality issues. The event now regularly attracts 50,000 people over the three days of the Pride Cymru Big Weekend.

Patrons have included rugby referee Nigel Owens, singer Charlotte Church and Welsh screenwriter and television producer Russell T. Davies.

5 SEPTEMBER

Was the original recipe for Jack Daniel's legendary American whiskey discovered in Wales?

Jasper Newton 'Jack' Daniel, founder of the eponymous Tennessee whiskey distillery, was probably born on 5 September 1850 in Lynchburg, Tennessee – but his grandfather Joseph 'Job' Daniel, was born in Wales before emigrating to the US.

In 2012, Mark Evans was researching his family history when he discovered a recipe, the ingredients of which match those which go into making the world's bestselling whiskey. It was written in 1853 by his great-great grandmother, a Llanelli herbalist who was also called Daniel. Her husband, John 'Jack the Lad' Daniel left Llanelli to move to Tennessee, where the Jack Daniel Distillery was opened three years later. However, the Jack Daniel's company have since denied that Jack the Lad is *the* Jack Daniel and as a fire destroyed the company's early records, there's no way to really know whether there is genuinely a link between the two.

> ## DID YOU KNOW?
> Jack Daniel died from blood poisoning in 1911, which was allegedly caused when he kicked his safe in anger when he could not get it open. He had always had trouble remembering the combination.

6 SEPTEMBER

The Welsh National Eisteddfod of 1917 was held on 6 September at Birkenhead and is remembered as 'The Eisteddfod of the Black Chair'.

When the winner of the Chair poetry competition was announced as Hedd Wyn from Trawsfynydd, there was silence and no one moved forward to collect the prize. This was because Ellis Evans, who wrote under his bardic name of Hedd Wyn, had been killed a few weeks earlier on the first day of the Battle of Passchendaele during the First World War. The chair was draped in black cloth for the remainder of the ceremony and was later taken to Evans's home farm of Yr Ysgwrn near Trawsfynydd.

7 SEPTEMBER

Born in Merthyr Tydfil on 7 September 1925, Laura Mountney Ashley (1925–85) was a fashion designer and businesswoman. She started making furnishing materials in the 1950s and expanded into manufacturing and designing clothes in the 1960s.

Laura left school at sixteen, to serve in the Women's Royal Naval Service and met her husband, engineer Bernard Ashley in Wallington at a youth club. Her early textile work involved designing napkins, table mats, headscarves and tea towels, which Bernard printed using a machine he designed. Her breakthrough came when she was looking for patches of Victorian design to make patchworks. Failing to find any at a display of traditional handicrafts by the Women's Institute at the Victoria and Albert Museum, she decided to make her own and used her creations as Victorian style headscarves. These became hugely popular after Audrey Hepburn wore one in the 1953 film *Roman Holiday*. The success encouraged the couple to move back to Wales in 1961 and go into full-time production. The first Laura Ashley shop opened in Machynlleth that same year.

8 SEPTEMBER

The government's decision to establish an RAF bombing school at the historic and cultural site of Penyberth on the Llŷn peninsula in 1936 was met with intense anger throughout Wales. With previous protests having been ignored, three Plaid Cymru members, Saunders Lewis, Lewis Valentine and D. J. Williams, decided that the only course of action remaining was to set fire to the bombing school. They did so 8 September 1936, giving themselves up immediately at Pwllheli police station. They were later sentenced to nine months' imprisonment. Upon their release, 15,000 people welcomed them as heroes at a pavilion in Caernarfon.

9 SEPTEMBER

On 9 September 1843, the toll gate at Hendy was set alight and, in the resulting melee, a shot was fired. Minutes later the gatekeeper, seventy-five-year-old Sarah Williams, lay dead. This incident occurred during the Rebecca Riots, a series of protests that took place between 1839 and 1843.

Since 1752, Acts of Parliament had enabled committees (known as Turnpike Trusts) made up of trustees – usually local businessmen and landowners – to set up a network of toll gates to finance the repair and maintenance of road systems in Wales. This was before the major industrialisation of south Wales when the economy was mainly reliant on agriculture. Tenant farmers were especially hard-hit by the tolls as they regularly had to use the roads to transport produce and livestock and also had to pay tithes (a tenth of all their produce each year) to the church, as well as their rent.

The harsh economic situation resulted in a civil disturbance on 13 May 1839, when the gate at Efailwen in north-west Carmarthenshire was destroyed and the adjoining toll house set alight. For the following four years, the protests continued regularly, mainly in Pembrokeshire, Cardiganshire and Carmarthenshire. They were typically carried out by groups of dissenters dressed in women's clothing who set about destroying toll gates and attacking workhouses. The participants called themselves 'Rebecca and her daughters' – most likely referring to a passage in the Bible where Rebecca talks of the need to 'possess the gates of those who hate them' – and so, the protests became known as the Rebecca Riots.

Initially there was wide-scale public support for the riots, and when the government sent in troops to try to prevent the outbreaks, they were often sent on wild goose chases. However, this diminished following the death of Sarah Williams. After this three Rebecca rioters were transported to Australia and others were detained in prison.

However, the riots did force the government to call a Commission of Enquiry to explore the grievances of the Welsh farmers. As a result, in 1844 the Turnpike Trusts within each county were consolidated, with tolls on commodities such as lime being reduced by half. 'Rebecca and her daughters' eventually won their victory when the rapid spread of railways throughout Wales forced many of the Turnpike Trusts into bankruptcy and in 1888 the responsibility for roads was handed back to local councils.

10 SEPTEMBER

The last recorded fatal duel with pistols in Wales took place near Newcastle Emlyn on 10 September 1814. Thomas Heslop was killed by solicitor John Beynon following a drink-fuelled quarrel over the affections of a barmaid.

The story goes that Heslop, a mysterious man of West Indian origin and a recent arrival to Wales, had been invited to a partridge shoot by Beynon. At the end of the day, the shooting party retired to the Old Salutation Inn at Adpar for an evening of drinking and it was here that the two men fell out, resulting in Beynon being challenged to a duel by Heslop.

They stood with their backs towards each other on either side of a stream, armed with flintlock pistols and were sup-

posed to walk ten paces before turning and firing. However, it is said that Beynon only walked five paces before turning and shooting Heslop in the back. Heslop died instantly and was buried at nearby Llandyfriog Church, with the inscription 'Alas Poor Heslop' on his grave.

Beynon was initially convicted of manslaughter, but a number of powerful and well-known county figures spoke up on his behalf and he escaped with a fine. Although we can't say for certain, it could be that his mild punishment was due to Heslop's West Indian origins, an example of racial injustice.

11 SEPTEMBER

The first Women's Institute (WI) meeting in Britain was held in Llanfairpwllgwyngyllgogerychwyrndrobwllllanty-siliogogogoch on 11 September 1915.

The WI movement began in Canada in 1897 for the wives of members of the Farmers' Institute. In the UK, it was originally set up to revitalise rural communities and to encourage women to become more involved in producing food during the First World War. After the first year, there were forty WIs across the UK. It has since grown to become the UK's largest women's organisation with over 200,000 members in more than 6,500 branches.

12 SEPTEMBER

The Wales and Lions rugby player Ray Gravell was born in Kidwelly on 12 September 1951. He played club rugby for Llanelli and was a member of the team that beat the

All Blacks in 1972, eventually going on to captain the club from 1980–2. He made twenty-three appearances for Wales and played in two Grand Slam winning sides. In his later career, he would become a respected broadcaster and was also the Grand Sword Bearer of the Gorsedd of Bards, known by his bardic name Ray o'r Mynydd.

Gravell died on 31 October 2007. His public funeral at Stradey Park was attended by up to 10,000 mourners from all over Wales. Gravell's coffin was carried on to the field by six Llanelli players and, during the ceremony, the scoreboard read 'Llanelli 9–Seland Newydd 3', just as it did at the end of the famous All Blacks match in 1972.

At the Wales versus France Six Nations match at the Millennium Stadium in March 2008, Gravell's daughters led the Wales team onto the pitch carrying the Triple Crown plate. In the same match, members of the coaching staff wore shirts bearing Gravell's name and shirt number: thirteen.

13 SEPTEMBER

Roald Dahl (1916–90) is one of the most successful children's writers in the world; it is estimated that his books have sold more than 250 million copies worldwide.

Roald Dahl was born in Llandaff, Cardiff to Norwegian parents on 13 September 1916. After finishing school, Dahl worked for Shell Petroleum in Africa before joining the RAF as a pilot during the Second World War. The moment he was shot down in Libya inspired his first story, 'A Piece of Cake'.

After the war, Dahl married an American actress,

Academy Award winner Patricia Neal, and settled in Great Missenden, Buckinghamshire. It was here that in 1961, inspired by the bedtime stories he told his daughters, he wrote *James and the Giant Peach*. He followed this with *Danny the Champion of the World*, *The BFG* and *Charlie and the Chocolate Factory*, among many others. Dahl wrote for four hours every day in his little hut in the garden and was particular in using the same brand of pencil and special yellow paper.

Dahl's private life was struck by the tragedy with the death of his daughter, Olivia. And Patricia nearly died during the pregnancy of their fifth child, after which Dahl devoted himself to nursing her back to health. They later separated and Dahl married Llandaff-born film producer Felicity D'Abreu in 1983.

14 SEPTEMBER

On 14 September 1914 the 'Cardiff Pals' marched to war.

At the end of August 1914, it was decided that the British Army needed an additional 100,000 volunteers in the war against Germany. So, in an experimental move, they allowed groups of friends to enlist and serve in units together. These units proved extremely popular, becoming known as the Pals Battalions. On 14 September 1914, the Cardiff Pals were seen off to war by hundreds of people lining the streets. The Cardiff Pals went on to fight in Salonika for three years, defending Macedonia, northern Greece and the Aegean ports from German and Bulgarian forces. Tragically they suffered almost a hundred casualties in one assault on 18 September 1918, barely two months before the war ended. The devastating impact of such huge losses to single communities led to the disbanding of Pals Battalions for future conflicts.

15 SEPTEMBER

The Gleision Colliery mining accident occurred on 15 September 2011, in a drift mine at Cilybebyll near Pontardawe in the Tawe Valley.

The accident occurred while seven miners were working underground with explosives. An initial explosion caused the tunnel in which the miners were working to begin to fill with water. Three of the men managed to escape but a rescue operation to discovered the remaining four men dead the following day. This disaster was the worst to occur in Wales for three decades.

16 SEPTEMBER

On 16 September 1400, Owain Glyndŵr was proclaimed as Prince of Wales. It is now celebrated annually as Owain Glyndŵr Day. The day has been celebrated in modern-day Wales with re-enactments at historical castles connected to Glyndŵr, talks and events designed to educate people about his impact on the country.

Owain Glyndŵr's uprising began with a dispute during 1399 and 1400 over a piece of land that Glyndŵr claimed had been stolen by his neighbour, the Marcher Lord Sir Reginald de Grey. When Glyndŵr received no justice from

King Henry IV and his repeated appeals were ignored, he felt that he was left with no option other than to rebel against the unjust and oppressive rule of the English.

Word of Glyndŵr's stance struck a chord with other disaffected Welsh people and he became the symbolic leader of the resistance movement against the crown and the arrogant Marcher Lords. On 16 September 1400, Glyndŵr raised his banner on the outskirts of Ruthin and was proclaimed by his followers as Prince of Wales.

As word of the revolt spread, the men of Wales flocked to Owain's banner in droves and many exiled Welsh people returned to join what had become a widespread national uprising.

However in 1409, Glyndwr became besieged at Harlech Castle and this in effect was the end of the rebellion. He did, however, make his escape and remained unbetrayed and uncaptured until his death in c.1416.

17 SEPTEMBER

The man-made sea wall at Porthmadog known as The Cob was opened on 17 September 1811. It was built by William Alexander Madocks and was instrumental in the emergence of the towns of Porthmadog and Tremadog.

Crossing the estuary of the River Glaslyn had always been very dangerous, and people would engage guides in order to cross safely. Madocks had begun building the town of Tremadog in 1798 and when the Act of Union, combining the Kingdoms of Britain and Ireland came into force in 1800, it was anticipated that traffic in north Wales would increase as links with Ireland were developed.

Madocks saw an opportunity to increase the accessibility of Tremadog and to reclaim thousands of acres of land by building the sea wall across the River Glaslyn estuary. The project began in March 1805 and employed approximately 400 people. The Cob was opened on 17 September 1811 with a four-day celebration including an Eisteddfod.

18 SEPTEMBER

Gwynfynydd Gold Mine near Ganllwyd, Dolgellau was discovered on 18 September 1860 and remained active until 1998, when it was closed due to health and safety problems regarding the discharge from the mine into the River Mawddach. The largest and richest mine in the area, Clogau near Dolgellau, closed in 1911.

Welsh gold is prized because of its quality. It is found in two areas of Wales, the area around Dolgellau, and in Dolaucothi, Carmarthenshire. The Dolaucothi mine is thought to have been active since the late Bronze Age, perhaps as early as 600 BC. However, large-scale excavation has uncovered artefacts dating to approximately 75 AD, during the Roman rule of Britain.

The earliest gold artefact found in Wales was discovered on 16 October 2002, at Cwmystwyth, Ceredigion. Thought to be over 4,000 years old, the Banc Ty'nddôl sun-disc is a small, decorated, gold ornament that was most likely part of a funerary garment.

Welsh gold became fashionable when the Queen Mother chose it for her wedding ring in 1923. The ring was fashioned from a gift of Clogau gold, with enough left over for the wedding rings of Queen Elizabeth II, Princess Margaret, Princess Diana and the Duchess of Cambridge, Catherine Middleton. A kilogramme of the gold was also gifted to Queen Elizabeth II on her sixtieth birthday.

DID YOU KNOW?
In Welsh legend, King Arthur's sword, known as Caledfwlch, had a hilt crafted of Welsh gold.

---

19 SEPTEMBER

Today marks 'International Talk Like a Pirate Day', and there are a number of historical Welsh connections to piracy.

- Possibly from Wales, St Patrick (find out more on 17 March) was kidnapped by pirates and taken to Ireland where he was sold into slavery c.432.

- Prior to his conversion to Christianity, St Gwynllyw, King of Gwynllwg c.450 is the patron saint of Welsh pirates and the city of Newport. He led a life of violence and piracy causing terror across the Bristol Channel.

- In 1275, Edward I of England hired pirates to seize Eleanor de Montfort as she sailed from France to meet her future husband Llywelyn ap Gruffydd. Llywelyn was forced to make concessions to secure her release.

- John Callis was a sixteenth-century pirate who was active for decades on the Welsh side of the Bristol Channel. His most well-known base was the Point House at Angle in Pembrokeshire and he would often sell his bounty in Laugharne and Carew. He was captured and hanged at Newport in 1576.

- From c.1650 until the 1720s, the Caribbean was a prime target for piracy attacks: the English, French and Dutch were developing their competing empires and there was a lot of seaborne trade with valuable cargo and vast sums of money in the area. Notable Welsh pirates of this era include: Captain Morgan, a farmer's son from Llanrumney, Hywel Davies from Milford Haven and Black Bart from Casnewydd-Bach (Little Newcastle) near Fishguard.

Towards the mid-eighteenth century, the improved efficiency of country's navies made piracy far more difficult and there were fewer safe bases from which pirates could operate. This ended the 'Golden Age of Piracy' but resulted in an increase in smuggling, with the isolated beaches and hidden coves of Anglesey, the Llŷn Peninsula and the islands in the Bristol Channel such as Lundy, Flat Holm and Caldey Island being popular landing sites for illicit goods.

20 SEPTEMBER

On 20 September 1891, 'Buffalo Bill' Cody (1846–1917) and his Wild West Show performed at Cardiff – the first of many visits to Wales.

From 1863, he served for the Union during the American Civil War. After the war, he worked as a buffalo hunter for the Kansas Pacific Railway, which the government encouraged to transport Native Americans onto reservations. It's said he shot more than 4,000 buffaloes and this is how he got the name Buffalo Bill.

Bill came to international attention when he gave Grand Duke Alexis of Russia a guided a tour of the wild. The visit featured in a news report, and was followed by a series of novels based on his adventures.

In 1883, Bill set up his famous Wild West show, which was invited to Britain in 1887 as part of Queen Victoria's Golden Jubilee celebrations. His party comprised 500 people including cowboys and Native Americans as well as backstage workers and grooms for the 180 horses. In addition there were eighteen buffalo as well as elks and Texas Longhorn cattle. One of the group was the famous Annie Oakley, who shot a cigar from the mouth of the German Kaiser William I, the grandson of Queen Victoria.

The visit was a great success and Buffalo Bill returned in 1891 to tour many cities, including Cardiff where he performed at Sophia Gardens for three nights. Each show attracted over 20,000 people. Bill returned again in 1902 on a tour that lasted until 1904.

21 SEPTEMBER

J. R. R. Tolkien's novel *The Hobbit* was published on 21 September 1937. It achieved wide critical acclaim and is recognised as a classic in children's literature. He later wrote *The Lord of the Rings* trilogy, which is one of the bestselling works of literature ever written.

Tolkien (1892–1973) was heavily influenced by Wales, and especially the Welsh language. The Elvish language, Sindarin, sounds very much like Welsh and many of his place names have similar Welsh equivalents – for example Crickhollow (Crickhowell). Tolkien's fascination with the Welsh began during his childhood in Birmingham where he would see Welsh words on coal trucks arriving from Wales. He later studied the Welsh language and read a lot of medieval Welsh literature. He is quoted as saying, 'Welsh is of this soil, this island, the senior language of the men of Britain; Welsh is beautiful.'

22 SEPTEMBER

One of Britain's worst ever coal mining disasters occurred on 22 September 1934 at the Gresford Colliery near Wrexham where 266 men and boys died when a massive explosion ripped through the mine. There were only six survivors and just eleven of the victims' bodies were ever recovered. The cause of the The Gresford Disaster was never proven, but the inquiry suggested many contributory factors, which included poor mine management and safety procedures.

23 SEPTEMBER

Twin sisters Heidi and Jo Munro were born on 23 September 1976. However, Heidi was born in Welshpool in Wales and Jo was born in Shrewsbury in England. They claim to be the first pair of twins to be born in different countries. Their mother, Carol Munroe, was unaware she was carrying twins. She gave birth to Heidi at 9 a.m. in Welshpool but went into labour again later. For the second birth, she was taken to Shrewsbury Hospital, giving birth to Jo at 10:45 a.m.

24 SEPTEMBER

William Frost from Saundersfoot, arguably the true inventor of the flying machine, flew the 'Frost Airship Glider' for the first and only time on 24 September 1896.

Described as a balloon-powered hang-glider, with helicopter-style blades operated by foot pedals, Frost's flying machine was witnessed to fly for 500 metres before crashing into bushes. However, the event was not officially recorded and an overnight storm destroyed what remained of the craft. Frost died in 1935 without receiving the recognition his achievement surely deserved.

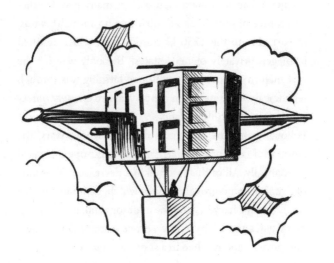

25 SEPTEMBER

The Carmarthen Cheese Riot occurred on 25 September 1818, when a crowd prevented a consignment of cheese from being loaded onto a ship docked at Carmarthen.

Cheese had become a vital part of many people's diet as a source of protein and a substitute for meat. This was, in part, due to the 1750 Enclosure Acts, which resulted in bigger, privately owned estates. The only way for the vast majority of people to continue farming was through tenancy. By the nineteenth century, approximately ninety per cent of agricultural land was being farmed this way. Following Britain's victory in the Napoleonic Wars, the amount of farm produce arriving from Europe increased dramatically. All of this resulted in a decrease in the value of Britain's home-grown produce which, combined with a series of poor harvests and the additional financial burden of toll gates and Church tithes, drove many tenant farmers into poverty and resulted in a shortage of food.

Consequently seeing cheese being sent for export instead of being made available to the people of Carmarthen enraged the crowd. A second attempt to load the cheese was made two days later. However, this time not only were the goods stopped from going on board, the vessel was also ransacked. Order was only regained when the merchants decided to distribute the cheese locally.

26 SEPTEMBER

The European Day of Languages is observed on 26 September.

Welsh is one of the oldest languages in Europe. It developed from the Brythonic language spoken in most of Britain before the Roman occupation. Following the Anglo-Saxon colonisation of England, the Brythonic speakers in Wales were cut off from those in those in the north and south-west of England, resulting in the separate development of the Welsh, Cumbric and Cornish languages.

A timeline of the Welsh language:

1536 The Act of Union of Henry VIII prohibited the use of Welsh in public administration and the legal system.

1567 The New Testament was translated into Welsh by William Salesbury.

1588 The complete Bible was translated into Welsh by Bishop William Morgan.

1847 A Royal Commission on the state of education in Wales controversially concluded that education was failing because people continued to speak Welsh. (Find out more on 1 July.)

1937 Following pressure from Plaid Cymru, the BBC established a Welsh regional broadcasting channel with limited Welsh-language content.

1942 The Welsh Courts Act established limited rights to use the Welsh language in a court of law.

1947 Ysgol Gymraeg Llanelli opened, the first Welsh-medium school to be fully maintained by an education authority.

1962 A radio broadcast by Saunders Lewis entitled *Tynged yr Iaith* (*The Fate of the Language*) foresaw the demise of Welsh and urged Welsh people to use it and insist on it for official purposes. This led to the establishment of *Cymdeithas yr Iaith Gymraeg* (the Welsh Language Society).

1967 A Welsh Language Act granted the right to testify in Welsh in a court of law, and the right to have official forms in Welsh.

1964 BBC Cymru Wales was launched.

1977 Radio Cymru was established.

1982 The Welsh-language television channel, S4C first broadcast. (Find out more on 14 July.)

1993 A Welsh Language Act confirmed the equal status of English and Welsh in Wales.

2003 The Welsh Assembly published *Iaith Pawb*, a national plan for a bilingual Wales.

27 SEPTEMBER

Born in Glynneath on 27 September 1943, Max Boyce is a singer and entertainer who rose to international fame with an act that combined musical comedy with his passion for rugby union and his origins in the mining communities of south Wales. Boyce began writing songs about the mining community whilst studying for a mining engineering degree in Trefforest in the early 1970s and then began performing in local clubs, where he developed the humorous element to his act.

Boyce became a household name in Wales and beyond thanks to the unexpected success of his album *Live at Treorchy*. Recorded on 23 November 1973, the album contains a mixture of songs and poems along with Boyce's interactions with the crowd at Treorchy Rugby Club. 'Hymns and Arias', one of the album's songs, has become an anthem of Welsh popular culture and is often heard at Wales international matches.

28 SEPTEMBER

Alexander Fleming discovered penicillin, the world's first antibiotic, on 28 September 1928. One of Fleming's research students was Merlin Pryce from the village of Troedyrhiw near Merthyr Tydfil. According to reports, it was Pryce, who, whilst tidying up the laboratory, first noticed that there was no sign of any bacteria surrounding mould in the now-famous Petri dish containing the staphylococci culture, which had accidentally been left out of an incubator while Fleming was on holiday. Fleming would later discover that the mould produced a bacteria-killing chemical, which he named penicillin.

29 SEPTEMBER

The statue of Betty Campbell was unveiled in Cardiff on 29 September 2021. Betty was Wales's first Black head teacher, a community activist and an inspirational champion of race equality in education.

Betty was born in Butetown, Cardiff in 1934. Her dream was always to become a teacher and, despite negative social stereotyping and the lack of encouragement she received from her teachers, she was determined to fulfil this. Betty excelled at school and was successful in winning a place at Cardiff Teacher Training College, after which she got her first job in Llanrumney, before returning to Butetown and Mount Stuart Primary School, where she later became headmistress.

At first, Betty's appointment attracted hostility from some parents, but she was able to prove herself more than capable – introducing innovative ideas of how children should be educated and being actively involved in the community. She became known as a leading authority on education and attracted attention from outside Wales. Betty was invited to meet Nelson Mandela during his visit to Wales in 1998 and Prince Charles made a personal visit to her school.

Over the course of her career, Betty served on the Home Office's Race Advisory Committee and was appointed to the Commission for Racial Equality. She represented her community as a councillor from 1999 to 2004 and was awarded an MBE in 2003 for services to education and community life. In 2015 Betty was awarded a lifetime achievement award by Unison Cymru's Black Members' group for her contribution to Welsh education and to the recognition of Black history.

30 SEPTEMBER

On 30 September 1913, John Jones – also known as *Coch Bach y Bala* (The Little Redhead of Bala) – made his final escape from prison.

Coch Bach's numerous escapes from prisons, police cells and holding jails have seen him go down in Welsh folklore as 'The Welsh Houdini'. It is said that he spent time in and escaped from every prison in north Wales, with his exploits being followed by national newspapers and becoming the subject of many postcards.

Coch Bach was born in 1853 in Bala and began his life of crime at an early age, stealing eggs from farmers. He soon graduated to taking unguarded property from local people. He made his first escape from Ruthin Gaol whilst awaiting trial for the theft of twelve watches.

He made his most famous escape in 1900 while waiting to be transferred to Dartmoor Prison from Caernarfon. Here he barricaded his cell door and dug an escape tunnel while the prison guards tried to break in to his cell. For his final escape, Coch Bach had broken through his cell wall, climbed the prison wall and lowered himself to freedom using a knotted blanket as a rope. However, he was shot in the leg during the attempt to recapture him and died six days later from his injuries.

1 OCTOBER

The thirty-eighth Ryder Cup was held on 1–4 October 2010 at the Celtic Manor Resort in Newport. The Celtic Manor's owner, Sir Terry Matthews, was the driving force in bringing the Ryder Cup to Wales for the first time: he and his team created a new world-class golf course in less than ten years, and they even built a £2 million bridge over the River Usk that led to a new practice ground.

The Ryder Cup is the world's third biggest sporting event, and the tournament in Newport was broadcast to 180 countries and more than 750 million homes across the globe. As professional golfer Colin Montgomerie said, 'the world was watching and Wales delivered'.

Although the weather wasn't good for the event, Sir Terry saw this as a positive: 'We got an extra day of coverage for all the sponsors. Can you imagine signing up for an event as big as the Ryder Cup and getting thirty-three per cent extra for free!'

Matthews started his working life as an apprentice with the General Post Office (now British Telecom (BT)), before studying engineering at Swansea. Whilst on holiday in Canada he landed a job and decided to stay. He borrowed £1,800 and started the firm Mitel, which offered the first affordable push-button tone phones. This proved a phenomenal success and he subsequently sold the business to BT. Matthews then founded Newbridge Networks, which he sold to Alcatel of France for close to £5 billion, becoming Wales's first billionaire. Interestingly, Wesley Clover, the name of Matthew's international investment company, is named after a Wesleyan chapel in the Newport area where, as a child, he says he found a four-leaf clover.

2 OCTOBER

Life-saving dog Swansea Jack died on 2 October 1937.

The black retriever from the North Dock area of Swansea regularly responded to cries of help from anyone in difficulty in the waters of the docks and riverbanks of the city, bringing them to the safety of the dockside.

It's documented that his first rescue was in June 1931 when he saved the life of a young boy. A few weeks later, in front of a crowd of people, Swansea Jack rescued another swimmer who had run into trouble. Over his lifetime he went on to save the lives of twenty-seven people and, in 2000, he was named 'Dog of the Century'.

Swansea Jack died on 2 October 1937 after eating rat poison and his burial plot – which was paid for by public funds – was situated on the Swansea to Mumbles promenade by St Helens Rugby ground.

3 OCTOBER

On 3 October 1283, Dafydd ap Gruffydd, the brother of Llywelyn ap Gruffydd, become the first prominent person in recorded history to be hanged, drawn and quartered. He was also the first person known to have been tried and executed for high treason against the King, and Edward I ensured his death was slow and agonising. Dafydd was dragged through Shrewsbury attached to a horse's tail, then hanged until he was almost dead, revived, then disembowelled and his entrails burned before him for 'his sacrilege in committing his crimes' (one count of treason was committed during Easter 1282). Then his body was cut into four quarters 'for plotting the king's death'.

A timeline of events leading to Dafydd ap Gruffydd's execution:

1238   Dafydd was born to Gruffydd ap Llywelyn and his wife, Senena, and thus a grandson of Llywelyn Fawr.

1255   Dafydd joined in a challenge to Llywelyn at the Battle of Bryn Derwin. Llywelyn was victorious and imprisoned Dafydd but released him and restored him to favour the following year.

1263 Dafydd joined King Henry III of England against Llywelyn.

1267 At the Treaty of Montgomery, Llywelyn was recognised as Prince of Wales by King Henry III and Dafydd was again restored to Llywelyn's favour.

1272 Henry III died and was replaced on the throne by his son Edward I.

1274 Dafydd was involved in an unsuccessful assassination attempt on Llywelyn and forced to flee to England where he was maintained by King Edward I and assisted in further raids on Llywelyn's lands.

1276 Edward I declared Llywelyn a rebel and gathered a massive army to march against him.

1282 Around Easter, Dafydd, now reconciled with Llywelyn, attacked Hawarden Castle, thereby starting the final conflict with Edward I.

1282 On 11 December Llywelyn was killed and Dafydd, who had become Prince of Wales, went on the run.

1283 In January, Edward I had the heartland of independent Wales ringed with a massive army.

Dafydd was initially based at Dolwyddelan, but with limited resources this became indefensible and he moved to Castell y Bre.

1283   On 22 June Dafydd was eventually captured and taken to King Edward at Rhuddlan.

1283   On 3 October Dafydd was executed, with Edward ensuring that his death was slow and agonising.

4 OCTOBER

On 4 October 1976, British Rail began its Inter-City 125 mile-per-hour high-speed train service, with the first scheduled journey on the London to Cardiff via Bristol route.

British Rail didn't hold an official ceremony to mark the occasion and so most passengers on the 8.05 a.m. train from Paddington were unaware that they were making history. However, they would have appreciated some improvements in comfort, such as aircraft-like seating and sliding electric doors at the end of each carriage. Hot food was also served from an on-board kitchen with the aid of a state-of-the-art microwave oven.

Powered by two diesel motors, the Inter-City 125 recorded a top speed of more than 140 miles per hour, making it the fastest diesel-powered train in the world at the time. It reduced journey times across the UK and led to a marked increase in passengers.

5 OCTOBER

The 5 October 1839 saw the opening of West Bute Dock in Cardiff, which resulted in Cardiff becoming one of the biggest coal exporting docks in the world by 1913.

Following the discovery and development of coal found in the Cynon and Rhondda Valleys and the rapid expansion of Merthyr's iron operations in the wake of the Industrial Revolution, their export required a sea connection to the Bristol Channel.

The Glamorganshire Canal was opened in 1794, linking Cardiff with Merthyr. By the 1830s Cardiff was shipping almost half of Britain's iron exports. In 1839, John Crichton-Stuart, second Marquess of Bute and Cardiff's foremost landowner, became instrumental in the construction of the (West) Bute Dock.

Two years later, the Taff Vale Railway was opened and, with the construction of the new East Bute Dock from 1855, coal supplanted iron as the industrial foundation of south Wales. Coal exports increased from from 43,650 to 2.184 million tons between 1840 and 1870.

However, frustration at the lack of further development in Cardiff led to rival docks being opened in 1865 at Penarth and in 1889 at Barry. Cardiff responded by opening Roath Dock in 1887 and Queen Alexandra Dock in 1907, which saw coal exports from the South Wales Coalfields via Cardiff rise to 10,700,000 tons by 1913, making Cardiff the biggest coal exporting dock in the world.

6 OCTOBER

The memorial statue of Llywelyn ap Gruffydd Fychan in Llandovery was unveiled on 6 October 2001. Llywelyn ap Gruffydd Fychan was gruesomely executed on 9 October 1401 for thwarting the efforts of King Henry IV's forces to capture Owain Glyndŵr.

Glyndŵr had instigated an uprising against English rule and declared himself Prince of Wales in 1400. (Find out more on 31 March.) Henry sent a force into Wales to find Glyndŵr and they tracked him down to Llandovery. On his arrival in the town, Henry, who was accompanied by a huge army, looked for local help in locating Glyndŵr and local landowner, Llywelyn ap Gruffydd Fychan volunteered.

However, the sixty-year-old Llywelyn, who had two sons in Glyndŵr's army, had no intentions of betraying him. For weeks, he led the king and his forces on a wild goose chase through the uplands of Deheubarth, which allowed Glyndŵr and his men time to make their escape. The king's patience became taxed and he began to see that Llywelyn was not taking them to their man. Angrily, Henry ordered that Llywelyn was to be dragged through the town of Llandovery and executed in the town square in front of the castle gates. Glyndŵr remained uncaptured and was never betrayed.

7 OCTOBER

On 7 October 1567, William Salesbury published the first Welsh translation of the New Testament.

Translations of the New Testament and whole Bible in other languages had been produced earlier that century, and in 1563 Elizabeth I introduced legislation requiring all churches in Wales to have Welsh translations of the Book of Common Prayer and the Bible alongside the English versions. Welsh became the first non-state language of Europe to be used to convey the word of God after the Reformation.

The Welsh translation of the New Testament followed in 1567. William Salesbury was the principal translator but worked with Richard Davies (Bishop of St Davids) and Thomas Huet (Precentor of St Davids) to prepare the translation from the original Greek.

However, although his translation can be viewed as a monumental achievement, it wasn't universally well received at the time. The main fault was not the translation itself, but the confusing layout Salesbury used. He was determined to show the Latin word origins, included several different words for the same meaning and put dialect alternatives in the margins. This resulted in a text that was difficult to read and there were reports of congregations finding it agonising to listen to the clergymen struggling to get through the service. His translation was subsequently superseded by a translation of the whole Bible by Bishop William Morgan in 1588.

8 OCTOBER

On 8 October 1945, Rudolf Hess, Adolf Hitler's deputy in the Nazi Party, was flown to Nuremberg to face trial for war crimes, ending his three years of imprisonment at Maindiff Court Military Hospital in Abergavenny.

In 1941, Hess made a dramatic midnight flight to Scotland, in what is thought to have been an attempt to achieve peace between Britain and Nazi Germany. He had bailed out over Eaglesham and was subsequently arrested by members of the Home Guard. He then spent several weeks in the Tower of London (the last person to be imprisoned there) and then at Camp Z in Aldershot, undergoing interrogation and debriefing.

On 26 June 1942 he was transferred to Maindiff Court, where he had his own room, was allowed to keep journals, take walks around the grounds and was even taken on drives around the local countryside.

Hess was found guilty at Nuremberg and sentenced to life imprisonment at Spandau Prison in Berlin.

9 OCTOBER

The Washington Monument on the National Mall in Washington, US was opened on 9 October 1888. Halfway up, there is a stone that was donated by the people of Wales. Its inscription reads *Fy Iaith, Fy Ngwlad, Fy Nghenedl. WALES. Cymry am byth.* (My Language, My Country, My Nation. WALES. The Welsh Forever.)

The Washington Monument was built to commemorate George Washington, commander-in-chief of the Continental Army and the first American president, who once declared 'good Welshmen make good Americans'. The Washington National Monument Society invited countries, cities, states and patriotic societies to contribute 193 memorial stones to pay tribute to Washington's character and achievements, of which the Welsh stone is one.

10 OCTOBER

On 10 October 1551, William Herbert was created Baron Herbert of Cardiff. Herbert was a highly influential figure at the Tudor royal court and his son, Henry Herbert was responsible for an extensive programme of repairs and extensions to Cardiff Castle and gardens.

William Herbert (c.1501–17 March 1570) was probably born in Glamorgan. In his youth, he was described as a 'mad fighting fellow' and was forced to flee to France after he killed a man in a fight in Bristol. In France, he joined the service of King Francis I and earned the reputation of being a brave and courageous soldier. So much so that, when he decided to return to Britain, King Francis recommended him for a senior role in Henry VIII's court, where he met and married Anne Parr, the sister of Henry's sixth wife, Catherine Parr.

When Henry VIII died in 1547, Herbert acted as executor to Henry VIII's will and as a guardian of the young King Edward VI. He was created Baron Herbert of Cardiff and was given Caerphilly Castle, Castell Coch and extensive lands in south Wales. Following Edward VI's death, Herbert became involved in the plan to place the Protestant Lady Jane Grey on the throne but, when it became clear that Lady Mary Tudor would take the throne as Mary I, Herbert wisely switched his allegiance and acted as escort for Mary's future husband, King Philip of Spain, on his journey to London in 1554 as well as crushing Thomas Wyatt's rebellion against the marriage.

11 OCTOBER

The Mold Cape – a solid sheet-gold object – dating from approximately 1900–1600 BC was discovered on 11 October 1833. It was found in a Bronze Age burial mound at Bryn yr Ellyllon, between Mold and Buckley. It is thought to be part of a ceremonial dress.

During the Bronze Age (c.2100 BC–c.800 BC), it is thought that the population steadily increased and people became more skilled in metalworking, producing tools and weapons as well as decorative artefacts that demonstrated high status.

The Mold Cape is one of the most spectacular Bronze Age gold artefacts yet discovered and one of the finest prehistoric examples of its kind in the world.

12 OCTOBER

Christopher Columbus landed in what is now the Bahamas on 12 October 1842, as part of his famous 'voyage of discovery' to the New World. Columbus is often cited as the first European to make contact with what is now known as America; however, it is now known that the Vikings had arrived in what is now Newfoundland in the 10th century.

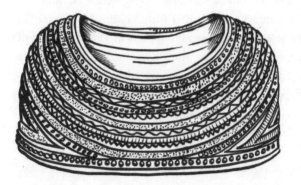

Wales has its own legend of a crossing of the Atlantic that predates Columbus when Madog, ab Owain Gwynedd, arrived in what is now Alabama in 1170. According to the story, Madog returned to Gwynedd to recruit settlers and left, never to be seen again. The settlers supposedly travelled up the great rivers before settling down in the Midwest and intermarrying with the indigenous people.

References to a seafaring Madog were used during the Elizabethan era to bolster British claims to America. The earliest surviving account appears in Humphrey Llwyd's unpublished *Cronica Walliae* written in 1559. John Dee used this manuscript when he submitted a treatise, *Title Royal*, to Queen Elizabeth I in 1580 citing a historic claim to America through King Arthur and Madog.

Some facts that support the legend:

- It's claimed that a site on Rose Island, Kentucky, was once home to a colony of Welsh-speaking Native Americans.

- During the first English navigation of the James River, Virginia, in 1607, Welshman Peter Wynne, wrote that some of the pronunciation of the Monacan language (the language of the first Jamestown settlers) resembled 'Welch'.

- Another encounter with a Welsh-speaking Indian was claimed by the Reverend Morgan Jones. Jones said that he had been captured in 1669 by a tribe of Tuscarora called the Deog, whose chief spared his life when he heard Jones speak Welsh, a language he understood.

· Francis Lewis, a signer of the American Declaration of Independence, is said to have had a conversation with a Native American chief who spoke Welsh.

· Thomas Jefferson, the third President of the United States, believed the 'Madoc (Madog) story' to be true.

· Llewellyn Harris, a missionary who visited the Zuni tribe in 1878, noted that they had many Welsh words in their language.

13 OCTOBER

On 13 October 1910, the crew of the St David's lifeboat on board the *Gem* went to rescue three crew stranded in terrible weather aboard the *Democrat*, a coal ship delivering to Ramsey Island. The rescue was a success, but *Gem* – a sail-assisted rowing boat – crashed onto the rocks on the return journey, killing three crew members. Yet somewhat miraculously given the conditions, the twelve remaining lifeboatmen and the three rescued sailors survived by clinging to rocks for over twelve hours. They were eventually rescued when Will Thomas managed to dry out matches sufficiently enough to set fire to his oilskins to alert help from nearby Porthclais Harbour.

In the aftermath of the disaster, sixteen-year-old Sydney Mortimer, who had sailed one of the Porthclais rescue boats and saved ten of the survivors, received the Royal National Lifeboat Institution's (RNLI) Silver Medal. Two years later he became the youngest coxswain of St David's lifeboat. The incident was instrumental in bringing about the use of petrol motorboats by the RNLI and also provided valuable lessons in how to improve the cork life jackets of the day.

14 OCTOBER

At 8 a.m. on Tuesday 14 October 1913, a huge explosion occurred at the Universal Colliery in Senghenydd. The explosion and subsequent release of poisonous gas claimed the lives of 439 of the 950 miners that were working underground at the time. It remains the worst mining disaster in British history.

It is thought that the explosion was caused by a spark from the electric signalling gear that ignited methane gas and was so violent that a pit cage was blown back up the shaft. It also caused coal dust lying on the mine floor to rise and catch fire and the flames were quickly followed by afterdamp – waves of poisonous carbon monoxide – that suffocated the miners who had escaped the explosion.

Rescue attempts were hampered by fires and fallen debris, but men and boys were found and rescued from among the wreckage. However, after three weeks all hope had long gone of finding further survivors as the victims' bodies were brought to the surface. Some could only be identified by their clothing: one young boy was identified by the patch on his jacket that his mother had sewn on a few days earlier.

The subsequent inquiry was critical of the owners and management for the poor safety standards at the colliery, especially as lessons had not been learned from a previous disaster in 1901 in which eighty-one men were killed. Yet only £24 in total was ever paid out in fines or as compensation and Universal Colliery was back in operation by the end of the following month. The colliery eventually closed in 1986.

There is a memorial to the men and boys who lost their lives in the disaster, at Nant y Parc Primary School, which now stands on the site of the mine, and another at the local comprehensive school as well as a clock on Senghenydd square.

15 OCTOBER

Traditionally, October 15 was the day of the Llangammarch Horse Fair which, by the 1890s, was the biggest pony fair in Wales and well known throughout Britain.

Llangammarch lies in the foothills of Mynydd Epynt, an area long-associated with horse-breeding where local farmers had the grazing rights of over 34,000 acres of mountain upland.

Early on the day of the fair, farmers would drive hundreds of horses off the Eppynt to Llangammarch. Horses and ponies were the main form of transport at the time, as well as being vital for farm work, driving livestock and for use as pit ponies. Dealers would come to the fair from all over Wales, Ireland as well as the Midlands and southern counties of England. Some horses were also destined for Belgium and France. There were no auctioneers and deals were struck by the clap of hands and payment in cash. The sold ponies and horses were then driven to Garth railway station where trains were laid on for their onward journey. There were also stalls selling clothes and anything and everything horse-related. Local residents sold refreshments to the fair-goers and there would be much celebration in Llangammarch's pubs and hotels.

In 1939, the Ministry of Defence purchased several thousand acres of Mynydd Epynt for use as a training area, resulting in the removal of the grazing land for the ponies. This, combined with the introduction of more efficient tractors for farm work saw the fair rapidly decline in popularity and it disappeared by the end of the 1940s.

16 OCTOBER

The 16 October marks World Food Day. Some traditional Welsh foods include:

Cawl The national dish of Wales is a broth that most often contains lamb, leeks and a selection of favourite vegetables. In the early sixteenth century, the most common recipes included salted bacon or beef with swedes, carrots and other seasonal vegetables, as well as potatoes.

Welsh cakes *Pice ar y maen* (cakes on the stone) are small sweet cakes that were the perfect size to be slipped into the working man's pocket. They are made from simple pantry items: flour, sugar, milk and butter. Traditionally they were made on a flat bakestone griddle and cooked with plain flour rather than self-raising flour and baking powder, which would have resulted in in a much flatter and crisper cake than the ones most people know today.

Bara brith This is a fruit loaf, which was traditionally eaten at Christmas or on St David's Day.

Welsh rarebit This dish is made with a melted cheese, mustard and ale or milk sauce poured over slices of toasted bread. The origin of the name is uncertain, but 'Welsh rabbit' first appeared as a dish in 1725. It is thought that the dish was attributed to the Welsh because of their historic fondness for cheese, which poorer people used as a source of protein instead of meat.

Laverbread (*Bara Lawr*) This bread is traditionally made by cooking purple laver seaweed (*Porphyra umbilicalis*) for up to ten hours to produce laver. The laver is then coated with oatmeal and fried to produce laverbread.

17 OCTOBER

The 17 October 1948 saw the opening of the Hoover washing machine factory at Pentrebach, Merthyr Tydfil.

The period following the Second World War had seen a decline in several of the traditional industries of south Wales, particularly the coal and steel industries. It was, therefore, a welcome boost to the Merthyr area when Hoover decided to build a manufacturing unit in the town to facilitate the growing white goods industry. Initially, 350 people were employed at the factory but this grew significantly to approximately 5,000 by the 1960s and expanded through the 1970s as business boomed. The factory became an iconic building and the Hoover Company became part of the community – running cricket, football, rugby and athletics teams as well as organising Christmas parties and pantomimes for local children.

In 1985, Sir Clive Sinclair's famous but ultimately unsuccessful Sinclair C5 electric car was produced at the factory. Then during the 1990s, business began to decline. In 1992, Hoover lost £20 million on a promotion offering two free flights to each customer that purchased £100 worth of electrical goods. In 1995, there were job cuts following Hoover's buyout by the Italian-based company, Candy. Then in 2002, a fire at the factory caused major disruption to production. Production ceased in 2009 when Candy moved it to the Czech Republic and China. The factory now operates as a warehouse and distribution centre for domestic goods for Hoover Candy.

18 OCTOBER

Lynn Davies won a gold medal in the long jump in Tokyo on 18 October 1964 with a jump of 8.07 metres. He was the first Welsh individual representing the British team to become an Olympic athletics champion.

Davies, from Nantymoel, near Bridgend, later became

the first athlete to hold Olympic, European and Commonwealth titles at the same time. He was Britain's flag bearer at the 1968 Olympics and was later elected President of the UK Athletics Members Council. He was also one of the first five athletes inducted into the Welsh Athletics Hall of Fame in 2007.

19 OCTOBER

The prolific campaigner for educational improvements Mary Jane Bridges-Adams was born on 19 October 1854 in Maesycwmmer.

Bridges-Adams initially pursued a career in teaching and in 1897 was elected to the London School Board. In 1900, she was instrumental in the opening of Britain's first free kindergarten in London. She later became the secretary to Daisy Greville, Countess of Warwick, with whom in 1905, she toured the country promoting the concept of free school meals. In 1907, she established Britain's first Open Air School for Recovery, which helped sick and feeble children recover from their ailments.

Bridges-Adams supported adult education for workers and founded the Working Women's Movement, which fought to improve conditions for working-class women. She also campaigned for improved sanitation and housing and for the provision of free cultural services such as libraries and art galleries. In 1917, she joined the campaign for asylum for refugees from tsarist Russia.

20 OCTOBER

The 20 October marks World Statistics Day. Here are a number of interesting stats about Wales:

- With a population of 2,000, St Davids in Pembrokeshire is the smallest cathedral city in the world.

- Llanwrtyd Wells in Powys, with a population of 850, claims to be the smallest town in Britain.

- Wales has over 600 castles – more per square mile than any other country in Europe. Caerphilly is the largest castle in Wales and is the second largest in Europe. Chepstow Castle is Britain's oldest surviving medieval stone castle, its construction having commenced in 1067.

- The village of Llanfairpwllgwyngyllgogerychwyrn-drobwllllantysiliogogogoch on Anglesey has the second-longest place name in the world. (Find out more on 1 August.)

- Snowdon (or Yr Wyddfa) is the highest peak in Wales at 1,085 metres (3,560 feet).

- Dan-yr-Ogof, near Ystradgynlais, is Britain's longest and largest show-cave and nearby Ogof Ffynnon Ddu is Britain's deepest cave.

- The Menai Bridge in Anglesey was the first and longest suspension bridge in the world constructed to take heavy traffic.

- The National Eisteddfod of Wales is the largest festival of competitive music and poetry in Europe.

- The glasshouse at the National Botanic Garden of Wales in Llanarthne, Carmarthenshire, is the world's largest single-span glasshouse.

- Conwy possesses the most complete medieval town walls in the United Kingdom, the smallest house in Britain (3.1 metres high and 1.8 metres wide), and the oldest house in Wales (the fourteenth-century Aberconwy House).

21 OCTOBER

At 9.15 a.m. on Friday 21 October 1966, a waste tip above the mining village of Aberfan began to slide down the mountainside, firstly destroying a farm cottage and killing all its occupants. It then engulfed Pantglas Junior School and about twenty houses in the village, killing 144 people, including 116 school children.

Workers in the mountain had seen the slide start, but could not raise the alarm because their telephone cable had been stolen and thick fog prevented people in the village from seeing what was happening.

News of the tragedy travelled fast and hundreds of people headed to Aberfan to try and help. It was futile: nobody was rescued alive after 11 a.m. and it was nearly a week before all the bodies were recovered.

A tribunal's report into the disaster found that the blame for the disaster rested entirely with the National Coal Board (NCB), and their 'total absence of a tipping policy'. On Mynydd Merthyr, directly above Aberfan, several tips containing mining debris from the Merthyr Vale Colliery had been deposited over the years, onto highly porous sandstone that contained numerous underground springs. The NCB's area management had been made aware of the concerns regarding the tipping of spoil above the primary school, but these were largely ignored. The report also showed the tips had never been surveyed and were continuously being added to in a chaotic manner. The disregard for the unstable geological conditions and the NCB's failure to act after previous smaller slides had occurred were found to have been major factors that contributed to the catastrophe.

The slide itself was caused after substantial bursts of heavy rain in the days leading up to the disaster, which had caused three to six metres of subsidence on one of the tips. This then led to more than 150,000 cubic metres of debris breaking away and flowing downhill at high speed.

22 OCTOBER

The Welsh Courts Act 1942 was enacted on 22 October of that year.

Since the Act of Union in 1536, English had been the

only language used in the law courts, ignoring the fact that most people in Wales only spoke Welsh. The 1942 act gave Welsh people the right to use Welsh in courts providing that the Welsh speaker would be at a disadvantage if compelled to speak English. This was by no means an ideal situation, as such a disadvantage had to be proven and there were problems finding judges or magistrates who understood the Welsh language. However, it can be seen as a slackening of legislation which ultimately led to the Welsh Language Act 1967, and gave rise to the concept of equal validity between the Welsh and English languages within the legal system.

23 OCTOBER

On 23 October 1863, the Ffestiniog Railway was the first public narrow-gauge railway in the world to introduce steam locomotives into general service.

The line was constructed between 1833 and 1836 to transport slate from the quarries around the inland town of Blaenau Ffestiniog to the coastal town of Porthmadog where it was loaded onto ships. The railway line was sloped, so that loaded wagons could be run by gravity downhill all the way from Blaenau Ffestiniog to the port. The empty wagons were then hauled back up by horses.

During the late 1850s, it became clear that the line was reaching its operational capacity while the output of the Blaenau Ffestiniog slate quarries continued to rise. In 1860, the board of the company began to investigate the possibility of introducing steam locomotives to increase the carrying capacity of the railway. In 1862 the company

advertised for manufacturers to tender to build the line's first locomotives. In February 1863, the bid of George England and Co. was accepted and production of the first locomotives was begun.

Steam locomotives allowed much longer slate trains to be run and also enabled the official introduction of passenger trains in 1865. Today, the Ffestiniog Railway is a major tourist attraction located mainly within the Snowdonia National Park, travelling through both forest and mountainous scenery.

24 OCTOBER

Founded on 24 October 1898, The South Wales Miners' Federation (SWMF), nicknamed 'The Fed', was a trade union for miners in south Wales.

The Fed was formed following the defeat of the south Wales miners' strike of 1898 and was almost unique among British unions in that it dominated not only the working life but also the social and cultural interests of the south Wales coal valleys. By 1914, the SWMF had 200,000 members, making it the largest union of any kind in the UK. It became the National Union of Miners (NUM (South Wales Area)) in 1945.

25 OCTOBER

On 25 October 1970, the Forty Martyrs of England and Wales were canonised by Pope Paul VI.

The Forty Martyrs of England and Wales comprise a

group of Catholic men and women who were executed for treason and related offences in the Kingdom of England between 1535 and 1679. Religious repression meant that faithful Roman Catholics were required to rebel against the English Crown. They were therefore considered by the Catholic Church to be Christian martyrs. Six of those canonised were Welsh and the Catholic Church in Wales keeps 25 October as the feast of the 'Six Welsh Martyrs and their companions'.

The six Welsh martyrs are the priests Philip Evans from Monmouth, John Lloyd from Breconshire, John Jones from Clynnog Fawr on the Llŷn Peninsula, David Lewis from Abergavenny, John Roberts from Trawsfynydd and the teacher Richard Gwyn from Montgomeryshire.

26 OCTOBER

On 26 October 1914, Ernest Shackleton's Trans-Antarctic expedition team of 1914–17 left Buenos Aires on the *Endurance*. Unbeknown to Shackleton, also onboard was a stowaway, Perce Blackborow, from Pill, Newport.

Blackborow was in the Merchant Navy, but had been rejected from the expedition for being too young and inexperienced. Undeterred, Blackborow hid on board until he was discovered after three days at sea. Shackleton gave him a furious dressing-down and told him stowaways were the first to be eaten in times of hardship. Blackborow's cheeky response that the expedition's leader had more meat on him endeared him to Shackleton who then agreed to take him on as a steward.

The *Endurance* became stuck in ice in February 1915 and drifted until she sank in November. After this, the crew spent two months living on shifting ice floes exposed to freezing winds. Blackborow made the mistake of wearing leather rather than the cold-weather felt boots and developed frostbite in his toes.

By April 1916 the ice floes started to split so Shackleton made the decision to try and get the lifeboats through to reach safety. This was frustratingly slow and perilous as they were exposed to mountainous seas and killer whales, but the team eventually made it to Elephant Island from where seven of the crew led by Shackleton sailed to get help. The remaining crew sheltered from howling gales and freezing temperatures, living off the meat from seals and penguins. By June, Blackborow's feet had become gangrenous and the toes of his left foot had to be amputated.

Shackleton's party eventually managed to reach South Georgia, some 750 miles away, from where they eventually managed to get a rescue ship through to the men on Elephant Island on 30 August 1916. Blackborow, who was awarded the Polar Medal for his service on the expedition, spent three months recovering in Chile before returning to Newport.

27 OCTOBER

Dylan Marlais Thomas was born on 27 October 1914, at 5 Cwmdonkin Drive in Swansea. His father was an English teacher at the local grammar school and recited Shakespeare to Thomas before he could read.

Thomas excelled in English and reading but neglected

other subjects and dropped out of school at sixteen to become a junior reporter for a local newspaper. In 1932, he decided to concentrate on poetry full time.

In 1934, Thomas moved to London and published his first book of poems, to great acclaim. Two years later, Thomas met the dancer Caitlin Macnamara and they married in 1937. The marriage was turbulent, but the couple left London together in 1944 and eventually settled at the Boat House in Laugharne.

On a tour of America in 1953, Thomas collapsed in the Chelsea Hotel, New York, after a long drinking bout at the White Horse Tavern. On 9 November, he died at St Vincent's Hospital, aged thirty-nine. He is buried in Laugharne and has a memorial plaque in Poet's Corner in Westminster Abbey.

28 OCTOBER

Cardiff achieved city status on 28 October 1905 in recognition of its great economic and industrial success.

Long barrows (Neolithic burial chambers) such as those at Tinkinswood and Coedkernew demonstrate the presence of people in the Cardiff area in Neolithic times. By the first century AD, the area was populated by the Silures tribe. The Romans began to settle the area c. AD 75 and built a fort on the banks of the River Taff, to protect the Severn estuary. (The origins of the name Cardiff most probably derive from the Welsh/Brythonic name *Caerdydd*, meaning 'fort on the Taff'.)

In 1081, the Normans built a castle on the site of the old

Roman fort. In the Middle Ages, Cardiff had developed into a port and trading centre, and had a population of approximately 1,500. Centuries later, its strategic position at the bottom of coal and iron valleys meant the town benefitted greatly from the Industrial Revolution and its first dock was built in 1830. By 1881 it was the most populous town in Wales.

Cardiff was proclaimed the capital city of Wales on 20 December 1955. Today it is the home of the Welsh Assembly Government and the largest waterfront development in Europe.

DID YOU KNOW?

In 1404, during the uprising of Owain Glyndŵr, the town and castle were burned.

---

29 OCTOBER

The 29 October 1929 became known as Black Tuesday, when investors traded some 16 million shares on the New York Stock Exchange in a single day. Billions of dollars were lost, wiping out thousands of investors.

Building on post-war optimism, the decade following the First World War was one of wealth and excess. However, by the end of the 1920s, too much debt, a decline in production and rising unemployment were combining to cause slowing economic growth. Panic selling in the United States stock market, centred in Wall Street, New York, began on Black Thursday, 24 October 1929, and continued until the market crashed spectacularly on 29 October. Investors lost billions of dollars and the vast majority were totally wiped out. It was the most devastating stock market crash in the history of the United States and triggered a severe worldwide economic depression referred to as the Great Depression.

This financial crisis was to become the longest, deepest, and most widespread depression in history; it began to overwhelm Britain in 1931 and a coalition National Government was formed to try and deal with the crisis.

The financial collapse had a devastating effect on the industrial areas of Wales, as demand for products collapsed and unemployment more than doubled. Low incomes resulted in poor health and substandard housing and the reduction in unemployment benefits led to massive protests. It also caused massive emigration, with Wales losing 390,000 people between 1925 and 1939.

30 OCTOBER

On 30 October 1799, the Llandovery Bank was established in Llandovery in the premises known as the King's Head on Stone Street, where it was locally known as the Black Ox Bank (Banc yr Eidon) because the banknotes were embellished with an engraving on the left-hand side of a Welsh black ox.

Historically, the Welsh hill farmers derived their main income from the breeding of black cattle, before taking them into eastern England to be fattened up before sale in

London markets. The long journey home meant that the travellers – or drovers – were vulnerable to attacks from highwaymen and armed gangs, so there grew a need to establish a way of transferring the proceeds from the sale to a bank near the home farm.

David Jones, a successful local drover who had married into a rich family, established the Black Ox Bank in Llandovery. David Jones's grandsons continued running the Llandovery Bank after his passing, and also opened branches at Lampeter and Llandeilo, under the title David Jones & Co. The company was sold to Lloyds Bank Ltd in 1909, thus ending the last surviving private bank in west Wales.

31 OCTOBER

With the rugby results reading 'Llanelli 9–New Zealand 3', 31 October 1972 became known as 'the day the pubs ran dry'.

On this day, Llanelli became one of the few clubs to beat the New Zealand All Blacks. Under the expert coaching of Carwyn James and the inspirational leadership of Delme Thomas, Llanelli won this bruising and hard-fought encounter at a packed Stradey Park, with Roy Bergiers scoring a try converted by Phil Bennett, and Andy Hill adding a long range penalty.

Llanelli are not the only Welsh club to have beaten the All Blacks, however. On 28 September 1935, Swansea RFC became the first club side to ever beat them, winning 11–3 – two of Swansea's half backs were still schoolboys at

Gowerton Grammar.

On 21 November 1953, Cardiff RFC beat the New Zealand All Blacks 8–3. Bleddyn Williams, the club captain, had toured New Zealand with the British Lions in 1950 and had a strategy to make the heavier New Zealand players run and tire out quickly. Ten years later, on 30 October 1963, Newport RFC beat New Zealand 3–0. It was the touring team's only defeat on the tour. Newport, captained by Brian Price, dominated the forward battle and David Watkins at outside half kept New Zealand pinned back with his tactical kicking and darting runs. The only score of the game was a drop goal by John 'Dick' Uzzell.

1 NOVEMBER

S4C, a Welsh language television channel, was launched on 1 November 1982.

Prior to the launch of S4C, Welsh language television programmes had been limited to occasional broadcasts on BBC Wales or HTV Cymru, often at inconvenient or off-peak times. This was highly unsatisfactory to audiences in Wales, who wanted a full service in Welsh throughout the broadcasting schedule.

The 1970s saw vigorous campaigning for a TV service in Welsh, and by the 1979 election, both major parties had pledged to introduce a Welsh-language fourth channel if they won the election. Shortly after the Conservative victory, the Home Secretary William Whitelaw decreed that Wales would not be granted its Welsh language channel after all.

Much civil unrest and disobedience ensued. People risked prosecution and even prison by refusing to pay TV licence fees, or took part in sit-ins at BBC and HTV studios. More extreme action included attacking television transmitters. Then in 1980, Gwynfor Evans, a former president of Plaid Cymru, threatened to go on hunger strike if the Conservative government didn't fulfil its promise to establish a Welsh-language TV service. (Find out more on 14 July.) S4C started broadcasting on 1 November 1982, the night before Channel 4.

The first programme to broadcast on S4C was the cartoon series *SuperTed* created by Welshman Mike Young. It was later dubbed into English and broadcast on BBC1 throughout the UK.

2 NOVEMBER

On 2 November 1925, the failure of two dams caused a flood that swamped the village of Dolgarrog, near Conwy, killing sixteen people.

The cause of the disaster was the collapse of the Eigiau Dam – a gravity dam owned by the Aluminium Corporation. The floodwater breached the Coedty Dam further downstream – an embankment dam – which failed to hold back the weight of water, releasing a huge volume of water that flooded Dolgarrog. Many more villagers would have been killed had they not been in the local theatre watching a film that night.

The disaster at Dolgarrog led Parliament to pass the Reservoirs (Safety Provisions) Act in 1930 that introduced laws on the safety of reservoirs, which has since been replaced by the 1975 Reservoirs Act. In 2004, a £60,000 memorial trail was opened by the last survivor of the dam disaster, Fred Brown, who on that night lost his mother and his younger sister.

3 NOVEMBER

On 3 November 2006, Jones Jones Jones, an event held at the Wales Millennium Centre in Cardiff, succeeded in breaking the world record for the largest gathering of people with the same surname in one place.

Jones is a surname of medieval origins, derived from the given name John which is derived from the Hebrew name Yochanan (Johanan). It remains the most popular surname in Wales, is the second most common surname in England after Smith, and the fifth most common in the United States.

4 NOVEMBER

The Newport Rising took place on 4 November 1839.

In the early 1800s, calls to reform to the elitist electoral system resulted in the Reform Act of 1832. However, many working-class people felt this act did not go far enough as voters were still required to possess property to the value of £10, a substantial sum at that time. This division gave rise to the Chartist movement, which wanted to see:

- The right to vote for men aged over twenty-one.

- The implementation of secret balloting.

- No requirement for MPs to own property.

- Payment for MPs, so that the poor were not debarred from the role.

- Equally sized constituencies.

- Annual Parliamentary elections.

In May 1839, Henry Vincent, a leading Chartist, was arrested for making inflammatory speeches and later sentenced to twelve months in prison. Furious outbreaks of violence ensued, and another Chartist, John Frost, called for a mass demonstration demanding Vincent's release.

This took place on 4 November 1839, with 3,000 men marching with pikes, clubs and firearms from Pontymister to Newport. Troops were called in and, when the chanting crowd arrived at the Westgate Hotel, the order was given to open fire. At least twenty men were killed and fifty more were seriously injured.

Frost, along with other Chartist leaders, was found guilty of high treason and sentenced to be hanged, drawn and quartered. The ensuing outcry at the brutality of the sentences forced Prime Minister Lord Melbourne to commute them to life transportation.

The convicts were granted a total pardon in 1856 and Frost received a hero's welcome on his return to Newport. By the time of his death, aged ninety-one, most of the reforms for which the Chartists had campaigned were enshrined in law.

5 NOVEMBER

The Gunpowder Plot of 1605 was a failed attempt by a Catholic group to kill King James I by blowing up the House of Lords during the State Opening of England's Parliament. On 5 November, one of the conspirators, Guy Fawkes, was discovered guarding thirty-six barrels of gunpowder beneath the Houses of Parliament. He was sentenced, along with seven other conspirators, to be hanged, drawn and quartered.

It's believed that the plot was masterminded by Welsh spymaster Hugh Owen (1538–1618) a fervent Catholic who had vowed to destroy the Protestant order. He had helped plan the Spanish Armada and had been implicated in the 1571 Ridolfi plot to assassinate Queen Elizabeth I, after which he had fled to Europe from where continued to coordinate his network.

It is thought that Owen originally introduced Guy Fawkes to the other conspirators, and he was also named in Fawkes's trial as the man 'whose finger hath been in every treason which hath been of late years detected'. Owen escaped retribution, enjoying the safe haven of Catholic Europe. Several assassination attempts against him failed, and Owen died peacefully of old age in Rome.

6 NOVEMBER

The 6 November is the feast day of St Illtud (Illtyd), one of the most significant figures of early Christianity.

Reputedly born in Brittany and from a military background, it is said that Illtud travelled to Britain as a skilled warrior serving Arthur in the defence of Britain against a Saxon invasion. Illtud's band raided Llancarfan Abbey but the monks pursued them into a bog where 'the earth swallowed all of them except Illtud'.

After this, St Cadog reminded Illtud of his religion and the humbled warrior took up a monastic life, founding the abbey at Llanilltud Fawr (Llantwt Major) where in AD 508, he re-established the monastery school known as Cor Tewdus, which had reputedly been burnt down by Irish pirates in AD 446. This monastic complex became a centre of learning, with students studying the Bible, philosophy, science, geometry, rhetoric, grammar and arithmetic. It reputedly had seven halls, 400 houses and more than 2,000 students, which included St David, St Patrick, Paul Aurelian, Taliesin, Gildas and Samson. Illtud himself is said to have been a disciple of Germanus of Auxerre who visited Llanilltud on his mission to Britain.

As well as Llanilltud, there are churches dedicated to Illtud in Breconshire, Glamorgan, Carmarthenshire, Llanelltyd, Brittany and on Gower. In Merthyr, there are also holy wells dedicated to him and the legendary place of his burial is Bedd Gwyl Illtud, Breconshire.

7 NOVEMBER

On 7 November 1916, Charles Evans Hughes lost narrowly to Woodrow Wilson in the United States presidential election when he failed to win California.

Hughes was the son of a Welsh-speaking minister who had emigrated to the US from Tredegar. He was highly regarded with a reputation for intelligence, personal integrity, and moderation and is regularly listed among the best presidents America never had.

Hughes was a successful lawyer when he was elected as the Governor of New York in 1906 and he was appointed as an Associate Justice of the Supreme Court of the United States in 1910. He resigned in 1916 to accept the Republican presidential nomination and was widely viewed as the favourite to win the presidency. However, the 1916 campaign was dominated by the ongoing Mexican Revolution and the impending threat of the First World War which was underway in Europe. Wilson campaigned on the policy of avoidance of American involvement in the European conflict and it was ultimately successful with voters.

Hughes remained a popular politician and was encouraged to run again in 1920 but refused to allow his name to be considered following the death of his daughter from tuberculosis. Nevertheless, the Republicans won by a landslide and Hughes was appointed as Secretary of State. Between 1930 and 1941 he served as Chief Justice of the Supreme Court of the US and is considered to be one of the most distinguished holders of that position.

8 NOVEMBER

Did you know that Big Ben is named after a Welshman? Born on this day, Sir Benjamin Hall, first Baron Llanover (1802–67) was a civil engineer who was responsible for the British government's building projects. His work included the rebuilding of the Houses of Parliament and the installation of the bell in the clock tower. The nickname 'Big Ben' was given to the Great Bell in honour of Sir Benjamin, whose name is inscribed on it.

As MP for Monmouth, Sir Benjamin campaigned to have religious services in Welsh. He was also outspoken on the issue of the state of the Anglican church in Wales and deplored the exploitation of church revenues. He was married to Augusta Hall, Baroness Llanover, a committed patron of the Welsh arts. (Find out more on 21 March.)

9 NOVEMBER

On 9 November 1961, Rosemarie Frankland (1943–2000) from Rhosllanerchrugog, Wrexham, became the first British woman to win the Miss World title.

When she was crowned, the compère, Bob Hope, said that she was the most beautiful girl he had ever seen. As Miss World, she joined Hope at a United Service Organizations concert in Alaska and the pair reportedly had an affair that lasted many years. Frankland later became Hope's personal assistant and she later embarked on an acting career which included a role in the 1965 film, *I'll Take Sweden,* in which Hope also starred.

Helen Morgan, from Barry, became the second Welsh

woman to win the Miss World title when she was crowned on 22 November 1974. However, she was encouraged to resign four days after her victory on the discovery that she had an eighteen-month-old child, even though she did not break the competition rules (which stipulated only that entrants must be unmarried). In the same year, she won the Miss Wales and Miss United Kingdom titles and came second in the Miss Universe pageant.

10 NOVEMBER

'Dr Livingstone, I presume?' This now famous greeting was allegedly uttered by Henry Morton Stanley on 10 November 1871, upon finding missionary and explorer David Livingstone in Tanzania.

Born as John Rowlands in Denbigh in 1841, Stanley was brought up in a workhouse, as his parents were not married. In 1859, he found work on a boat sailing to America and jumped ship in New Orleans where he was befriended by Henry Hope Stanley, a wealthy trader whose name he adopted. He fought on both sides in the American Civil War, before becoming a journalist with the *New York Herald*, for whom he travelled widely in Asia as an overseas correspondent.

In 1869, Stanley persuaded the paper's editor to commission him to find David Livingstone, the Scottish missionary and explorer, who had travelled to Africa but had not been heard from for some time. Stanley travelled to Zanzibar and kitted an expedition accompanied by 200 porters. During the 700-mile expedition through the trop-

ical forest, his horse died after a bite from a tsetse fly, many of his porters abandoned him (it's said he flogged and possibly shot his men), and most of those who remained were stricken with tropical diseases.

On 10 November 1871, Stanley came across Livingstone near Lake Tanganyika in what is now Tanzania, greeting him with the now classic line. Stanley then joined Livingstone's exploration of the region, and came to public attention with the publication of his book about his adventures, entitled *How I Found Livingstone. Travels, Adventures, and Discoveries in Central Africa.*

Stanley went on to explore vast areas of central Africa, following the Congo River from its source to the sea. With the support of King Leopold II of Belgium, he returned with plans to develop the region and worked to open the lower Congo to commerce with the construction of roads. His methods of using forced labour, corporal punishment and brutality during this time have, however, stained his reputation in recent histories. His statue in St Asaph has always been controversial: over fifty people, including Jan Morris and Benjamin Zephaniah, campaigned against its erection in 2010, and after 7,000 people petitioned for its removal, a public vote was held for locals on the subject in 2021, though they voted for it to remain.

On his return to Europe in 1890, Stanley began a worldwide lecture tour. He became the Member of Parliament for Lambeth and was knighted in 1899. Stanley died in London on 10 May 1904.

11 NOVEMBER

Able Seaman Richard Morgan died on Armistice Day, 11 November 1918, while serving on the destroyer HMS *Garland*. He was twenty-six years old and was probably the last British serviceman to die in the First World War. He is buried in the village of Defauden in Monmouthshire and is one of 40,000 Welsh servicemen to be killed during the conflict.

12 NOVEMBER

On 12 November 1983, Mark Brown became the first Black person to play rugby union for Wales.

Brown was born in Pillgwenlly, Newport, in 1988, to a Jamaican father and a mother from Yorkshire. He was raised in Cwmbran and did not play any rugby until he was seventeen. After spells with Cwmbran RFC and Ebbw Vale, Brown came to prominence with Pontypool RFC during their golden era of the 1970s and 1980s. Despite Brown's first test match ending in a surprise 24–6 defeat to Romania, Brown earned a further five international caps.

Controversially, Brown's international appearance is also notable in the fact that it took so long for a Black player to be selected to play rugby union for Wales, with many talented Black players having been previously overlooked. This has led to the charge of institutionalised racism being levelled at the Welsh Rugby Union.

In contrast, George Bennett and Alex Givvons became the first Black men to play rugby league for Wales in 1935. Not only was rugby league more racially tolerant, it was also a professional sport, based predominantly in the north of England, that had split from the amateur Rugby Football Union over the issue of payments to the players. This prompted players overlooked for international union selection in Wales to 'go north' to pursue their ambitions. Many of them subsequently became highly respected figures and enjoyed successful rugby league careers:

- In 1972, Clive Sullivan was made captain of the Great Britain national rugby league team. This made him the first Black captain of any national British sporting side.

- Roy Francis became the sport's first ever Black Great Britain international and the first Black British professional coach in any sport.

- Johnny Freeman made 395 appearances for Halifax scoring 290 tries (a club record).

- Billy Boston is a legend at Wigan Rugby League Club, where he scored a record 478 tries and also has a stand named in his honour at the DW Stadium in Wigan.

- Colin 'Dicko' Dixon, who is Wales's longest serving international, making his debut in 1963 and his final appearance in 1981. He also played in the 1972 World Cup winning side for Great Britain.

The Union game has also been slow to recognise these players' achievements and they are still regarded as the forgotten heroes of Welsh rugby. However, the city of Cardiff announced in 2020 that a statue depicting Billy Boston, Clive Sullivan and Gus Risman will be erected to represent all the Black Welsh players who headed north.

13 NOVEMBER

Gareth Bale won his hundredth Welsh cap on 13 November 2021, in the World Cup qualifying football match between Wales and Belarus. Bale is Wales's all-time record goal scorer and was the captain of the team that qualified for the UEFA Euro 2020 Championship and the 2022 FIFA World Cup tournament. He was also a key member of Wales's memorable Euro 2016 campaign, in which they lost in the semi-final to the eventual winners, Portugal. At club level, he has won five Champions League titles with Real Madrid and was awarded the PFA Players' Player of the Year award for the 2012–13 season.

Bale attended Whitchurch High School in Cardiff, where he played football alongside Wales rugby captain Sam Warburton. His talent was clear even then, and the school's PE teacher, Gwyn Morris, had to take measures to ensure that other pupils had a chance to compete during lessons, such as restricting Bale to playing with his non-dominant foot. Morris said of him, 'Gareth has a fierce determination to succeed and has the character and qualities to achieve his personal goals. He is one of the most unselfish individuals that I have had the pleasure to help educate.'

14 NOVEMBER

During the 1880s, due to the high demand for Welsh coal and the high cost of using the Bute docks at Cardiff, the industrialist David Davies decided to construct new docks at Barry with a railway connection from the Rhondda. Work began on the new dock on 14 November 1884, and it opened for trade in 1889. More docks were added later and, by 1903, exports had risen to over nine million tonnes. By 1913, Barry had become the largest coal exporting port in the country.

The docks gave rise to many subsidiary business enterprises, from repair yards and cold storage facilities to flour mills and shipping agents. Even when a worldwide depression in the 1920s began to decimate the Welsh coal trade, there were still more than fifty companies trading out of Barry docks. Eventually, the collapse of the Welsh coal trade left Barry and its docks redundant. The arrival of the Geest Company in 1959, importing bananas from the West Indies, provided a temporary reprieve to the town, but when the company withdrew in the 1990s, the port of Barry went into terminal decline.

Today, like many other dockland areas, the old waterfront has been redeveloped. Parts of the old docks have been used as locations for TV shows like *Doctor Who* and *Torchwood* and, perhaps most famously, the television series *Gavin and Stacey*, which was set and filmed in Barry.

Wales on this Day

15 NOVEMBER

On 15 November 2020, the first episode of the twentieth series of the British popular television series *I'm a Celebrity... Get Me Out of Here!* was broadcast. Due to Covid-19 regulations, for the first time in the show's history it was not filmed in Australia, but at the imposing remains of Gwrych Castle, which towers above the coastal resort of Abergele on the north Wales coast.

The ancient site features the remains of an Iron Age hill fort, a Roman shrine, lead and silver mines, and is reputedly the site of a medieval battle. In the nineteenth century, Lloyd Hesketh Bamford-Hesketh had the castle constructed in the Victorian Gothic style as a memorial to his ancestors, the Lloyds of Gwrych, who trace their ancestry to Llywelyn the Great.

During the Second World War, the castle was a place of refuge for 200 Jewish refugee children who were rescued from Nazi Germany by the *Kindertransport* programme. The castle was subsequently used as a training venue for world middleweight boxing champion Randolph Turpin and as an occasional venue for the Dragon Rally, one of the UK's toughest and longest-running motorcycle events. The castle's current high profile is much thanks to architectural historian Dr Mark Baker, who has dedicated himself to its preservation and restoration since he was twelve.

16 NOVEMBER

On 16 November 1326, Edward II along with his close friend and probable lover, Hugh Despenser the Younger, were captured by the forces of his wife, Queen Isabella at Pant-Y-Brad (The Hollow of Treason) near Tonyrefail and imprisoned at Llantrisant Castle.

This was the end of the disastrous reign of Edward II, which had begun in 1307. The following year, he married Isabella of France and became unpopular due to the disastrous defeat at the Battle of Bannockburn in 1314 and his constant quarrelling with his barons. His close friendship with the much-hated Hugh Despenser the Younger damaged his relationship with Isabella, who fled to France and then returned with an army, led by her ally Roger de Mortimer, to overthrow Edward. Isabella's army marched on London and when Edward realised the support she had, he fled to Caerphilly Castle with Despenser.

Then the news came through that Isabella's forces had taken Bristol Castle from Despenser's father, who had been executed. Edward and Despenser apparently panicked and left Caerphilly for Neath Abbey, from where they attempted to negotiate for peace with Isabella. When they were unable to reach an agreement with the queen, Edward and Despenser attempted to return to Caerphilly, but they were intercepted and detained at Llantrisant Castle.

The king was deposed and sent to Berkeley Castle. His son, Edward III, was proclaimed king on 25 January 1327. Despenser was hanged, drawn and quartered, with his head placed on top of London Bridge. There were unsuccessful attempts to rescue Edward, but in September 1327, it was announced that he too was dead.

17 NOVEMBER

The Suez Canal opened on 17 November 1869, and is one of the world's most important shipping routes. It runs across the Isthmus of Suez in Egypt and reduces the sailing distance between Britain and India by some 4,500 miles as ships no longer needed to travel around southern Africa.

A French vessel *L'Aigle* was supposed to have the honour of being the first ship to pass through the canal. However, a cheeky night time manoeuvre by George Strong Nares, from Monmouthshire, ensured that his ship *Newport* was ahead at the time of the official opening. To avoid a diplomatic incident, the Admiralty were obliged to give Nares an official reprimand for his actions, but he also got an unofficial vote of thanks and was promoted to captain.

Nares had followed his father in taking up a career in the Royal Navy. After qualifying from the Royal Naval School in 1845, Nares served as midshipman and mate, before qualifying as a lieutenant. He served as second mate of an expedition to try and find John Franklin who had disappeared on an Arctic exploration to navigate the Northwest Passage. Nares then served as a lieutenant in charge of cadet training and wrote the highly regarded training manual *The Naval Cadet's Guide*. He was promoted to commander in 1862 and was involved in surveying firstly on the east coast of Australia and the Great Barrier Reef and then the Gulf of Suez.

In 1872, Nares was appointed as captain of HMS *Challenger* for an expedition circumnavigating the globe to investigate the deep ocean for scientific purposes for the first time. The expedition discovered about 4,700 new species of marine life and has been described as one of the greatest advances in the knowledge of our planet. In 1875, the Admiralty sent Nares to lead the British Arctic Expedition in an attempt to reach the North Pole. The mission was ultimately unsuccessful as Nares turned back when many of his men contracted scurvy; however, large amounts of scientific data were still collected. He was promoted to vice-admiral in 1892.

18 NOVEMBER

On 18 November 1840, the paddle steamer, *The City of Bristol*, was shipwrecked off the Gower Peninsula. She was washed on to Llangennith Sands, where her engines can still be seen at low tide. Twenty-seven crew and passengers were drowned, although three bullocks and seventy-five pigs managed to swim ashore.

Because of its treacherous tides, 250 ships have been wrecked along this coastline over the centuries, prompting the Whiteford Lighthouse to be built in 1865 in an attempt to protect shipping in the seas around Swansea, Llanelli and Burry Port.

19 NOVEMBER

Welsh was spoken officially at the European Union for the first time on 19 November 2008 when Wales's Culture Minister Alun Ffred Jones spoke in Welsh to the Council of Ministers at Brussels.

Some other firsts for the Welsh language include:

- The Welsh language was officially spoken for the first time on 22 November 1987 in the Vatican by Pope John Paul II.

- From 22 February 2017, MPs were permitted to use the Welsh language in parliamentary debates for the first time.

- On 17 July 2010, the Welsh language was used for the first time in a ceremony at Westminster Cathedral, to honour the martyred saint, John Roberts.

20 NOVEMBER

Jan Morris (2 October 1926–20 November 2020) was an acclaimed historian, author and travel writer, and one of the world's most famous transgender women.

Born to an English mother and Welsh father, Jan Morris was born and largely raised in England but always identified as Welsh and became a dedicated Welsh nationalist.

After serving in the Second World War, Morris became a newspaper correspondent with *The Times* and *Guardian*. In 1953, she was the only journalist accompanying the British Mount Everest expedition and it was she who reported Edmund Hillary and Tenzing Norgay reaching the summit. In 1956, she reported on the Suez Crisis and was the first to provide irrefutable proof of collusion between France and Israel in the invasion of Egyptian territory. She also travelled to Havana to interview Che Guevara, and to Moscow to interview the British intelligence defector Guy Burgess.

As an author, Morris is best known for the *Pax Britannica* trilogy (1968–1978), a history of the British Empire and for her many essays on travel. Her 1985 novel *Last Letters from Hay* was nominated for that year's Booker Prize for fiction.

In 1949, Morris married Elizabeth Tuckniss and the couple settled in Llanystumdwy. In 1972, she became one of the first high-profile figures to transition and have surgery. She described it in detail in *Conundrum* (1974), which *The Times* chose as one of the '100 key books of our time'.

Morris was a fellow of the Royal Society of Literature. She was elected to the Gorsedd Cymru in 1992 as well as receiving the Glyndŵr Award for Outstanding Contribution to the Arts in Wales in 1996.

21 NOVEMBER

The 21 November marks World Television Day.

Some Welsh television facts:

- The first television signals in Wales came from the newly constructed Wenvoe transmitter in 1952 (the first BBC broadcast was made in 1929).

- The first all Welsh-language television programme was broadcast in 1953 – a service from Cardiff's Tabernacle Baptist Church.

- Set up in 1958, Wales's first independent television service was 'Television Wales and the West' (TWW) and broadcast from the village of St Hilary near Cowbridge. It was replaced by Harlech Television in 1967, which operated from bases in Cardiff and Bristol.

- BBC Cymru Wales was launched in 1964.

- BBC Cymru Wales's first colour programme was coverage of the Llangollen Eisteddfod in 1970.

- In 1974, *Pobl y Cwm* became the first Welsh language soap opera broadcast and is the BBC's longest-running television soap opera. It is now transmitted on S4C and is regularly its most watched programme of the week.

- S4C was launched in 1982 and has since played an important role in the survival of the Welsh language. (Find out more on 1 November.)

22 NOVEMBER

A three-year dispute began on 22 November 1900, when 2,800 men walked out of the Penrhyn Quarry in Bethesda. Most of the quarrymen held out for the entire three years, by which time they had been crippled by hardship.

The dispute was the result of years of ongoing dissatisfaction in the quarrying industry. An agreement or 'bargain', which had protected the quarrymen's earnings against working with rock of variable quality, had not been honoured and therefore the entire workforce went on strike.

The quarry owner, Lord Penrhyn, was determined to break the tradition of 'bargain' because of the autonomy it afforded the workers. He vigorously opposed unionisation, and it was the right to an effective union that became the main principle during the strike.

By 1902, 1,300 had left the area in search of other work, mainly to the South Wales Coalfields. Tensions between strikers and returning workers were high, with notices being displayed in the houses of striking men bearing the words *'Nid oes Bradwr yn y Tŷ Hwn'* ('There is no traitor in this house'). The atmosphere became increasingly severe when it became obvious that Lord Penrhyn would not compromise. Facing starvation, the quarrymen were gradually forced back to work.

The strike was a devastating blow to the slate industry. Penrhyn's labour force had been decimated, and a depression in the building industry meant the gradual disintegration of slate quarrying in Wales.

23 NOVEMBER

Gangster Llewellyn Morris Humphreys, known as Murray the Hump, whose parents came from a hill farm in Carno, near Newtown, died of a heart attack while doing the vacuuming on 23 November 1965.

Murray the Hump was one of the most successful gangsters of all time and one of the most powerful men in the Chicago underworld. He was one of the organisers of the infamous St Valentine's Day Massacre in 1929 when seven members of Bugs Moran's gang were machine-gunned to death. On the death of Al Capone in 1947, Murray the Hump succeeded him at the head of the organisation. He introduced money laundering to the mob, and was responsible for introducing gambling to Las Vegas. By 1965, the FBI was beginning to catch up with him and he was involved in a fist fight with them on 23 November 1965. He was found dead later that evening.

Murray the Hump never forgot his roots and visited Wales in 1963 under an assumed name.

24 NOVEMBER

On 24 November 1816, a twenty-seven-metre column was unveiled in Llanfair PG (Llanfairpwllgwyngyll) on Anglesey commemorating the courage and heroism at the Battle of Waterloo of Henry William Paget, first Marquess of Anglesey, who lived nearby at Plas Newydd on Menai Strait.

When war broke out with France, Paget raised a regiment of volunteers and began a military career that saw him rise quickly to the rank of major general. During the Battle of Waterloo on 18 June 1815, Paget was assigned as the Duke of Wellington's second in command and led the charge of the heavy cavalry, destroying General d'Erlon's corps in the centre of the French line. Paget reportedly had eight horses shot from under him, each time calling for another so he could carry on fighting. However, one of the last shots fired hit Paget's right leg, necessitating its amputation above the knee. There are many widely repeated anecdotes regarding

the circumstances in which Paget lost his leg. According to one, when Paget was hit by the bullet, he exclaimed, 'By God, sir, I've lost my leg!', to which Wellington replied, 'By God, sir, so you have!' According to another legend, his only comment throughout the amputation was, 'The knives appear somewhat blunt.' The amputated leg became a tourist attraction in Waterloo.

Five days after the battle, Paget was created Marquess of Anglesey and appointed a Knight of the Garter. He had an artificial leg fitted – the world's first articulated wooden leg with moveable joints at the knee, ankle and toe and later known as the 'Anglesey leg'. (This can still be seen at Plas Newydd.) The loss of his leg did not impede Paget's career and he went on to lead a distinguished public life, twice becoming Lord Lieutenant of Ireland.

25 NOVEMBER

The murder-mystery play *The Mousetrap* opened in London's West End on 25 November 1952. As a ninth birthday present, the play's author, Agatha Christie, signed world rights to the work over to her Welsh grandson, Mathew Prichard. Prichard – now chairman of Agatha Christie Ltd, which manages the literary and media rights to all of Christie's works around the world – set up the Colwinston Charitable Trust (named after the village in the Vale of Glamorgan), which uses royalties to promote the arts in Wales. The Welsh National Opera, Wales Millennium Centre and Chapter Arts have all benefited from the trust's financial support.

26 NOVEMBER

Built by William Jessop and Thomas Telford, the Pont-cysyllte Aqueduct, which carries the Llangollen branch of the Shropshire Union Canal over the Dee Valley, was opened on 26 November 1805. It is the highest and longest aqueduct in Britain and the first aqueduct in the world to use a cast-iron trough. It is also a Grade 1 Listed Building and a World Heritage Site.

27 NOVEMBER

On 27 November 1874, quartermaster Hence Thomas Lewis (also known as Twm Pen Stryd) from Moelfre was just one of five people out of 477 rescued from a disastrous shipwreck.

The emigration ship *Cospatrick* was sailing from England to New Zealand and had reached the Cape of Good Hope when a fire broke out on board. A passenger carrying a candle had entered the cargo area of the ship with the intention of stealing some of its contents and had accidentally set fire to some tar used for the ship's maintenance. The fire spread quickly and, in the resulting panic, only two of the lifeboats were able to be launched, with the remainder of the passengers being lost with the ship which was destroyed. Next, a storm moved in and one of the lifeboats sank with no survivors. Most of the occupants of the other lifeboat died due to exposure to the elements and lack of food and the last of the survivors were forced to drink the blood and eat the livers of the dead. After seven days adrift, only five were alive when they were rescued by a passing ship and two of these died shortly afterwards. The surviving three men, including Tem Pen Stryd, were later put on trial for cannibalism.

28 NOVEMBER

On 28 November 2021, during Storm Arwen, a Kemp's Ridley sea turtle was washed up on Talacre beach, Flintshire. The Kemp's Ridley is the world's rarest turtle and an endangered species. They are normally found in the Gulf of Mexico, some 4,000 miles from Wales. The turtle was taken in by Anglesey Sea Zoo, who named it Tally and began the process of nursing it back to health, with the aim of returning them to the Gulf of Mexico.

Storm Arwen was named by the Met Office and was one of three names of Welsh origin designated to storms during the 2021–22 storm season, the others being Gladys and Olwen. Despite sounding Welsh, the name Arwen was invented by J.R.R Tolkien for an Elvish princess in the *Lord of the Rings* trilogy. However, Tolkien's invented language is heavily influenced by Welsh.

29 NOVEMBER

On 29 November 2021, it was reported that Traffic Wales would be renaming some their road gritters with suggestions by public.

Among the puns under consideration were: Huw Sledgewards, Rob Brrr-ydon, Alun Wyn-ter Jones, I'M4Gritting, Geraint Thom-ice, Ian Slush, National Ice-steddfod, The Grit Redeemer, Gareth Hale, Nigel Snowins, George

North Pole, Snow Ledley, Catherine Sleeta-Jones, Dame Shirley Bass-sleet and Grit Rhys Jones.

Welsh language versions include Huwie Halen, The Ei-radicator, Llywelyn Ein Lluwch Olaf, Halen Robson Kanu, Rhewi Sant, Tanny Graean Thompson, Shirley Iâssey and Ieti George.

30 NOVEMBER

The Blaenavon industrial landscape became a World Heritage Site on 30 November 2000, the first 'cultural landscape' to be recognised in the United Kingdom. The landscape includes the Blaenavon Ironworks, the Big Pit coal mine, surrounding mines and quarries, transport infrastructure, workers' housing and other aspects of early industrialisation.

Blaenavon lies at the upper end of the River Lwyd valley and is on the north-eastern rim of the South Wales Coalfield. In pre-industrial times, the area only consisted of scattered farmsteads. Its growth into an industrial community resulted from the area's rich deposits of iron ore, coal and limestone. The Industrial Revolution in Britain was based on iron, steel and coal which was used to build and fuel railways, factories and engines all over the world.

There is evidence of small-scale mining in the Elgam area of Blaenavon in 1325. From 1565, iron ore was extracted here by the Hanbury family, who were ironmasters and tinplate manufacturers in Pontypool.

In 1787, the lease of the land that was known locally as Lord Abergavenny's Hills was taken out by three businessmen from the Midlands – Thomas Hill, Benjamin Pratt and Hill's brother-in-law Thomas Hopkins – and they opened an ironworks the following year. The venture was an immediate success and Blaenavon became an important producer of iron products. This was boosted by the demand for cannon and weapons due to Britain's involvement in various naval conflicts at the time.

By 1821, Hill's son, also named Thomas, had built a tram-road to connect the Blaenavon works to the Brecknock and Abergavenny Canal and therefore to the Newport Docks, the limestone quarries at Pwll Du and Tyla, the forge in Cwm Llanwenarth on the west flank of the Blorenge mountain. Skilled workers came to Blaenavon from all over Britain and Ireland and its population rose from approximately 1,000 in 1800 to 5,115 in 1840.

In 1836, the works were bought by the Blaenavon Iron and Coal Company, which was subsequently involved in the building and the running of St Peter's Church, the town hall and a hospital in the town.

The railway line from Blaenavon to Brynmawr was completed in 1869 and connected the area to the English Midlands via the Heads of the Valleys line. In 1877 it was extended to meet the Great Western Railway line to Pontypool and Newport Docks.

In 1870, the company added steel production to its activities. This proved very successful and was aided by the revolutionary method of eliminating phosphorus from iron introduced by Sidney Gilchrist Thomas and his cousin Percy Gilchrist.

In 1880, local supplies of iron ore were becoming

exhausted and the company opened Big Pit coal mine. Another boom period for the town followed and the population rose to over 20,000.

The railway line was closed to passengers in 1941. The line from Blaenavon to Pontypool was used for coal trains from Big Pit until the colliery closed in 1980.

1 DECEMBER

On 1 December 1865, Llandrindod Wells was linked to the rail network for the first time.

The beneficial effects of Llandrindod's local waters were known about from as far back as Roman times, but the development of the town only began after the arrival of the railway in 1865, when it became a fashionable Victorian tourist destination.

The first attempt at developing the area was in 1749 when a Mr Grosvenor built a large hotel on the banks of the present lake. However, his venture was unsuccessful, as the hotel acquired a dubious reputation and closed in 1787. But when the railway arrived, bringing visitors from London, Liverpool, Manchester and Birmingham, the town flourished, with hotels and guesthouses springing up to cater for the 80,000 visitors that visited the town every year.

The depression that followed the First World War, coupled with the rising popularity of seaside holidays, brought a dramatic decline in the number of visitors to the town, though these have started to increase again in more recent years.

2 DECEMBER

On 2 December 2002, Dr Rowan Williams from Ystradgynlais was confirmed as being the 104th Archbishop of Canterbury. He was enthroned on 27 February 2003 and was the first Welsh successor to the position; in fact, as Bishop of Monmouth and Archbishop of Wales, he was the first Archbishop of Canterbury since the Reformation not to be appointed from within the Church of England. His attendance at the services for Pope John Paul II also made him the first Archbishop of Canterbury to attend a Pope's funeral since the Protestant Reformation.

Apart from Welsh, Dr Rowan Williams speaks or reads nine other languages. He was criticised for allegedly supporting a pagan organisation, the Welsh Gorsedd of Bards, which promotes Welsh language and literature and uses Druidic ceremonial traditions but is not religious in nature. In 2010, in an address he gave to the congregation of a service to honour the martyred Welsh saint John Roberts, Williams spoke in both English and Welsh. This was the first time the Welsh language had been used in a ceremony at Westminster Cathedral.

Williams's ten year term as Archbishop of Canterbury came to an end on 31 December 2012. At a ceremony at Lambeth Palace, he gave the official robes that he had worn on his enthronement to the president of the National Museum Wales, where they are now on display and are considered the property of the people of Wales.

3 DECEMBER

On 3 December 1935, Felinfoel Brewery produced Britain's first ever canned beer, transforming the country's buying habits.

Founded in 1878 by German immigrants trying to recreate their local lager, Felinfoel is based in the eponymous village near Llanelli (spelt Llanelly until 1966) and is the oldest brewery in Wales. It was the first brewery outside the US to commercially can beer. The cans were made from tinplate produced in south Wales which, from the late eighteenth century until the early twentieth, dominated the world's production, so much so that in the early 1890s, eighty per cent of all tinplate was produced in south Wales.

4 DECEMBER

The daguerreotype of Margam Castle taken in 1841 by Calvert Jones is credited with being the first photograph ever taken in Wales.

Calvert Jones was born in Swansea on 4 December 1804. He was a mathematician, painter and photographer who came from a wealthy Swansea family and was educated

THE FELINFOEL BREWERY CO.LTD. PALE ALE

PR CO.LTD.

canned at
the Brewery

LLANELLY

at Eton and Oriel College, Oxford. He became rector of Loughor where he developed a great interest in photography, taking many photographs of the Swansea area as well as France and Italy. Jones also discovered a technique for taking panoramic photographs by overlapping images.

In 1847, Jones inherited the Heathfield estate in Swansea, which he developed and named Mansel Street after his brother. He died in Bath and was buried at St Mary's Church, Swansea, but his grave was bombed during the Second World War and destroyed.

5 DECEMBER

On 5 December 1931, in an international match against Northern Ireland at Belfast, Eddie Parris became the first Black player to represent Wales in a football international. He is also generally considered to be only the second British Black or mixed-race player to play international football, the first being Scotsman Andrew Watson in the 1880s. At the time, Parris was one of only two Black players who were regulars in the Football League, the other being Jack Leslie of Plymouth Argyle who was controversially withdrawn from an England squad in 1925.

Eddie Parris was born in Pwllmeyric, near Chepstow in 1911, the son of a Barbadian father and a white mother. He began his playing career with Chepstow Town at the age of sixteen and was described as a pacy, goal-scoring left-winger. He later played for Bradford Park Avenue, AFC Bournemouth, Luton Town, Bath City, Northampton Town and Cheltenham Town.

After his international call-up, Parris was not selected to represent Wales again, which, at a time of racial tension and prejudice, was likely due to his mixed-race heritage. However, the fact that Wales had lost heavily and the fact that he was injury prone and considered talented but inconsistent would not have helped his case.

6 DECEMBER

David Lloyd George replaced Herbert Asquith as British Prime Minister on 6 December 1916, making him the first – and to date the only – Welshman to hold the position.

Lloyd George was born to Welsh parents in Manchester in 1863. His father died when he was three, prompting David's mother to move the family back to her native Caernarfonshire. Here David, a lifelong Welsh nationalist, was strongly influenced by his uncle Richard Lloyd, a minister and political activist.

In 1890, Lloyd George was elected Liberal MP for Caernarfon and was appointed Chancellor of the Exchequer in 1908.

During the early stages of the First World War, Lloyd George was put in charge of the Ministry of Munitions then made secretary for war and finally prime minister. His achievements in persuading the Royal Navy to introduce the convoy system and the unification of the Allied military command under the French general Ferdinand Foch were both instrumental in him being acclaimed as the man who had won the war.

After the war, he became politically untouchable, even

though he was a Liberal leading a predominantly Conservative party. From 1919 to 1922, however, his government steadily weakened and there was increased Conservative hostility towards him that finally forced him to resign in 1922.

Although Lloyd George is remembered mostly for his contribution to winning the First World War, he is also regarded as one of the great reforming British chancellors of the twentieth century and his legacy includes laying the foundation of the welfare state, increasing council house building, improving pensions and raising the school leaving age to fourteen. For opposition parties, he was a revered and well-respected opponent in the Houses of Parliament where he was nicknamed the 'Welsh Wizard'.

7 DECEMBER

At a meeting of the Religious Tract Society on 7 December 1802, a story about a young girl's quest to get her own Bible helped set in motion the founding of the British and Foreign Bible Society. The Bible society is not limited to a particular religious group, and encourages the use of the Scriptures throughout the world.

The story was that of fifteen-year-old Mary Jones from Llanfihangel-y-Pennant. In 1800, she walked for twenty-five miles, barefoot, over rugged land and mountains to purchase a Bible in Bala. Mary came from a very religious family and was educated in a circulating school (schools that rotated around rural areas of Wales for set periods of the year), in which the Bible was used as the central part of learning. She was therefore keen to obtain her own copy and reportedly saved for nearly six years to buy one. One of the only people in north Wales who had copies of the Bible at that time was the Calvinistic Methodist clergyman Thomas Charles from Bala, so Mary set out on her long journey – but on her arrival, she discovered that Charles had sold out. Charles, though, was so impressed with her determination that he found somewhere for her stay for the two days before new supplies arrived, and then sold her three copies for the price of one.

During that meeting in December 1802, inspired by Mary's story, the Reverend Joseph Hughes stressed the need for reduced-price Bibles for Welsh speakers. He asked, 'If for Wales … why not for the world?'

8 DECEMBER

The film *The Greatest Showman* premiered on 8 December 2017. The musical drama was inspired by the story of P. T. Barnum's creation of Barnum's American Museum and the Barnum & Bailey Circus in 1870, which was billed as 'The Greatest Show on Earth'. The film also depicts the lives of its star attractions, among them was George Auger, who at eight feet and three inches tall, was known as both The Tallest Man In The World and The Cardiff Giant.

Born in Cardiff in 1882, George was already over six-foot-tall by the time he was fourteen. He began his career as a police officer in Cardiff and was soon promoted to Queen Victoria's personal escort squad. He got his big break into show business when he was spotted while visiting Barnum and Bailey's circus. He quickly became a celebrity and, in

1906, he wrote his own play, *Jack the Giant Killer*, which ran for almost ten years – he brought it to Cardiff in 1908. George died suddenly in 1922, just before he was to star alongside Harold Lloyd as the giant Colosso in the film *Why Worry?*

Although award-winning, *The Greatest Showman* has been highlighted by some as not presenting a well-rounded perspective of P. T. Barnum, who was 'more interested in exploiting people than empowering them' (Steve Rose, *Guardian*, 2017), particularly when it came to Indigenous and African-American people.

9 DECEMBER

At 7 p.m. on 9 December 1960, Neath-born Maudie Edwards spoke the very first lines on *Coronation Street*, which would go on to become the world's longest-running television soap opera. She was playing corner shop owner Elsie Lappin. The opening words were, 'Now the next thing you've got to do is get a sign writer in. That thing above the door'll have to be changed.' She was addressing Florrie Lindley, a barmaid who would be taking over the shop.

10 DECEMBER

Sir Hugh Myddelton was the Welshman who enabled clean drinking water to come to London. He died on 10 December 1631.

Myddelton (1560–1631) was the son of Richard Myddelton, governor of Denbigh Castle. When he came of age, he left home to seek his fortune in London. There, he embarked on an entrepreneurial career that took in textiles, mining, engineering, jewellery and politics. He later succeeded his father as the Denbigh Boroughs MP and was also appointed as the Royal Jeweller by King James I.

In the early seventeenth century, London's population exploded and sanitation was a serious problem. It was decided that the answer was to construct an artificial river to bring clean drinking water into the heart of London. Myddleton's idea was to divert the water from the River Lea in Hertfordshire to Clerkenwell in the City of London, and he was able to persuade King James to invest fifty per cent of the capital backing, which swept away all objections from landowners along the route.

Myddleton's thirty-five-mile long artificial New River took five years to construct, but had an almost instantaneous benefit and by 1614, deaths due to water-borne infections had halved from the previous year.

11 DECEMBER

The death of Llywelyn ap Gruffydd on 11 December 1282 ended the aspiration of an independent Wales and resulted in the subjugation of Wales by Edward I.

Llywelyn was born c.1223, the grandson of Llywelyn ap Iorwerth (Llywelyn the Great), King of Gwynedd. He overcame rivalries with his brothers Owain and Dafydd to become the sole ruler of most of Gwynedd by 1258 and was confirmed as the dominant prince in Wales by Henry III in 1267. However, Henry III died in 1272 and

Llywelyn's relationship with the English crown deteriorated under the new king, Edward I. Ultimately Llywelyn had to acknowledge the English king as his sovereign.

Then, in 1282, Dafydd attacked the English at Hawarden Castle and Rhuddlan and Llywelyn felt obliged to support his brother. (Find out more on 3 October.) After some fierce battles with the English, according to one version of the story, Llywelyn was tricked into attending a meeting with the English commander, Edmund Mortimer, at Aberedw Castle. Here he was ambushed and killed. His head was sent to Edward, who placed it on the gate of the Tower of London. Resistance continued for a while under Dafydd, but by June of the following year he too had been captured and executed, and his head was displayed next to Llywelyn's.

Nobody knows for sure the whereabouts of Llywelyn's final resting place, though most historians suggest it is the Cistercian abbey at Abbeycwmhir. (Find out more about Llewelyn on 24 June.)

12 DECEMBER

On 12 December 1965, the Beatles concluded their last live UK tour with two performances at the Capitol Theatre, Cardiff.

The Capitol Theatre opened in 1921, with a capacity of 3,158. It was purchased by the Rank Organisation in 1964 and has seen performances from acts such as Tom Jones, Queen and Bob Dylan. The theatre was closed in 1978 and demolished the following year.

13 DECEMBER

Llandovery College first opened on 1 March 1848, but the foundation stone of the current college building was laid on 13 December 1849.

The college was founded by surgeon Thomas Phillips, initially as a school for boys, to cultivate the promotion of the Welsh language, Welsh literature and history. Girls were first admitted in the 1960s. Llandovery was chosen as its location because of its accessibility from all parts of south Wales and the absence of manufacturing industries in the area.

The college is known for its sporting tradition and for its involvement in the formation of the Welsh Rugby Union in Neath in 1881. It was one of the very first teams in Wales to play rugby. Former pupils include two players for the very first Welsh international team and its second captain, Charles Lewis. Other former pupils who have represented Wales at rugby include Alun Wyn Jones, Cliff Jones, George North, Andy Powell and Craig Quinnell.

14 DECEMBER

Born on 14 December 1892, Alfred 'Fred' Bestall (1892–1986) is remembered as the writer and illustrator of the Rupert Bear stories in the *Daily Express,* which appeared between 1935–65. Most of the landscapes that Bestall used in his illustrations were inspired by his childhood holidays in Snowdonia, an area he revisited regularly as an adult. He eventually settled in a cottage on Mynydd Sygun, in Beddgelert in 1956.

15 DECEMBER

Swansea (Welsh name, Abertawe) was officially granted city status on 15 December 1969. Swansea's population in 2020 was 246,600, making it the second largest city in Wales and the twenty-fifth largest city in the United Kingdom.

It is believed that Swansea – in the sheltered waters of Swansea Bay, with access inland along the River Tawe – was established as a trading post by the Vikings. The Normans established control of the area when Henry de Beaumont built Swansea Castle in 1107, in his position as the caput (chief) of the lordship of Gower. The town of Swansea developed around the castle and it was granted its first town charter around 1158.

Swansea developed as the centre of the local fishing industry but, from the early eighteenth century, metallurgical industries also became established due to its central position between the tin mines of Cornwall and Devon and the industrial centres of the English Midlands. (Find out more on 14 February.) Industrialisation brought improved transport and urban growth and Swansea was made a borough with a mayor in 1835, and three docks were built between 1852 and 1881. Swansea's population also grew rapidly – from around 1,000 in the seventeenth century to 6,831 in 1801, 16,000 in 1841 and 134,000 in 1901. The first official bid for city status was made in 1911. However, at the time Swansea's industries were in decline and Cardiff had become Wales's premier exporting dock.

Swansea continued to suffer from the depression and economic hardships following the First World War. The town was further devastated by the Swansea Blitz during the Second World War – a three-day bombing campaign from 19–21 February 1941. Swansea's town centre became a blazing inferno as the Luftwaffe unleashed 1,273 high explosive bombs and 56,000 incendiary devices, targeting the port, docks, and the oil refinery at Llandarcy. The town centre was almost completely obliterated: 857 properties were destroyed and 11,000 damaged, while 230 people were killed and 409 injured.

Swansea survived. The determination of its people to regenerate the town resulted in new industries being established and it was also promoted as a tourist centre – all of which helped to bring a degree of prosperity back to the town. Swansea continued to campaign for city status throughout the 1960s, highlighting its cultural history and the sporting successes of its football and rugby teams. These efforts were finally recognised in 1969.

16 DECEMBER

On 16 December 1905, Wales defeated New Zealand at rugby union for the first time, winning three points to nil.

The New Zealand team arrived in Cardiff for the last game of their tour of Britain and Ireland, unbeaten, to face Wales, who had just won the Triple Crown. The only score of a hard, fast and uncompromising match was a try by Welsh winger Teddy Morgan. However, later in the game, Welsh centre Rhys Gabe prevented an almost certain score by New Zealander Bob Deans. Interestingly, during the scrums, Wales used four men in the front row, against New Zealand's three, ensuring that they won the ball at every scrum.

The match is also notable for being the first time a nation's national anthem was sung before a sporting event. After the All Blacks had performed their customary haka, the Welsh team, in a pre-planned response, started to sing the national anthem. The home supporters soon joined in, with the result that 'Hen Wlad Fy Nhadau' echoed around the stadium.

17 DECEMBER

Sarah Jacobs, the 'Welsh Fasting Girl', died on 17 December 1869.

Sarah was born in 1857 on a farm near Llanfihangel-ar-Arth in Carmarthenshire. When she was nine, she became seriously ill and was confined to bed for a considerable period of time. She passed the time by composing poems and reading the Bible. Then, according to her parents, Evan and Hannah, she suddenly began to refuse food. However, she did not suffer any ill effects and seemed to be thriving. Word got out, and Sarah became famous, with people travelling from all over Wales and England to see her lying in her bed, surrounded by flowers and reading the Bible. They considered themselves to be witnessing a miracle and were encouraged to give gifts and money to Sarah.

Some people, however, were sceptical and Dr Phillips of Guy's Hospital decided to arrange for six nurses to carry out a twenty-four-hour vigil, in which they would observe, but offer no treatment or help unless Sarah asked for food. Sarah did not, however, and she slowly lapsed into semi-consciousness, before dying on 17 December. An autopsy later found food in Sarah's stomach and groove marks on her toes, where it was supposed she had been trying to open a stone water bottle in a desperate attempt to get water.

People were outraged when news of the cruel experiment and Sarah's death became public and her parents were imprisoned for manslaughter. However, none of the doctors or nurses were prosecuted.

18 DECEMBER

On 18 December 2018 a mural entitled 'Season's Greetings' was discovered on a backstreet garage at Taibach, an area of Port Talbot. It was later confirmed to be the work of graffiti artist Banksy.

The poignant image depicts a joyful child embracing falling snow; however, the adjacent wall reveals that the flakes are emitting from a burning skip. Art dealer John Brandler bought the work and loaned it to Neath Port Talbot council for a period of three years. The Welsh Government, supported by contributions from Port Talbot-born actor Michael Sheen, paid for it to be moved to an unoccupied building where it could be viewed by the public.

Despite campaigns to keep the work in Wales, Neath Port Talbot stated that the ongoing cost of housing and insuring the installation was prohibitive, and in February 2022 the work was transported to a storage facility in England. The Banksy Preservation Society hopes to raise funds to ensure that the mural will be on display to the public in future.

19 DECEMBER

On 19 December 1958, the first purpose-built supermarket in Wales opened in Market Street, Llanelli. The Co-operative shop was declared as 'the most modern and hygienic food store in the principality' and as the first 'one-stop shop' for food and hygiene products. Then in September 1972, the French retail giant Carrefour opened Britain's first hypermarket in Caerphilly, some twenty years after it first appeared in France.

20 DECEMBER

Frances Elizabeth Hoggan (née Morgan; 1843–1927) was born in Brecon on 20 December 1843. She was the first British woman to receive a doctorate in medicine from a European university and the first female doctor to be registered in Wales.

Frances's father was a curate and she was raised and educated in Cowbridge and Windsor. She obtained her doctorate from Zurich University in 1870, after which she married Dr George Hoggan. The couple then operated the first husband-and-wife medical practice in the UK. Francis was also an active campaigner for social reform and was particularly involved in racial issues.

21 DECEMBER

Daleks first appeared on British televisions on 21 December 1963. The Daleks were the menacing opponents of Doctor Who and were invented by scriptwriter and novelist Terry Nation.

Nation was born in Cardiff in 1930 and was one of British television's most prolific and successful writers during the 1960s and 1970s. He began his professional career as a stand-up comedian but soon switched to scriptwriting, writing for comedians such as Harry Worth, Eric Sykes and Frankie Howerd. He also wrote for a number of television series including *The Saint, The Baron, The Avengers* and *The Persuaders,* later becoming a script editor and an associate producer.

Terry Nation is just one of many notable Welsh connections to *Doctor Who*. The prolific television actor Peter Halliday, born in Cefn Mawr, Denbighshire and brought up in Welshpool, gained cult status for his many appearances in *Doctor Who* in the 1960s and 1970s. Russell T. Davies from Swansea was the head writer and executive producer from 2005–10, is returning for the sixtieth anniversary episodes in 2023. These twenty-first-century series were produced by BBC Wales and based in Cardiff. Julie Gardner from Neath, who was Head of Drama at BBC Wales, was its executive producer.

22 DECEMBER

Stephen of Blois claimed the throne of England on 22 December 1135 during a breakdown in law and order in England referred to as 'The Anarchy'. The Anarchy originated towards the end of the reign of Henry I. Henry's attempts to install his daughter, Empress Matilda, as his successor were unsuccessful and on Henry's death on 1 December 1135, his nephew Stephen of Blois seized power. The ensuing succession crisis lasted until 1154, when Matilda's son, Henry II, became King of England and began launching campaigns to regain lost territories.

During this time, many native Welsh lords took advantage of the opportunity to recover lands previously lost to the Normans. On New Year's Day 1136, Hywel ap Maredudd, a warrior chieftain from Brycheiniog, raised an army and marched on south Gower. When the Normans intercepted them between Loughor and Swansea there was a violent clash on the common of Garn Coch, referred to as the Battle of Llwchwr (Battle of Gower). The Norman force was routed and lost 500 men. This victory inspired more rebellions and Gruffydd ap Rhys, lord of Deheubarth, journeyed to meet with Gruffydd ap Cynan of Gwynedd to enlist his aid in the revolt. In his absence, his wife Gwenllian raised an army and attacked the Norman castle of Kidwelly (Cydweli). However, she was defeated, captured and beheaded. Two of her sons, Morgan and Maelgwyn, also died – one slain in battle and one captured and executed.

In response, Cadwaladr and Owain, the brothers of Gwenllian, invaded Deheubarth, taking Llanfihangel, Aberystwyth and Llanbadarn. Subsequently, the two Gruffydds engaged a massive Norman army drawn from all the lordships of south Wales at the Battle of Crug Mawr, two miles outside Cardigan, in October 1136. After some hard fighting, the Norman forces were forced to retreat and were pursued as far as the bridge over the River Teifi. The bridge collapsed under the weight of the fleeing Normans and hundreds are said to have drowned. Others fled into Cardigan, which was taken and burned by the Welsh. However, they were unable to take the castle and it remained the only one still under Norman control until the end of the rebellion.

In Deheubarth in 1146, Cadell ap Gruffydd took the castles of Carmarthen and Llansteffan. His campaigns are also notable for the inclusion of Cadell's brother Rhys ap Gruffydd, then aged thirteen, who was later to become known as the Lord Rhys and one of the most prominent Welsh rulers of his generation. In 1149, Oswestry was captured by Madog ap Maredudd of Powys and it remained in Welsh hands until 1157.

23 DECEMBER

Saturnalia (17–23 December) was a pagan festival held in honour of the agricultural god Saturn. On the last day of celebrations it was traditional to give friends and loved ones gifts of small terracotta figurines known as *sigillaria*. Many of the traditions of Saturnalia are the basis of ones we now associate with Christmas.

Some Christmas traditions originating from Wales:

- Some parts of Wales enjoyed *Noson Gyflaith* (Toffee Evening), when families would invite friends to their homes for an evening of making toffee and storytelling. Women would also sell their toffee, which was also called *taffi*, *dant*, *fanny* or after the name of the person who made it – for example *losin Mag* (Mag's sweets).

- The Plygain carol service was held on Christmas morning, sometimes as early as 3 a.m. but more often at 6 a.m. It was a custom for many to stay up all night before attending, making *cyflaith* (treacle toffee) or singing, dancing and playing the harp. The bringing in of the candles was seen as an important part of the service as it symbolised the coming of the Light of the World. As part of the service people were invited to sing *plygains* – a type of Welsh carol.

- Holly-Beating or 'holming' was a Boxing Day tradition in some parts of Wales, in which young men would beat the arms and legs of young women with sprigs of holly until they bled. In others areas, the custom was for the last person in bed in the morning to get the beating. Thankfully, these customs died out by the end of the nineteenth century.

- The Mari Lwyd (Grey Mare) involved a horse figure being carried from door to door by a group of Mari Lwyd singers, often wearing traditional dress. The group performed a series of rap battle-like rhyming insults in Welsh, to which the family would respond to try and outwit the horse. Ultimately, though, the singers would often be invited into the house as the Mari Lwyd is said to bring good luck for the coming year. The group would be given food, beer or money and then entertain the household with a farewell song. The tradition is still performed in some parts of Glamorgan. Some regions also traditionally waited until January to perform the custom.

24 DECEMBER

The Red Bandits of Mawddwy (*Y Gwylliaid Cochion*) were a band of outlaws, robbers and highwaymen from the area of Dinas Mawddwy in the mountains above Dolgellau, an area where there were great difficulties in preserving law and order. These outlaws became famous in folk literature and are remembered through a number of place names in the area, such as Llety'r Gwylliaid (bandits lodging), Llety'r Lladron (robbers lodging) and also the bandits' reputed meeting place, the Brigand's Inn at nearby Mallwyd.

The bandits were eventually captured, and on 24 December 1555, a staggering eighty of them were executed. There is a burial mound at Rhos Goch (the Red Moor), where it's said their bodies are buried.

25 DECEMBER

On Christmas Day 1914, the 2nd Battalion, Royal Welsh Fusiliers were involved in one of the most moving events of any conflict, whilst fighting on the front line in northern France during the First World War. In his memoirs, Private Frank Richards from Blaina recalled how two men put up a board with 'Merry Christmas' written on it and then climbed up the trench with their hands up. Two German soldiers did likewise and the two pairs of soldiers then walked into no man's land and shook hands. Then soldiers from both sides threw down their arms and joined them. They exchanged gifts such as beer, cigarettes, plum puddings and chocolate and sang carols, and organised a football match.

The following morning, Captain Stockwell of the Welsh

Fusiliers climbed up the trench and held up the sign with 'Merry Christmas' on it. A German commander then appeared on the other side with a sign saying 'Thank You'. Both men saluted each other, fired three shots into the air and then climbed back into their positions and the war recommenced.

26 DECEMBER

The animated children's television series *Fireman Sam* was first broadcast as *Sam Tân* in Welsh on S4C on 26 December 1985.

Fireman Sam is about the adventures of a fireman called Sam, his fellow firefighters and other townspeople in the fictional Welsh rural town of Pontypandy. The series has been sold to over forty countries, from Australia to Norway, and is used across the United Kingdom to promote fire safety. It has even been adapted into a live musical theatre show. Mal Pope, a musician and composer from Swansea, sang the theme song.

27 DECEMBER

The Dan yr Ogof Caves were first discovered on 27 December 1912 by Tommy and Jeff Morgan, who were trying to find the source of the River Llynfell, which flowed through their farmland.

The brothers had searched for the source previously but a large lake had prevented them from going far into the mountain. Undeterred they returned with coracles, candles, a piece of rope and an old revolver, using arrows in the sand to find their way back. They crossed not one lake but four and discovered a labyrinth of caves, passages and chambers – a 330-million-year-old wonderland of stalactites and stalagmites. They were eventually stopped by a passage that was too small to crawl through. Not long afterwards, they started charging a small entrance fee to take people into the caves by candlelight.

The caves were properly opened to the public in 1939. However, during the Second World War the government closed the caves down and used them to store ammunition and works of art. Water from the caves was also piped to Swansea when the water mains were damaged by bombs during the blitz on the city.

In 1963, a local girl called Eileen Davies, a member of the South Wales Caving Club, managed to crawl further into the caves to discover over ten more miles of caves and passages. Expert cavers believe that there are still more to discover.

28 DECEMBER

Ivor the Engine was first released on television on 28 December 1959.

Ivor the Engine is a children's television series that tells the story of a little green locomotive living in the 'top left-hand corner of Wales'. His friends include Jones the Steam, Evans the Song and Dai Station. The series was later revived in 1975 when new episodes in colour were produced for the BBC.

The series was written and narrated by Oliver Postgate,

with his friend Peter Firmin providing the artwork, which originally consisted of cardboard cut-outs painted with watercolours. It was produced in a disused cowshed at Firmin's home near Canterbury. The sound effects were endearingly low-tech, for example, the sound of Ivor's puffing was made vocally by Postgate himself.

Postgate's inspiration for the series came from an encounter with Welshman Denzyl Ellis, a former railway fireman, who had described to him how steam engines came to life when starting them up in the morning. Postgate decided to locate the story in the mountainous area of north Wales, as he considered it a more inspirational place than the flat terrain of the English Midlands.

29 DECEMBER

Llywd ap Iwan, the son of the founder of Y Wladfa, the Welsh settlement in Patagonia, was murdered on 29 December 1909. (Find out more about Y Wladfa on 28 May.) Some say that he was killed by Butch Cassidy and Sundance Kid but it's more likely that it was members of their gang. He was shot dead in the cooperative store, where he was the supervisor, close to his home at Nant y Pysgod and about thirty miles from Esquel in the foothills of the Andes.

After pursuing a career in crime for several years in the United States, the pressures of being pursued had forced Cassidy and Sundance to flee with Etta Place (Sundance's girlfriend), to Welsh speaking Patagonia in Argentina. They purchased a ranch on the east bank of the Rio Blanco near

Cholila, Chubut Province and lived there amongst Welsh settlers, breeding horses. By 1905, they had outstayed their welcome there and were aided in their escape to Bolivia by Sheriff Edward Humphreys, a Welsh settler who was friendly with Cassidy and enamoured of Etta Place. Butch Cassidy and the Sundance Kid were killed in 1908 following a shootout in Bolivia.

30 DECEMBER

On 30 December 2020, Michael Sheen revealed that he had returned his OBE to Buckingham Palace.

Sheen was awarded the accolade in 2009 for his services to drama. He changed his mind about accepting it because he began researching Welsh history after he was invited to speak at the Raymond Williams Memorial Lecture in 2017. Raymond Williams famously wrote a piece called *Who Speaks For Wales?* in 1971 and Sheen said that he took that as his starting point for the lecture. He learned about the history of the royal title, Prince of Wales, which Edward I created in 1301 as part of his subjugation of Wales. He realised that he could not deliver the lecture and also accept the OBE without compromising his principles.

Sheen decided that he wanted to do the lecture so he gave the OBE back adding: 'I didn't mean any disrespect but I just realised I'd be a hypocrite if I said the things I was going to say in the lecture about the nature of the relationship between Wales and the British state.'

31 DECEMBER

Rasys Nos Galan is an event held in memory of Griffith Morgan – better known as Guto Nyth Brân (1700–1737), 'the fastest man of his time'. He hailed from Llwyncelyn, near Porth. A race is run every year on New Year's Eve at Mountain Ash, using the course that Guto ran on his first ever race. It has become a tradition for a mystery runner to compete and over the years this has included Iwan Thomas, Linford Christie and Alun Wyn Jones. At the conclusion of the race, a wreath is then placed on Guto's grave in Llanwynno graveyard. There is also a commemorative statue of Guto in Mountain Ash.

It was said that Guto's speed was first noticed when he managed to catch a wild hare. Another legend has it that he could run the seven miles to the local town of Pontypridd and back home again before his mother's kettle had boiled. Seeing his potential, the local shopkeeper, *Siân o'r Siop* (Siân from the shop), became his trainer and manager and organised a race on Hirwaun Common against an unbeaten English captain for a £400 prize. Guto won the race easily and he kept on winning – remaining unbeaten until he was thirty. Over the years, Guto and Siân fell in love and Guto decided to retire to enjoy a quiet life with Siân.

However, in 1737, a new champion runner had emerged, called the 'Prince of Bedwas' and Siân persuaded Guto to have one last race against him, for a prize of 1,000 guineas. The race was run over the twelve miles from Newport to Bedwas and was a very even contest. Nearing the finish, Prince held a slender lead; however, one last lung-bursting effort from Guto saw him cross the line first. In the celebrations after, Guto collapsed and died in Siân's arms.

ACKNOWLEDGEMENTS

With thanks to our publisher Amy Feldman.

Calon would like to thank Professor Charlotte Williams, OBE and Dr Lucy Taylor for their invaluable input on the manuscript, as well as Abbie Headon and the many other people who made this book happen.

ABOUT THE AUTHORS

Huw Rees and Sian Kilcoyne run 'The History of Wales' Facebook page. They are a brother and sister team, dedicated to improving their knowledge of their country and sharing it with a wider audience. Their aim is to provide objective and (hopefully!) interesting information, to help them and their readers better understand who we are as a nation, highlighting major past events, items of interest and the famous Welsh people that have shaped us into what we are today.

Wales on this Day is their first book.

ABOUT CALON

Calon

Calon is the University of Wales Press's non-fiction imprint that brings the many varied and fascinating stories of Wales to readers across the world. Our books cover a vast range of subjects; whether you're interested in food or folklore, music or memoir, travel or nature writing, then Calon's books are for you.

MORE BOOKS FROM CALON

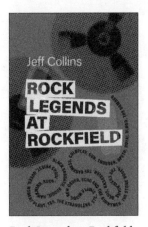

Rock Legends at Rockfield
by Jeff Collins
978-1-91527-904-0 £16.99

Welsh Food Stories
by Carwyn Graves
978-1-91527-900-2 £14.99

An Indigo Summer
by Ellie Evelyn Orrell
978-1-91527-907-1 £14.99

Return to My Trees
by Matthew Yeomans
978-1-915279-14-9 £18.99